RECOLLI

OI

TOUR MADE IN ꜱᴄᴏᴛ𝘓𝘈...

A.D.1803

By

Dorothy Wordsworth

Edited by J. C. Shairp

This edition: text restoration and graphic restoration from the second edition 1874, by the publisher, A. MacKay Ltd, Scotland.

This is an edited compilation of the second edition, published by Edmonston and Douglas, EDINBURGH, 1874.

Restoration/Graphics: C. E. Mac Kay   **Editor:** Iain C. MacKay

ISBN: 978-0-9573443-2-7   **This publication:** 2014

Printed and bound in Scotland by Clydeside Press,
37 High Street, Glasgow, G1 1LX

Cover: The Falls at Inversnaid. Dorothy first saw them on Friday, August 26th 1803

CONTENTS

Dorothy Wordsworth

William Wordsworth

*A Twentieth Century "Car," a refined version
of the one used by Dorothy and William in Scotland*

INTRODUCTION TO THIS EDITION

Over the years I have ventured out on day trips around Scotland enjoying its beautiful scenery and friendly people. I was given a copy of the previous edition of Dorothy's journeying in Scotland and I was delighted to see how many places I recognised were in it. I enjoyed reading of her experiences at the places I had visited, but wanted a smaller version and when I was told that there was going to be an updated edition of the book, with pictures and photos of the places she visited, I was delighted. I could instantly imagine people who had bought the book taking sojourns around Scotland, following the journey Dorothy had taken and reading her diary, learning of her experiences at these same places and getting a sense of history.

I find that the way the format of the book has been changed makes it so much easier to read; the size and style of the print has also been changed and the weeks are supported by familiar photos and prints pertaining to the relevant journey, at the end of the appropriate chapter.

Dorothy Wordsworth was an amazing, resilient and strong young woman. I believe she was in her early thirties when she, her brother, William Wordsworth and their friend Samuel Coleridge undertook the journey by "car" along roads unlike those of today, but of familiar routes.

When I was little my father took us on trips to Loch Lomond and the Trossachs in our Riley and, although the car had suspension (unlike the carriages of Dorothy's day), I recall how long the journeys felt because of the bumping around in the back seat and making one feel a little squeamish. In Dorothy's day even the roads we took did not exist. At one point Dorothy mentions having to alight from the carriage and trundle up the muddy, waterlogged pathway because the rain was falling so heavily that the horse was struggling to get up the hill. From the comfort and warmth of my centrally heated home I read of her arriving at lodgings where, even in summer, it was damp in the houses and the sheets they were to sleep in were also damp. I can imagine that she often had to wear clothes that had not properly dried. Despite these hardships she loved being in Scotland, meeting the people and writing about these in her diary. Even after a long journey, sometimes laborious, cold wet and uncomfortable, Dorothy took time to write her diary diligently and prolifically.

The journey that Dorothy and her companions undertook in 6 weeks would probably be easily and comfortably done in 4 days. However travelling by modern car would prevent the scenery and ambience from being fully experienced, as journeying slowly gives more opportunity to hear the wind, birds, trees and other sounds of nature.

I am so glad that the photo of "The Falls at Inversnaid" is the picture on the front cover. It is a beautiful journey to reach them, driving down a road which ends abruptly at a pier on Loch Lomond; literally "The end of the road." I remember parking, walking past the hotel and there were the Falls ... so beautiful... and, looking up at the awesome sight of the falls, realising that Dorothy and William once stood on the same spot. I look forward to the adventure of doing just that again – following Dorothy's actual journey. I am sure there will be many people who will enjoy doing the same.

Louise Mackie   *Irvine, 11th January 2014*

PREFACE TO SECOND EDITION

I cannot allow a Second Edition of this Journal to appear without expressing my grateful sense of the lively interest it has awakened. It has met with a welcome, not warmer than it deserves, but warmer than I had ventured to hope for. Private persons, most qualified to judge, have found in it enjoyment more even than they had anticipated. Writers in the daily and weekly press have vied with each other in their commendations of it. To these last,—my unknown friends,—I will not offer any thanks in behalf of the Journal. To have received it coldly would have been to have done injustice, not so much to it, as to themselves. But I do tender them my thanks for the kind way in which they have spoken of the little I have done in editing it. I rejoice to find that the estimate I had formed of its merit has been fully acknowledged by most writers who have noticed it. One or two, indeed, I regret to say, have gone out of their way to speak harshly of the poet's treatment of his sister. Of their rude and ill-natured comments I will offer no refutation. To do so would be an injustice to the poet's character, as if it needed such defence. This only I will say, that the remarks to which I allude are founded on misconceptions as groundless as they are unkind.

There is the less need to notice these, because they are but as one jarring note in what has otherwise been a harmony of approval. So hearty has been the reception which the Journal has met, that it seems to prove, either that the circle of Wordsworth's admirers must be wider than I had believed, or that the sister's feeling narrative must have touched many whom her brother's poetry has failed to reach. Either way, I cannot but rejoice in the result. For I am sure that none can read the Journal carefully and sympathetically without gathering from the perusal, not merely a passing pleasure, but some more permanent good.

Among the many kindly comments that have been made on the Journal, some few facts have been noticed to which I have not in the former Preface adverted. It would have been easy, had it been desirable, to have expanded that sketch to a much greater length. But the facts noticed as omissions do not seem to me to have much bearing on the purpose I had in view. There is, however, one fact I have observed since the Preface was written, too characteristic not to find a place here:- In the note which the Poet in his later years dictated to the second 'Evening Voluntary' written in 1833, this incident is thus mentioned:—'. . . My sister, when she first heard the voice of the sea from this point (the high ground of the coast of Cumberland overlooking Whitehaven and the sea beyond it), and beheld the scene spread before her, burst into tears. Our family then lived at Cockermouth, and this fact was often mentioned among us, as indicating the sensibility for which she was so remarkable.' This was when she was a child. It is the maturity of the same sensibility, tender and deep, which meets us at every turn in the Tour, and makes the record of it so attractive.

Again, it has been noted, not perhaps without a sense of disappointment, that the Journal records not a word of the talk which must have flowed forth from the two great poets. 'Though Coleridge and Wordsworth were with her, the first for a part, the other for the whole of the journey, they don't say a noticeable thing, except perhaps a poorish Coleridgian joke at Leadhills.' They may, however, have dropped good sayings by the way, and yet Miss Wordsworth left them unrecorded. For she was familiar with their talk, and would not stare even at their best sayings, as some lionizing stranger might have done. Besides, it must be remembered that Coleridge was, during this journey, out of sorts, and probably did not flow. As for Wordsworth, I hardly think it would be his way to discourse at large in the presence of the grand and solitary forms of nature. Rather, I believe, his feeling would be—silence is best. Has he not reminded us that -

> *'There are powers,*
> *Which of themselves our minds impress;*
> *That we can feed this mind of ours,*
> *In a wise passiveness'?*

It was just because he could present to nature so broad and tranquil an expanse of receptive silence that he took in so much of it and learned so deeply both its outward appearances and its inner spirit. And Wordsworth and his sister were as much in sympathy with each other as with nature. And therefore I can well imagine that, in a state of pure receptivity, they may have dreamed away mile after mile without interchanging a word. It is to this large power of silent sensibility, in brother and sister alike,—the tongue still, the eye and heart awake,— that we owe most of what is best in the Journal of the sister, as well as in the Poems of the brother.

Having read again, since its publication, most of the Journal, I am more than ever impressed with the suggestive and educating power that is in it. I do not remember any other book more capable of training heart and eye to look with profit on the face of nature, as it manifests itself in this, our northern land. And the ordinary run of men need such teaching. They need to have their eyesight purged, that seeing, they may truly see, and feeling, may rightly feel; at this season especially, when so many of our countrymen are gazing, too often in hopeless vacancy, on the very scenes described in this Journal, and thousands flying at post-speed through the usual tourist rounds, hardly knowing what to look for or how to look. Many have left their city abodes to bivouack for weeks; it may be for months, together, in the glens, on the moors, or by the loch-shores of the Highlands. For this century has brought with it no greater social change than the increased

7

desire for enjoying nature among all ranks of the people, combined with the increased means of gratifying it. The inward and the outward change fit into each other, and mutually react.

With this thirst for external nature so vastly increased, were it not well that all persons should gather from it, if possible, something more than fresh air and exercise. Air and exercise are well, but the relish and benefit of these would not be lessened, but enhanced, if heart and imagination were being fed at the same time. More than half the enjoyment gathered from any special day among the mountains, comes from the certainty that 'these things it will delight us to remember.' But if the memory is to be stored with images which will rise on after-hours of dreariness to gladden us, must not the eye that gazes be informed by the imagination and the heart? Perceptive eye and imaginative heart are no doubt natural gifts, not to be gained in the schools. But where they exist by nature, they may be quickened and expanded by education. And I know no book more fitted to educate them than this Journal. Therefore, to all to whom nature and true human-hearted-ness are dear, I once more commend it not only for rapid perusal, but for close and loving study.

CUILALUINN   *August 1874*

PREFACE TO THE FIRST EDITION

Those who have long known the poetry of Wordsworth will be no strangers to the existence of this Journal of his sister, which is now for the first time published entire. They will have, by heart, those few wonderful sentences from it, which here and there stand at the head of the Poet's 'Memorials of a Tour in Scotland in 1803.' Especially they will remember that 'Extract from the Journal of my Companion' which preludes the 'Address to Kilchurn Castle upon Loch Awe,' and they may sometimes have asked themselves whether the prose of the sister is not as truly poetic and as memorable as her brother's verse. If they have read the Memoirs of the Poet published by his nephew the Bishop of Lincoln, they will have found there fuller extracts from the Journal, which quite maintain the impression made by the first brief sentences. All true Wordsworthians then will welcome, I believe, the present publication. They will find in it not only new and illustrative light on those Scottish poems which they have so long known, but a faithful commentary on the character of the poet, his mode of life, and the manner of his poetry. Those who, from close study of Wordsworth's poetry, know both the poet and his sister, and what they were to each other, will need nothing more than the Journal itself. If it were likely to fall only into their hands, it might be left without one word of comment or illustration. But as it may reach some who have never read Wordsworth, and others who, having read, do not relish him, for the information of these something more must be said. The Journal now published does not borrow all its worth from its bearing on the great poet. It has merit and value of its own, which may commend it to some who have no heart for Wordsworth's poetry. For the writer of it was in herself no common woman, and might have secured for herself an independent reputation, had she not chosen rather that other part, to forget and merge herself entirely in the work and reputation of her brother.

Dorothy Wordsworth was the only sister of the poet, a year and a half younger, having been born on Christmas Day 1771. The five children who composed the family, four sons and one daughter, lost their mother in 1778, when William was eight, and Dorothy six years old. The father died five years afterwards, at the close of 1783, and the family home at Cockermouth was broken up and the children scattered. Before his father's death, William, in his ninth year, had gone with his elder brother to school at Hawkshead, by the lake of Esthwaite, and, after the father died, Dorothy was brought up by a cousin on her mother's side, Miss Threlkeld, afterwards Mrs. Rawson, who lived in Halifax. During the eight years which Wordsworth spent at school, or, at any rate, from the time of his father's death, he and his sister seem seldom, if ever, to have met. The first college vacation in the summer of 1788 brought him back to his old school in the vale of Esthwaite, and either this or the next of his undergraduate summers restored him to the society of his sister at Penrith. This meeting is thus described in the 'Prelude:'—

'In summer, making quest for works of art,
Or scenes renowned for beauty, I explored
That streamlet whose blue current works its way
Between romantic Dovedale's spiry rocks;

Pried into Yorkshire dales, or hidden tracts
Of my own native region, and was blest
Between these sundry wanderings with a joy
Above all joys that seemed another morn
Risen on mid-noon; blest with the presence, Friend!
Of that sole sister, her who hath been long
Dear to thee also, thy true friend and mine,
Now, after separation desolate
A gift then first bestowed.'

They then together wandered by the banks of Emont, among the woods of Lowther and, "climbing the Border Beacon, looked wistfully towards the dim regions of Scotland." Then and there too, Wordsworth first met that young kinswoman who was his wife to be.

During the following summers the Poet was busy with walking tours in Switzerland and North Italy, his residence in France and his absorption in the French Revolution, which kept him some years longer apart from his sister. During those years Miss Wordsworth lived much with her uncle Dr. Cookson, who was a canon of Windsor and a favourite with the Court, and there met with people of more learning and refinement, but not of greater worth, than those she had left in her northern home. In the beginning of 1794 Wordsworth, returned from his wanderings, came to visit his sister at Halifax, his head still in a whirl with revolutionary fervours. He was wandering about among his friends with no certain dwelling-place, no fixed plan of life, his practical purposes and his opinions, political, philosophical, and religious, all alike at sea. But whatever else might remain unsettled, the bread-and-butter question, as Coleridge calls it, could not. The thought of orders, for which his friends intended him, had been abandoned; law he abominated; writing for the newspaper press seemed the only resource. In this seething state of mind he sought once more his sister's calming society and the two travelled together on foot from Kendal to Grasmere, from Grasmere to Keswick, 'through the most delightful country that was ever seen.'

Towards the close of this year (1794) Wordsworth would probably have gone to London to take up the trade of a writer for the newspapers. From this however he was held back for a time by the duty of nursing his friend Raisley Calvert, who lay dying at Penrith. Early in 1795 the young man died, leaving to his friend, the young

Poet, a legacy of £900. The world did not then hold Wordsworth for a poet, and had received with coldness his first attempt, 'Descriptive Sketches and an Evening Walk,' published two years before. But the dying youth had seen farther than the world, and felt convinced that his friend, if he had leisure given him to put forth his powers, would do something which would make the world his debtor. With this view he bequeathed him the small sum above named. And seldom has such a bequest borne ampler fruit. 'Upon the interest of the £900, £400 being laid out in annuity, with £200 deducted from the principal, and £100 a legacy to my sister, and £100 more which "The Lyrical Ballads" have brought me, my sister and I have contrived to live seven years, nearly eight.' So wrote Wordsworth in 1805 to his friend Sir George Beaumont. Thus at this juncture of the Poet's fate, when to onlookers he must have seemed both outwardly and inwardly well-nigh bankrupt, Baisley Calvert's bequest came to supply his material needs, and to his inward needs his sister became the best earthly minister. For his mind was ill at ease. The high hopes awakened in him by the French Revolution had been dashed, and his spirit, darkened and depressed, was on the verge of despair. He might have become such a man as he has pictured in the character of 'The Solitary.' But a good Providence brought his sister to his side and saved him. She discerned his real need and divined the remedy. By her cheerful society, fine tact, and vivid love for nature she turned him, depressed and bewildered, alike from the abstract speculations and the contemporary politics in which he had got immersed, and directed his thoughts towards truth of poetry, and the face of nature, and the healing that for him lay in these.

> *'Then it was*
> *That the beloved sister in whose sight*
> *Those days were passed—*
> *Maintained for me a saving intercourse*
> *With my true self; for though bedimmed and changed*
> *Much, as it seemed, I was no further changed*
> *Than as a clouded or a waning moon:*
> *She whispered still that brightness would return,*
> *She, in the midst of all, preserved me still*
> *A Poet, made me seek beneath that name,*
> *And that alone, my office upon earth.'*

By intercourse with her and wanderings together in delightful places of his native country, he was gradually led back

> *'To those sweet counsels between head and heart*
> *Whence genuine knowledge grew.'*

The brother and sister, having thus cast in their lots together, settled at Racedown Lodge in Dorsetshire in the autumn of 1795. They had there a pleasant house, with a good garden, and around them charming walks and a delightful country, looking out on the distant sea. The place was very retired, with little or no society, and the post only once a week. But of employment there was no lack. The brother now settled steadily to poetic work; the sister engaged in household duties and reading, and then when work was over, there were endless walks and wanderings. Long years afterwards, Miss Wordsworth spoke of Racedown as the place she looked back to with most affection 'It was,' she said, 'the first home I had.'

The poems which Wordsworth there composed were not among his best,—'The Borderers,' 'Guilt or Sorrow,' and others. He was yet only groping to find his true subjects and his own proper manner. But there was one piece there composed which will stand comparison with any tale he ever wrote. It was 'The Ruined Cottage' which, under the title of the 'Story of Margaret,' he afterwards incorporated in the first Book of 'The Excursion.' It was when they had been nearly two years at Racedown that they received a guest who was destined to exercise more influence on the self-contained Wordsworth than any other man ever did. This was S. T. Coleridge. One can imagine how he would talk, interrupted only by their mutually reading aloud their respective Tragedies, both of which are now well-nigh forgotten, and by Wordsworth reading his 'Ruined Cottage,' which is not forgotten. Miss Wordsworth describes S. T. C, as he then was, in words that are well known. And he describes her thus, in words less known,—'She is a woman indeed, in mind I mean, and in heart; for her person is such that if you expected to see a pretty woman, you would think her ordinary; if you expected to see an ordinary woman you would think her pretty, but her manners are simple, ardent, impressive. In every motion her innocent soul out-beams so brightly, that who saw her would say, "Guilt was a thing impossible with her."

Her information various, her eye watchful, in minutest observation of nature, and her taste a perfect electrometer.'

The result of this meeting of the two poets was that the Wordsworths shifted their abode from Racedown to Alfoxden, near Nether Stowey, in Somersetshire, to be near Coleridge. Alfoxden was a large furnished mansion, which the brother and sister had to themselves. 'We are three miles from Stowey,' the then abode of Coleridge, writes the sister, 'and two miles from the sea. Wherever we turn we have woods, smooth downs, and valleys, with small brooks running down them, through green meadows, hardly ever intersected with hedgerows, but scattered over with trees. The hills that cradle these valleys are either covered with fern and bilberries, or oak woods which are cut for charcoal. Walks extend for miles over the hill-tops, the great beauty of which is their wild simplicity—they are perfectly smooth, without rocks.' It was in this neighbourhood, as the two poets loitered in the sylvan combes, or walked along the smooth Quantock hilltops, looking seaward, with the 'sole sister,' the companion of their walks, that they struck each from the other his finest tones. It was with both of them the heyday of poetic creation. In these walks it was that Coleridge, with slight hints from Wordsworth, first chaunted the vision of the Ancient Mariner, and then alone, 'The rueful woes of Lady Christabel.' This, too, was the birthday of some of the finest of the Lyrical Ballads, of 'We are Seven,' 'Simon Lee,' 'Expostulation and Reply,' and 'The Tables Turned,'

'It is the first mild day in March, and I heard a thousand blended notes.' Coleridge never knew again such a season of poetic creation, and Wordsworth's tardier, if stronger, nature, received from contact with Coleridge that quickening impulse which it needed, and which it retained during all its most creative years.

But if Coleridge, with his occasional intercourse and wonderful talk, did much for Wordsworth, his sister, by her continual companionship, did far more. After the great revulsion from the excesses of the French Revolution, she was with him a continually sanative influence. That whole period, which ranged from 1795 till his settling at Grasmere at the opening of the next century, and of which the residence at Racedown and Alfoxden formed a large part, was the healing time of his spirit. And in that healing time she was the chief human minister.

Somewhere in the 'Prelude' he tells that, in early youth, there was a too great sternness of spirit about him, a high, but too severe, moral ideal by which he judged men and things, insensible to gentler and humbler influences. He compares his soul to a high, bare craig, without any crannies in which flowers may lurk, untouched by the mellowing influences of sun and shower. His sister came with her softening influence, and sowed in it the needed flowers, and touched it with mellowing colours.

> 'She gave me eyes, she gave me ears,
> And humble cares and delicate fears,
> A heart, the fountain of sweet tears
> And love, and thought and joy.'

Elsewhere in the 'Prelude' he describes how at one time his soul had got too much under the dominion of the eye, so that he kept comparing scene with scene, instead of enjoying each for itself— craving new forms, novelties of colour or proportion, and insensible to the spirit of each place and the affections which each awakens. In contrast with this temporary mood of his own he turns to one of another temper:—

> 'I knew a maid,
> A young enthusiast who escaped these bonds,
> Her eye was not the mistress of her heart,
> She welcomed what was given, and craved no more;
> Whate'er the scene presented to her view,
> That was the best, to that she was attuned
> By her benign simplicity of life.
> Birds in the bower, and lambs in the green field,
> Could they have known her, would have loved; methought
> Her very presence such a sweetness breathed,
> That flowers, and trees, and even the silent hills,
> And everything she looked on, should have had
> An intimation how she bore herself
> Towards them and to all creatures.
> God delights In such a being; for her common thoughts
> Are piety, her life is gratitude.'

But it was not his sister the Poet speaks of here, but of his first meeting with her who afterwards became his wife.

The results of the residence at Racedown, but especially at Alfoxden, appeared in the shape of the first volume of the 'Lyrical

Ballads,' which were published in the autumn of 1798 by Mr. Cottle at Bristol. This small volume opens with Coleridge's 'Rime of the Ancyent Marinere,' and is followed by Wordsworth's short but exquisite poems of the Alfoxden time, and is closed by the well-known lines on Tintern Abbey. Wordsworth reaches about the highest pitch of his inspiration in this latter poem, which contains more rememberable lines than any other of his, of equal length, save perhaps the Immortality Ode. It was the result of a ramble of four or five days made by him and his sister from Alfoxden in July 1798, and was composed under circumstances 'most pleasant,' he says, 'for me to remember.' He began it upon leaving Tintern, after crossing the Wye, and concluded it as he was entering Bristol in the evening.

Everyone will recollect how, after its high reflections he turns at the close to her, 'his dearest Friend,' 'his dear, dear Friend,' and speaks of his delight to have her by his side, and of the former pleasures which he read in 'the shooting lights of her wild eyes,' and then the almost prophetic words with which he forebodes, too surely, that time when 'solitude, or fear, or pain, or grief should be her portion.'

That September (1798) saw the break-up of the brief, bright companionship near Nether Stowey. Coleridge went with Wordsworth and his sister to Germany, but soon parted from them and passed on alone to Gottingen, there to study German, and lose himself in the labyrinth of German metaphysics. Wordsworth and Dorothy remained at Goslar, and, making no acquaintances, spent the winter—said to have been the coldest of the century—by the German stoves, Wordsworth writing more lyrical poems in the same vein which had been opened so happily at Alfoxden. There is, in these poems, no tincture of their German surroundings; they deal entirely with those which they had left on English ground. Early in spring they returned to England, to spend the summer with their friends, the Hutchinsons, at Sockburn-upon-Tees. There Dorothy remained, while in September, Wordsworth made with Coleridge the walking tour through the lakes of Westmoreland and Cumberland, which issued in his choice of a home at Grasmere for himself and his sister.

At the close of the year, Wordsworth and his Sister set off and walked, driven forward by the cold, frosty winds blowing from behind, from Wensleydale over Sedbergh's naked heights and the high range that divides the Yorkshire dales from the lake country. On the shortest day of the year (St. Thomas's Day) they reached the small two-storey cottage at the Townend of Grasmere, which, for the next eight years, was to be the poet's home, immortalized by the work he did in it. That cottage has, behind it, a small orchard-plot or garden ground shelving upwards toward the woody mountains above, and in front it looks across the peaceful lake with its one green island, to the steeps of Silver-how on the farther side. Westward it looks on Helm Craig, and up the long folds of Easedale towards the range that divides Easedale from Borrow-dale. In this cottage they two lived on their income of a hundred pounds a year, Dorothy doing all the household work, for they had then, it has been said, no servant. Besides this, she had time to write out all his poems—for Wordsworth himself could never bear the strain of transcribing—to read aloud to him of an afternoon or evening and to accompany him on his endless walks. At one such reading by her of Milton's Sonnets it was that his soul took fire and rolled off his first sonnets. Nor these alone—her eye and imagination fed him, not only with subjects for his poetry, but even with images and thoughts. What we are told of the poem of the 'Beggars' might be said of I know not how many more. 'The sister's eye was ever on the watch to provide for the poet's pen.' He had a most observant eye, and she also for him; and his poems are sometimes little more than poetic versions of her descriptions of the objects which she had seen; and which he treated as seen by himself. Look at the poem on the 'Daffodils' and compare with it these words taken from the sister's Journal. "When we were in the woods below Gowbarrow Park, we saw a few daffodils close by the water side. As we went along there were more and yet more; and at last, under the boughs of the trees, we saw there were a long belt of them along the shore. I never saw daffodils so beautiful. They grew among the mossy stones about them. Some rested their heads on the stones, as on a pillow; the rest tossed, and reeled, and danced, and seemed as if they verily laughed with the wind. They looked so gay and glancing." It may also be noted that the Poet's future wife contributed to this poem these two best lines—

'They flash upon that inward eye, Which is the bliss of solitude.'

Or take another description from Miss Wordsworth's Journal of a birch-tree, 'the lady of the woods,' which her brother has not versified:—'As we were going along we were stopped at once, at the distance, perhaps, of fifty yards from our favourite birch-tree: it was yielding to the gust of the wind, with all its tender twigs; the sun shone upon it, and it glanced in the wind like a flying sunshiny shower. It was a tree in shape, with stem and branches, but it was like a spirit of water.' The life, which the Poet and his sister lived, during the eight years at the Townend of Grasmere, stands out with a marked individuality which it is delightful ever so often to recur to. It was as unlike the lives of most literary or other men, as the most original of his poems are unlike the ordinary run of even good poetry. Their outward life was exactly like that of the dalesmen or 'statesmen'—for so the native yeomen proprietors are called—with whom they lived on the most friendly footing, and among whom they found their chief society. Outwardly their life was so, but inwardly it was cheered by imaginative visitings to which these were strangers. Sheltered as they then were from the agitations of the world, the severe frugality of the life they led ministered in more than one way to feed that poetry which introduced a new element into English thought. It kept the mind cool, and the eye clear, to feel once more that kinship between the outward world and the soul of man, to perceive that impassioned expression in the countenance of all nature, which, if felt by primeval men, ages of cultivation have long forgotten. It also made them wise to practise the same frugality in emotional enjoyment which they exercised in household economy. It has been well noted {*See Essays of R. H. Hutton, Esq., vol. ii.*} that this is one of Wordsworth's chief characteristics. It is the temptation of the poetic temperament to be prodigal of passion, to demand a life always strung to the highest pitch of emotional excitement, to be never content unless when passing from fervour to fervour. No life can long endure this strain. This is specially seen in such poets as Byron and Shelley, who speedily fell from the heights of passion to the depths of languor and despondency. The same quick using up of the power of enjoyment produces the too common product of the Hasi man and the cynic. Wordsworth early perceived that all, even the richest, natures have but a very limited capacity of uninterrupted enjoyment, and that nothing is easier than to exhaust this capacity. Hence, he set himself to husband it, to draw upon it sparingly; to employ it only on the purest, most natural, and most enduring objects, and not to speedily dismiss or throw them by and demand more, but to detain them till they had yielded him their utmost. From this, in part it, came that the commonest sights of earth and sky—a fine spring day, a sunset, even a chance traveller met on a moor, any ordinary sorrow of man's life— yielded to him an amount of imaginative interest inconceivable to more mundane spirits. The simple healthiness and strict frugality of his household life suited well, and must have greatly assisted that wholesome frugality of emotion which he exercised. During those seven or eight Grasmere years, the spring of poetry which burst forth at Alfoxden, and produced the first volume of ' Lyrical Ballads,' flowed steadily on and found expression in other poems of like quality and spirit,—'Hartleap Well,' 'The Brothers,' 'Michael,' which, with others of the same order, written in Germany, appeared in the second volume of 'Lyrical Ballads.' And, after these two volumes had gone forth, Grasmere still gave more of the same high order,— 'The Daffodils,' 'The Leech-Gatherer,' and, above all, the 'Ode on Immortality.' It saw, too, the conclusion of the 'Prelude,' and the beginning of the 'Excursion.' So, it may be said, that those Grasmere years, from 1800 to 1807, mark the period when Wordsworth's genius was at its zenith. During all this time, sister Dorothy was by his side, ministering to him, equally in body and in mind—doing the part of household servant, and not less that of prompter and inspirer of his highest songs.

But this life of theirs, retired and uneventful as it seems, was not without its own incidents. Such was the homecoming of their younger sailor-brother John, who, in the first year of their residence at Grasmere—

> *'Under their cottage roof, had gladly come*
> *From the wild sea a cherished visitant.'*

He was, what his brother calls him, 'a silent poet,' and had the heart and sense to feel the sterling quality of his brother's poems, and to foretell, with perfect confidence, their ultimate acceptance, at the time when the critic, wits, who ruled the hour, treated them with contempt. The two brothers were congenial spirits, and William's poetry has many affecting allusions to his brother John, whose intention it was, when his last voyage was over, to settle in 'Grasmere's happy vale,' and to devote the surplus of his fortune to his brother's use. On his last voyage he sailed as captain of the 'Earl of Abergavenny' East-Indiaman, at the opening of February 1805; and on the 5th of that month, the ill-fated ship struck on the Shambles of the Bill of Portland, and the captain and most of the crew went down with her. To the brother and sister this became a permanent household sorrow. But in time they found comfort in that thought with which the Poet closes a remarkable letter on his brother's loss, — 'So good must be better; so high must be destined to be higher.'

Another lesser incident was a short tour to the Continent, in which, as the brother and sister crossed Westminster Bridge, outside the Dover coach, both witnessed that sunrise which remains fixed for ever in the famous sonnet. Another incident, and more important, was Wordsworth's marriage in October 1802, when he brought home his young wife, Mary Hutchinson, his sister's long-time friend, to their cottage at Townend. This is she whom he has sung in the lines—'She was a phantom of delight;' of whom he said in plain prose, 'She has a sweetness all but angelic, simplicity the most entire, womanly self-respect and purity of heart speaking through all her looks, acts, and movements.' The advent of Mrs. Wordsworth brought no change to Dorothy. She still continued to fill to her brother and his wife the same place which she had filled when her brother was alone, sharing in all the household duties and family interests, and still accompanying him in his rambles when Mrs. Wordsworth was detained at home. The year after the marriage, that is, in the fourth year of the Grasmere residence, after the first son was born, the brother and sister, accompanied by Coleridge, set out on that tour, the Journal of which is here published. Portions of it have already appeared in the 'Memoirs' of Wordsworth, but it is now for the first time given in full, just as it came from the pen of Miss Wordsworth, seventy years ago. As I shall have to speak of it again, I may now pass on and note the few facts that still remain to be told in illustration of the writer's character.

In the years which followed the tour in Scotland, other children were added to Wordsworth's family, till the small cottage at the

Townend could no longer accommodate the household. The second child was the poet's only daughter, whom, after his sister, he called Dorothy, generally known as Dora, for, as he tells Lady Beaumont, he could not find it in his heart to call her by another name. This second Dora occupies in Wordsworth's later poetry the same place which the first Dorothy held in his earlier. Aunt Dorothy's love, as it expanded to take in each new comer, did not lose any of its intensity towards her brother. While the uneasiness which the act of writing had always occasioned him was not diminished, weakness of eyesight increased. Then she had to write for him, she read to him, she walked with him as of old, besides sharing in all household cares. In November 1806, Wordsworth removed with his family to Coleorton, in Leicestershire, to spend the winter there in a house of Sir George Beaumont's; 'Our own cottage,' he writes, 'being far too small for our family to winter in, though we manage well enough in it during the summer.' In the spring of 1807, Wordsworth and his wife visited London. Dorothy, who was left with the children, wrote the poem called 'The Mother's Return,' as a welcome to Mrs. Wordsworth when she came back. This, with two other poems, written by her for the children, one on 'The Wind,' the other called 'The Cottager to her Infant,' afterwards appeared in an edition of her brother's poems.

This seems the proper place to give the account of Miss Wordsworth, as she appeared to De Quincey, when in 1807 he first made the acquaintance of Wordsworth, just before the Poet and his family quitted their old home in the cottage at Grasmere Townend. After speaking of Mrs. Wordsworth, he continues:—

'Immediately behind her moved a lady, shorter, slighter, and perhaps, in all other respects, as different from her in personal characteristics as could have been wished for the most effective contrast. "Her face was of Egyptian brown." Rarely, in a woman of English birth, had I seen a more determinate gipsy tan. Her eyes were not soft as Mrs.Wordsworth's, nor were they fierce or bold; but they were wild and startling, and hurried in their motion. Her manner was warm, and even ardent; her sensibility seemed constitutionally deep; and some subtle fire of impassioned intellect apparently burned within her, which—being alternately pushed forward into a conspicuous expression by the irresistible instincts of her temperament, and then

20

immediately checked in obedience to the decorum of her sex and age and her maidenly condition—gave to her whole demeanour, and to her conversation, an air of embarrassment, and even of self-conflict, that was almost distressing to witness. Even her very utterance and enunciation often suffered in point of clearness and steadiness, from the agitation of her excessive organic sensibility. At times the self-counteraction and self-baffling of her feelings caused her even to stammer. But the greatest deductions from Miss Wordsworth's attractions, and from the exceeding interest which surrounded her, in right of her character, of her history, and of the relation which she fulfilled towards her brother, were the glancing quickness of her motions, and other circumstances in her deportment (such as her stooping attitude when walking), which gave an ungraceful character to her appearance when out of doors. . . .

'Her knowledge of literature was irregular and thoroughly unsystematic. She was content to be ignorant of many things; but what she knew, and had really mastered, lay where it could not be disturbed—in the temple of her own most fervid heart.'

It may not be amiss here to add from the same gossipy, but graphic pen, a description of the Townend home, and of the way of life there, which has often before been quoted:—

'A little semi-vestibule between two doors prefaced the entrance into what might be considered the principal room of the cottage. It was an oblong square, not above eight and a half feet high, sixteen feet long, and twelve broad; very prettily wainscoted from the floor to the ceiling with dark polished oak, slightly embellished with carving. One window there was—a perfect and unpretending cottage window —with little diamond panes, embowered at almost every season of the year with roses, and, in the summer and autumn, with a profusion of jasmine and other fragrant shrubs. From the exuberant luxuriance of the vegetation around it, this window, though tolerably large, did not furnish a very powerful light to one who entered from the open air. ... I was ushered up a little flight of stairs, fourteen in all, to a little drawing-room, or whatever the reader chooses to call it. Wordsworth himself has described the fire-place of this room as his

'Half kitchen and half parlour fire.'

It was not fully seven feet six inches high, and in other respects pretty nearly of the same dimensions as the rustic hall below. There was, however, in a small recess, a library of perhaps three hundred volumes, which seemed to consecrate this room as the poet's study and composing-room, and such occasionally it was.

'About four o'clock, it might be, when we arrived. At that hour in November the daylight soon declined, and in an hour and a half we were all collected about the tea-table.

'This, with the Wordsworths, under the simple rustic system of habits which they cherished then and for twenty years after, was the most delightful meal of the day, just as dinner is in great cities, and for the same reason, because it was prolonged into a meal of leisure and conversation. That night I found myself, about eleven at night, in a pretty bedroom, about fourteen feet by twelve. Much I feared that this might turn out the best room in the house; and it illustrates the hospitality of my new friends to mention that it was. . . .

'Next morning Miss Wordsworth I found making breakfast in the little sitting-room. No one was there, no glittering breakfast service; a kettle boiled upon the fire; and everything was in harmony with these unpretending arrangements.

'I rarely had seen so humble a ménage; and, contrasting the dignity of the man with this honourable poverty, and this courageous avowal of it, his utter absence of all effort to disguise the simple truth of the case, I felt my admiration increased.

'Throughout the day, which was rainy, the same style of modest hospitality prevailed. Wordsworth and his sister, myself being of the party, walked out, in spite of the rain, and made the circuit of the two lakes, Grasmere and its dependency, Eydal, a walk of about six miles.

'On the third morning after my arrival in Grasmere, I found the whole family, except the two children, prepared for the expedition across the mountains. I had heard of no horses, and took it for granted that we were to walk; however, at the moment of starting, a cart, the common farmer's cart of the country, made its appearance, and the driver was a bonny young woman of the vale. Accordingly we were all carted along to the little town or large village of Ambleside, three and a half miles distant. Our style of travelling occasioned no astonishment; on the contrary, we met a smiling salutation wherever we appeared; Miss Wordsworth being, as I observed, the person most familiarly known of our party, and the one who took upon herself the whole expenses of the flying colloquies exchanged with stragglers on the road.'

When the family had to leave this cottage home at Townend, they migrated to Allan Bank in 1808, and there remained for three years. In the spring of 1811 they moved to the Parsonage of Grasmere, and thence, in the spring of 1813, to Rydal Mount, their final abode. Their sojourn in the Parsonage was saddened by the loss of two children, who died within six months of each other, and were laid side by side in the churchyard of Grasmere. The Parsonage looks right across the road on that burial place, and the continual sight of this was more than they could bear. They were glad, therefore, to withdraw from it, and to exchange the Vale of Grasmere, now filled for them with too mournful recollections, for the sweet retirement of Rydal.

Through all these changes sister Dorothy went of course with them, and shared the affliction of the bereaved parents, as she had formerly shared their happiness. In 1814, the year of the publication of the 'Excursion,' all of which Miss Wordsworth had transcribed, her brother made another tour in Scotland, and this time Yarrow was not unvisited. His wife and her sister went with him, but Dorothy, having stayed at home probably to tend the children, did not form one of the party, a circumstance which her brother always remembered with regret.

In the summer of 1820, however, she visited the Continent with her brother and Mrs. Wordsworth, but of this tour no record remains. Another visit, the last but one, Wordsworth made to Scotland in 1831, accompanied by his daughter Dora. This time Yarrow was revisited in company with Sir Walter Scott, just before his last going from Tweedside. Wordsworth has chronicled his parting with Scott in two affecting Poems, which if any reader does not know by heart, I would recommend him to read them in the Appendix (del.) to this Journal. But by the time this expedition was made, Dorothy was an invalid confined to a sick-room. In the year 1829 she was seized by a severe illness, which so prostrated her, body and mind, that she never recovered from it. The unceasing strain of years had at last worn out that buoyant frame and fervid spirit. She had given herself to one work, and that work was done. To some it may seem a commonplace one,—to live in and for her brother, to do by him a sister's duty. With original powers which, had she chosen to set up on her own account, might have won for her high literary fame, she was content to forget herself, to merge all her gifts and all her interests in those of her brother. She thus made him other and higher than he could have been, had he stood alone, and enabled him to render better service to the world than without her ministry he could have done. With this she was well content. It is sad to think that when the world at last knew him for what he was, the great, original poet of this century, she who had helped to make him so was almost past rejoicing in it. It is said that during those latter years he never spoke of her without his voice being sensibly softened and saddened. The return of the day when they two first came to Grasmere was to him a solemn anniversary. But though so enfeebled, she still lived on, and survived her brother by nearly five years. Her death took place at Rydal Mount in January 1855, at the age of eighty-three. And now, beside her brother and his wife and others of that household, she rests in the green Grasmere churchyard, with the clear waters of Rotha murmuring by.

To return to the Journal. As we read it, let us bear always in mind that it was not meant for us, for the world, or 'the general reader,' but to be listened to by a small family circle, gathered round the winter fire. We should therefore remember that, in reading it, we are, as it were, allowed, after seventy years, to overhear what was not primarily meant for our ears at all. This will account for a fullness and minuteness of detail which, to unsympathetic persons, may perhaps appear tedious. But the writer was telling her story, not for unsympathetic persons, not for 'general readers,' much less for literary critics, but for 'the household hearts that were her own,' on whose sympathy she could reckon, even down to the minutest circumstances of this journey. And so there is no attempt at fine or sensational writing, as we now call it; no attempt at that modern artifice which they call word-painting. But there is the most absolute sincerity, the most perfect fidelity to her own experience, the most single-minded endeavour to set down precisely the things they saw and heard and felt, just as they saw and felt and heard them, while moving on their quiet way. And hence perhaps the observant reader, who submits himself to the spirit that pervades this Journal, may find, in its effortless narrative a truthfulness, a tenderness of observation, a 'vivid exactness,' a far-reaching and suggestive insight, for which he might look in vain in more studied productions.

Another thing to note is the historic value that now attaches to this Journal. It marks the state of Scotland, and the feeling with which the most finely gifted Englishmen came to it seventy years since, at a time before the flood of English interest and 'tourism' had set in across the Border. The Wordsworths were, of course, not average English people. They came with an eye awake and trained for nature, and a heart in sympathy with nature and with man in a degree not common either in that or in any other age. They were north-country English too, and between these and the Lowland Scots there was less difference of fibre and of feeling than there generally is between Cumbrians and Londoners. All their lives they had been wont to gaze across the Solway on the dimly-outlined mountains of the Scottish Border. This alone and their love of scenery and of wandering were enough, apart from other inducement, to have lured them northward. But that tide of sentiment, which in our day has culminated in our annual tourist inundation, was already setting in. It had been growing ever since 'The Forty-five,' when the sudden descent of the Highland host on England, arrested only by the disastrous pause at Derby, had frightened the Londoners from their propriety, and all but scared the Second George beyond seas. This terror in time subsided, but the interest in the northern savages still survived, and was further stimulated when, about fifteen years after, the portent of Macpherson's Ossian burst on the astonished world of literature. Then, about eleven years later, in 1773, the burly and bigoted English Lexicographer buttoned his great-coat up to the throat and set out on a Highland sheltie from Inverness, on that wonderful 'Tour to the Hebrides,' by which he determined to extinguish for ever Macpherson and his impudent forgeries. Such a tour seemed at that day as adventurous as would now be a journey to the heart of Africa, and the stories which Johnson told of the Hebrideans and their lives let in on his Cockney readers the impression of a world as strange as any which Livingstone could now report of. Then, in 1786, came Burns, whose poetry, if it did not reach the ordinary Englishman of the literary class, at least thrilled the hearts of English poets. That Wordsworth had felt his power we know, for, independent as he stood, and little won't to acknowledge his indebtedness to any, he yet confesses in one place that it was Burns who first set him on the right track. This series of surprises coming from beyond the Tweed had drawn the eyes of Englishmen towards Scotland. Especially two such voices—Ossian speaking from the heart of the Highlands, Burns concentrating in his song the whole strength and the weakness also of Lowland character—seemed to call across the Borders on Wordsworth to come and look on their land. And during all the first days of that journey the thought of Burns and his untimely end, then so recent, lay heavy on his heart.

Again, it were well, as we read, to remember the time when this Diary was written. It was before Scott was known as an original poet, before he had given anything to the world save 'The Border Minstrelsy.' We are accustomed to credit Scott with whatever enchantment invests Scotland in the eyes of the English, and of foreigners. And doubtless a large portion of it is due to him, but perhaps not quite so much as we are apt to fancy. We commonly suppose that it was he who first discovered the Trossachs and Loch Katrine, and revealed them to the world in 'The Lady of the Lake.' Yet they must have had some earlier renown, enough to make Wordsworth, travelling two years before the appearance even of Scott's 'Lay,' turn aside to go in search of them.

To Dorothy Wordsworth and Coleridge this was the first time they had set foot on Scottish ground. Wordsworth himself seems to have crossed the Border two years before this, though of that journey there is no record remaining. As they set forth from Keswick on that August morning one can well believe that,

> 'Their exterior semblance did belie
> Their soul's immensity.'

None of the three paid much regard to the outward man. Coleridge, perhaps, in soiled nankeen trousers, and with the blue and brass in which he used to appear in Unitarian pulpits, buttoned round his growing corpulency; Wordsworth in a suit of russet, not to say dingy, brown, with a broad flapping straw hat to protect his weak eyesight. And as for Miss Wordsworth, we may well believe that in her dress she thought more of use than of ornament. These three, mounted on their outlandish Irish car, with a horse, now gibbing and backing over a bank, now reduced to a walk, with one of the poets leading him by the head, must have cut but a sorry figure, and wakened many a smile and gibe in passers-by. As they wound their way up Nithsdale, one can well imagine how some Border lord or laird, riding, or driving past in smart equipage, would look on them askance, taking them for what Burns calls a 'wheen gangrel bodies,' or for a set of Dominie Sampsons from the other side the Border, or for some offshoot of the 'Auld Licht' Seceders. Poor Coleridge, ill at ease and in the dumps all the way, stretched asleep on the car cushions, while the other two were admiring the scenery, could not have added to their hilarity. And it must have been a relief to Wordsworth and his sister, though the Journal hints it not, when he left them at Loch Lomond. But, however grotesque their appearance may have been, they bore within them that which made their journey rich in delight to themselves, not to say to others. They were then both in their prime, Wordsworth and his sister being just past thirty. They had the observant eye and the feeling heart which money cannot buy. No doubt to them, accustomed to the cleanness and comfort of the farms and cottages of Westmoreland, those 'homes of ancient peace,' with their warm stone porches and their shelter of household sycamores, the dirt and discomfort of the inns and of the humbler abodes they entered, must have been repulsive enough. Even the gentlemen's seats had to them an air of neglect and desolation, and the new plantations of larch and fir with which they had then begun to be surrounded, gave an impression of rawness, barrenness, and lack of geniality. Nor less in large towns, as in Glasgow, were they struck by the dullness and dreariness in the aspect and demeanour of the 'dim common populations.' They saw and felt these things as keenly as any could do. But, unlike ordinary travellers, they were not scared or disgusted by them. They did not think that the first appearance was all. They felt and saw that there was more behind. With lively interest they note the healthy young women travelling barefoot, though well dressed, the children without shoes or stockings, the barefoot boys, some with their caps wreathed with wild flowers, others who could read Virgil or Homer. They pass, as friends, beneath the humble cottage roofs, look with sympathy on the countenances of the inmates, partake, when bidden, of their homely fare; enter feelingly into their pathetic human histories. They came there not to criticise, but to know and feel.

Again, their intense love for their Westmoreland dales and meres did not send them to look on those of Scotland with a sense of rivalry, but of brotherhood. They were altogether free from that vulgar habit of comparing scene with scene which so poisons the eye to all true perception of natural beauty,—as though the one great end were to graduate all the various scenes of nature in the list of a competitive examination. Hence, whatever new they met with, they were ready to welcome and enjoy. They could appreciate the long, bare, houseless, treeless glens, not less than the well-wooded lakes. And yet Miss Wordsworth's home-heartedness makes her long for some touches of home and human habitation to break the long bleak solitudes she passed through. The absolute desolation of the Moor of Rannoch, so stirring to some, was evidently too much for her:-

'The loneliness loaded her heart, the desert tired her eye.'

Again, throughout the Journal, we see how, to her eye, man and nature interact on each other. That deep feeling, so strong in her brother's poetry, of the interest that man gives to nature, and still more the dignity that nature gives to man, is not less strongly felt by her. It is man seen against a great background of nature and solitude that most stirs her imagination. The woman sitting sole by the margin of Daer Water, or the old man alone in the corn-field, or the boy solitary on the Moor of Crawford-john—these in her prose are pictures quite akin and equal to many a one that occurs in her brother's verse. This sense of man with 'grandeur circumfused,' 'the sanctity of nature given to man,' is as primary in her as in her brother. I cannot believe that she merely learnt it from him. It must have been innate in both, derived by both from one original source.

One is struck throughout by the absence of all effort at fine or imaginative writing. But this only makes more effective those natural gleams that come unbidden. After the dullness of Glasgow and the Vale of Leven comes that wakening up to very ecstasy among the— that new world, magical, enchanting. And then that plunge into the heart of the Highlands, when they find themselves by the shores of Loch Katrine, alone with the native people there,—the smell of the peat-reek within, and the scent of the bog-myrtle without; those 'gentle ardours' that awake, as they move along Lochawe-side and look into the cove of Cruachan, or catch that Appin glen by Loch Linnhe, at the bright sunset hour, enlivened by the haymaking people; or that new rapture they drink in at the first glimpse, from Loch Etive shores, of the blue Atlantic Isles. And then what a fitting close to such a tour was that meeting with Walter Scott; the two great poets of their time, both in the morning of their power, and both still unknown, joining hands of friendship which was to last for life!

But I have said more than enough. Those who care for the things which the Wordsworths cared for will find in this quiet narrative much to their mind. And they will find from it some new light shed on those delightful poems, memorial of that tour, which remain as an undying track of glory illuminating the path these two trod. These poems are printed in the Appendix, that those who know them well may read them once again, and that those who do not know them, except by Guide-book extracts, may turn to them, after reading the Journal, and try whether they cannot find in them something which they never found elsewhere. There is one entry, the last in the Journal, made as late as 1832, which alludes to a fact which, but for this note, might have been left without comment. *The following is the entry referred to:—*

'*October 4th, 1832—I find that this tour was both begun and ended on a Sunday. I am sorry that it should have been so, though I hope and trust that our thoughts and feelings were not seldom as pious and serious as if we had duly attended a place devoted to public worship. My sentiments have undergone a great change since 1803, respecting the absolute necessity of keeping the Sabbath by a regular attendance at church. D.W.'*

Throughout the whole tour no distinction seems to have been made between Saturday and Sunday. One would have thought that, if nothing else, sympathy at least, which they did not lack, would have led Wordsworth and his sister to turn aside and share the Sabbath worship of the native people. Even the tired jade might have put in his claim for his Sabbath rest; not to mention the scandal which the sight of Sunday travellers in lonely parts of Scotland must then have caused, and the name they must many a time have earned for themselves, of 'Sabbath-breakers.' This last entry of 1832, however, marks a change, which, if it came to Dorothy, came not less decidedly to her brother. This change has been often remarked on, and has been stigmatized by 'the enlightened ones' as 'the reaction.' They say that the earlier nature-worship, which they call Pantheistic, speaks the true and genuine man; the later and more consciously Christian mood they regard as the product, not of deepened experience, but of timidity, or at least as the sign of decreasing insight. It is not so that I would interpret it. Wordsworth and his sister, with their rare gift of soul and eye, saw further into nature, and felt it more profoundly than common men can, and had no doubt found there something which the gross world dreams not of. They recovered thence a higher teaching, which men for ages had lost. They learnt to think of God as being actually very near to them in all they saw and heard; not as the mechanical Artificer, who makes a world and then dwells aloof from it, but as

'The Being that is in the clouds and air,
That is in the green leaves among the groves.'

In nature, which to most eyes is but a dull lifeless mass, impelled by dead mechanic movements, their finer spirits were aware of a breathing life, a living Presence, distinct, yet not alien from, their own spirits, and thence they drank life, and strength, and joy. And not in nature alone, but from their own hearts, from the deep places of their moral nature, and from their minglings with their fellow-men, they could oftentimes overhear

'The still sad music of humanity,
Nor harsh nor grating, though of ample power
To chasten and subdue.'

And through this they learned to feel for themselves, and not conventionally, the upholding presence of One on whom the soul's 'dark foundations rest.' Likely enough in the prime of their strength they may have imagined that these teachings coming from nature and from man were in themselves enough.

But when sorrow and bereavement came, and with them the deepened sense of sin and of utter need, they learned that in nature alone was nothing which in the end they could abide by. They had been true to the lights they had, and they were led on to higher. They were led to go beyond nature and man for their ultimate support, and to overhear from that higher region another, 'diviner tone, into which all the strains of this world's music are ultimately to be resolved.' The Poet, nor less his sister, came at length to feel, what philosophers find so hard to believe,—that The Being whom he had long known as near him in the solitudes of nature, as close to the beatings of his own heart, was He who had so loved him as to die for him. True it is that this later and more distinctly Christian experience is but faintly reflected in Wordsworth's poetry, compared with the earlier naturalistic mood. But this is explained by the fact that, before the later experience became prominent; the early fervour of poetic creation had already passed. Not the less for this, however, was the poet's later conviction; a riper, more advanced wisdom—not a etrogression.

CUILALUINN, June, 1874.   J. C. SHAIRP

PUBLISHER'S NOTE AND ACKNOWLEDGEMENT

We had been asked to have a look at the book by one of our clients, to see if it could be republished in some way, to make it more readable, possibly illustrated and edited to make it fit the pocket for a journey, such as a tour of Scotland. The original appendix was removed and footnotes were brought up to the original phrase and placed within brackets to help with the pace of reading. It was also felt that the illustrations should not be put within Dorothy's text, in order to retain the flow of her thoughts and respect her words; these are placed at the end of each week's travels. (We find in Haldane's, "The Drove Roads of Scotland," that Dorothy is constantly mentioned as an historical reference.)

Many of us are familiar with the poem, "Solitary Reaper," and it is remarkable to find it here in its original context in the Highlands of Scotland. Who can imagine travelling in a Scotland with few metalled roads and little communication, apart from the canals? Travelling in ordinary clothes, with ordinary footwear, Dorothy and William made their Scottish journey of over 600 miles in six weeks. Today, if you were driving it would take around eight hours.

At the beginning of the journey we find Coleridge and William appearing in the narrative, but as the journey progresses, the people of Scotland and nature come to the fore: the manager of the hotel at Arrochar who refuses them lodgings, the Highland chief at Loch Katrine on his horse with his servant, the greatly obese woman with her feet in a basin and the power of Loch Lomond at Inversnaid. Dorothy manages to bring in the most human of pictures on this journey. She also meets a stubborn servant who does not give them entrance to a castle, even though this has been arranged. In Glasgow she peeps into the Tontine at Glasgow Cross and sees the Glaswegian men chattering over coffee and as she goes through Partick four boys get a "hudgie" on her cart. She notices everything about them and how well educated they are; their rich clothes - and their bare feet! She enjoys their company and their conversation.

In the Highlands she remarks on the majesty and the power of the land. When going through Tyndrum she notices the people at worship at a prayer/mass rock. At the Inveroran Hotel she meets the Highland drovers and is struck by the atmosphere and the excitement of the situation (they were in the kitchen) - and the dogs! Later she meets them again at Falkirk where they greet her as a friend. This overpowers her emotionally. She had never been introduced to them but was greeted as an old acquaintance. (They actually saw her from the Black Hills at Glen Etive.p168) When in Appin she meets the tinkers with their fishing rods – a poor man's feeding tools. In the context of Appin we are reminded of the Appin murder and James of the Glens and Alan Breck Stewart. The latter was seen at the murder site with a fishing rod.

Her diet seems to have been mainly oats, milk, eggs and the occasional 'fowl'. When she is out in the rain she gets drenched through. When it is wet everything is wet, including the sheets and blankets. In the Lowlands she goes through Roslin and mentions the chapel. Above all, she meets Walter Scott who has done so much to romanticise Scotland; then she is home.

This is, indeed, a recollection, because she lost her original notes and recounted the journey from memory. What she wrote was intended to be read out to the family in an evening around the fire. She never forgot her journey and the people and families she met.

Dorothy came back to Scotland in the 1820s, but sadly we know very little of this journey.

This book was set up in Claris Works 5, took over 40 working hours to initially prepare and the illustrations are from the publisher's collection and those of the family. We would like to record our special thanks to Clydeside Press and the librarian and staff of the Mitchell Library, Glasgow, for their enthusiastic, professional help in the research and printing of this publication.

Netherton, Glasgow   *20th January 2014*

RECOLLECTIONS

OF

A TOUR MADE IN SCOTLAND.

A.D. 1803.

FIRST WEEK

William and I parted from Mary on Sunday afternoon, August 14th, 1803; and William, Coleridge, and I left Keswick on Monday morning, the 15th, at twenty minutes after eleven o'clock. The day was very hot; we walked up the hills, and along all the rough road, which made our walking half the day's journey. Travelled under the foot of

Carrock, a mountain covered with stones on the lower part; above, it is very rocky, but sheep pasture there. We saw several where there seemed to be no grass to tempt them. Passed the foot of Grisdale and Mosedale, both pastoral valleys, narrow, and soon terminating in the mountains—green, with scattered trees and houses, and each a beautiful stream. At Grisdale our horse backed upon a steep bank where the road was not fenced, just above a pretty mill at the foot of the valley; and we had a second threatening of a disaster in crossing a narrow bridge between the two dales; but this was not the fault of either man or horse. Slept at Mr.Younghusband's public-house, Hesket-Newmarket. In the evening walked to Caldbeck Falls, a delicious spot in which to breathe out a summer's day—limestone rocks, hanging trees, pools, and water breaks—caves and caldrons which have been honoured with fairy names, and no doubt continue in the fancy of the neighbourhood to resound with fairy revels.

Tuesday, August 16th—Passed Rose Castle upon the Caldew, an ancient building of red stone, with sloping gardens, an ivied gateway, velvet lawns, old garden walls, trim flower-borders with stately and luxuriant flowers. We walked up to the house and stood some minutes watching the swallows that flew about restlessly, and flung their shadows upon the sunbright walls of the old building; the shadows glanced and twinkled, interchanged and crossed each other, expanded and shrunk up, appeared and disappeared every instant; as I observed to William and Coleridge, seeming more like living things than the birds themselves. Dined at Carlisle; the town in a bustle with the assizes; so many strange faces known in former times and recognised, that it half seemed as if I ought to know them all, and, together with the noise, the fine ladies, etc., they put me into confusion. This day Hatfield was condemned. (1) I stood at the door of the gaoler's house, where he was; William entered the house, and Coleridge saw him; I fell into conversation with a debtor, who told me in a dry way that he was 'far over-learned,' and another man observed to William that we might learn from Hatfield's fate 'not to meddle with pen and ink.' We gave a shilling to my companion, whom we found out to be a friend of the family, a fellow-sailor with my brother John 'in Captain Wordsworth's ship.'(2) Walked upon the city walls which are broken down in places and crumbling away, and most disgusting from filth.

The city and neighbourhood of Carlisle disappointed me; the banks of the river quite flat, and, though the holms are rich, there is not much beauty in the vale from the want of trees—at least to the eye of a person coming from England, and, I scarcely know how, but to me the holms had not a natural look; there was something townish in their appearance, a dullness in their strong deep green. To Longtown—not very interesting, except from the long views over the flat country; the road rough, chiefly newly mended. Reached Longtown after sunset, a town of brick houses belonging chiefly to the Graham family. Being in the form of a cross and not long, it had been better called Crosstown. There are several shops, and it is not a very small place; but I could not meet with a silver thimble, and bought a halfpenny brass one. Slept at the Graham's Arms, a large inn. Here, as everywhere else, the people seemed utterly insensible of the enormity of Hatfield's offences; the ostler told William that he was quite a gentleman, paid every one genteelly, etc. etc. He and 'Mary' had walked together to Gretna Green; a heavy rain came on when they were there; a returned chaise happened to pass, and the driver would have taken them up; but 'Mr. Hopes' carriage was to be sent for; he did not choose to accept the chaise-driver's offer.

Wednesday, August 17th—Left Longtown after breakfast. About half-a-mile from the town a guide-post and two roads, to Edinburgh and Glasgow; we took the left hand road, to Glasgow. Here saw a specimen of the luxuriance of the heath-plant, as it grows in Scotland; it was in the enclosed plantations—perhaps sheltered by them. These plantations appeared to be not well grown for their age; the trees were stunted. Afterwards the road, treeless, over a peat-moss common—the Solway Moss; here and there an earth-built hut with its peat stack, a scanty growing willow hedge round the kail-garth, perhaps the cow pasturing near,—a little lass watching it,—the dreary waste cheered by the endless singing of larks.

We enter Scotland by crossing the river Sark; on the Scotch side of the bridge the ground is unenclosed pasturage; it was very green, and scattered over with that yellow flowered plant which we call grunsel; the hills heave and swell prettily enough; cattle feeding; a few corn-fields near the river. At the top of the hill opposite is Springfield, a village built by Sir William Maxwell—a dull uniformity in the houses, as is usual when all built at one time, or belonging to one individual, each just big enough for two people to live in, and in which a family, large or small as it may happen, is crammed. There the marriages are performed. Further on, though almost contiguous, is Gretna Green, upon a hill and among trees. This sounds well, but it is a dreary place; the stone houses dirty and miserable, with broken windows. There is a pleasant view from the churchyard over Solway Firth to the Cumberland Mountains. Dined at Annan. On our left, as we travelled along, appeared the Solway Firth and the mountains beyond, but the near country dreary. Those houses by the roadside which are built of stone, are comfortless and dirty; but we peeped into a clay 'biggin' that was very 'canny,' and I daresay will be as warm as a swallow's nest in winter. The town of Annan made me think of France and Germany; many of the houses large and gloomy, the size of them outrunning the comforts. One thing which was like Germany pleased me: the shopkeepers express their calling by some device or painting; bread-bakers have biscuits, loaves, cakes painted on their window-shutters; blacksmiths horses' shoes, iron tools, etc. etc.; and so on through all trades.

Reached Dumfries at about nine o'clock—market-day; met crowds of people on the road and every one had a smile for us and our car. . .

The inn was a large house, and tolerably comfortable; Mr. Rogers and his sister, whom we had seen at our own cottage at Grasmere a few days before, had arrived there that same afternoon on their way to the Highlands; but we did not see them till the next morning, and only for about a quarter of ah hour.

Thursday, August 18th—Went to the churchyard where Burns is buried. A bookseller accompanied us. He showed us the outside of Burns's house, where he had lived the last three years of his life, and where he died. It has a mean appearance, and is in a bye situation;whitewashed, dirty about the doors, as almost all Scotch houses are; flowering plants in the windows.

Went on to visit his grave. He lies at a corner of the churchyard, and his second son, Francis Wallace, beside him. There is no stone to mark the spot (3) but a hundred guineas have been collected, to be expended on some sort of monument. 'There,' said the bookseller, pointing to a pompous monument, 'there lies Mr. Such-a-one'—I have forgotten his name,—'a remarkably clever man; he was an attorney, and hardly ever lost a cause he undertook. Burns made many a lampoon upon him, and there they rest, as you see.' We looked at the grave with melancholy and painful reflections, repeating to each other his own verses:—

'Is there a man whose judgment clear
Can others teach the course to steer,
Yet runs himself life's mad career
Wild as the wave?
Here let him pause, and through a tear
Survey this grave.

The poor Inhabitant below
Was quick to learn, and wise to know,
And keenly felt the friendly glow
And softer flame;
But thoughtless follies laid him low,
And stain'd his name.'

The churchyard is full of grave-stones and expensive monuments in all sorts of fantastic shapes—obelisk-wise, pillar-wise, etc. In speaking of Gretna Green, I forgot to mention that we visited the churchyard. The church is like a huge house; indeed, so are all the churches, with a steeple, not a square tower or spire,—a sort of thing more like a glass-house chimney than a Church of England steeple; grave-stones in abundance, few verses, yet there were some—no texts. Over the graves of married women the maiden name instead of that of the husband, 'spouse' instead of 'wife,' and the place of abode preceded by 'in' instead of 'of.' When our guide had left us, we turned again to Burns's house. Mrs. Burns was gone to spend some time by the sea-shore with her children. We spoke to the servant-maid at the door, who invited us forward, and we sat down in the parlour. The walls were coloured with a blue wash; on one side of the fire was a mahogany desk, opposite to the window a clock, and over the desk a print from the 'Cotter's Saturday Night,' which Burns mentions in one of his letters, having received as a present. The house was cleanly and neat in the inside, the stairs of stone, scoured white, the kitchen on the right side of the passage, the parlour on the left. In the room above the parlour the Poet died, and his son after him in the same room. The servant told us she had lived five years with Mrs. Burns, who was now in great sorrow for the death of 'Wallace.' She said that Mrs. Burns's youngest son was at Christ's Hospital.

We were glad to leave Dumfries, which is no agreeable place to them who do not love the bustle of a town that seems to be rising up to wealth. We could think of little else but poor Burns, and his moving about on that unpoetic ground. In our road to Brownhill, the next stage, we passed Ellisland at a little distance and on our right his farmhouse. We might there have had more pleasure in looking round, if we had been nearer to the spot; but there is no thought surviving in connexion with Burns's daily life that is not heart-depressing. Travelled through the vale of Nith, here little like a vale, it is so broad, with irregular hills rising up on each side, in outline resembling the old-fashioned valances of a bed. There is a great deal of arable land; the corn ripe; trees here and there—plantations, clumps, coppices, and a newness in everything. So much of the gorse and broom rooted out that you wonder why it is not all gone, and yet there seems to be almost as much gorse and broom as corn; and they grow one among another you know not how. Crossed the Nith; the vale becomes narrow, and very pleasant; corn fields, green hills, clay cottages; the river's bed rocky, with woody banks. Left the Nith about a mile and a half, and reached Brownhill, a lonely inn, where we slept. The view from the windows was pleasing, though some travellers might have been disposed to quarrel with it for its general nakedness; yet there was abundance of corn. It is an open country— open, yet all over hills. At a little distance were many cottages among trees that looked very pretty. Brownhill is about seven or eight miles from Ellisland. I fancied to myself, while I was sitting in the parlour, that Burns might have caroused there, for most likely his rounds extended so far, and this thought gave a melancholy interest to the smoky walls. It was as pretty a room as a thoroughly dirty one could be—a square parlour painted green, but so covered over with smoke and dirt that it looked not unlike green seen through black gauze. There were three windows, looking three ways, a buffet ornamented with tea-cups, a superfine largeish looking-glass with gilt ornaments spreading far and wide, the glass spotted with dirt, some ordinary alehouse pictures, and above the chimney-piece a print in a much better style—as William guessed, taken from a painting by Sir Joshua Reynolds—of some lady of quality, in the character of Euphrosyne. 'Ay,' said the servant girl, seeing that we looked at it, 'there's many travellers would give a deal for that. It's more admired than any in the house.' We could not but smile; for the rest were such as may be found in the basket of any Italian image and picture hawker.

William and I walked out after dinner; Coleridge was not well, and slept upon the carriage cushions. We made our way to the cottages among the little hills and knots of wood, and then saw what a delightful country this part of Scotland might be made by planting forest trees. The ground all over heaves and swells like a sea; but for miles there are neither trees nor hedgerows, only 'mound' fences and tracts; or slips of corn, potatoes, clover—with hay between, and barren land; but near the cottages many hills and hillocks covered with wood. We passed some fine trees, and paused under the shade of one close by an old mansion that seemed, from its neglected state, to be inhabited by farmers. But I must say that many of the 'gentlemen's' houses which we have passed in Scotland have an air of neglect, and even of desolation. It was a beech, in the full glory of complete and perfect growth, very tall, with one thick stem mounting to a considerable height, which was split into four 'thighs,' as Coleridge afterwards called them, each in size a fine tree. Passed another mansion, now tenanted by a schoolmaster; many boys playing upon the lawn. I cannot take leave of the country which we passed through to-day, without mentioning that we saw the Cumberland mountains within half a mile of Ellisland, Burns's house, the last view we had of them. Drayton has prettily described the connexion which this neighbourhood has with ours when he makes Skiddaw say—

'Scurfell {Criffel} from the sky,
That Anadale {Annandale} doth crown, with a most amorous eye,
Salutes me every day, or at my pride looks grim,
Oft threatning me with clouds, as I oft threatning him.'

These lines recurred to William's memory, and we talked of Burns, and of the prospect he must have had, perhaps from his own door, of Skiddaw and his companions, indulging ourselves in the fancy that we *might* have been personally known to each other, and he have looked upon those objects with more pleasure for our sakes. We talked of Coleridge's children and family, then at the foot of Skiddaw, and our own new-born John, a few miles behind it; while the grave of Burns's son, which we had just seen by the side of his father, and some stories heard at Dumfries respecting the dangers his surviving children were exposed to, filled us with melancholy concern, which had a kind of connexion with ourselves. In recollection of this, William long afterwards wrote the following Address to the sons of the ill-fated poet:—

Ye now are panting up life's hill,
Tis twilight time of good and ill,
And more than common strength and skill
Must ye display,
If ye would give the better wil
Its lawful sway.
Strong-bodied if ye be to bear
Intemperance with less harm,
beware,
But if your Father's wit ye share,
Then, then indeed,
Ye Sons of Burns, for watchful care
There will be need.

For honest men delight will take
To shew you favour for his sake,
Will flatter you, and Fool and Rake
Your steps pursue,
And of your Father's name will make
A snare for you.
Let no mean hope your souls enslave,
Be independent, generous, brave;
Your Father such example gave,
And such revere,
But be admonished by his grave,
And think and fear.

Friday, August 19th—Open country for a considerable way. Passed through the village of Thornhill, built by the Duke of Queensberry; the 'brother-houses' so small that they might have been built to stamp a character of insolent pride on his own huge mansion of Drumlanrigg, which is full in view on the opposite side of the Nith. This mansion is indeed very large; but to us it appeared like a gathering together of little things. The roof is broken into a hundred pieces, cupolas, etc., in the shape of casters, conjuror's balls, cups, and the like. The situation would be noble if the woods had been left standing; but they have been cut down not long ago, and the hills above and below the house are quite bare. About a mile and a half from Drumlanrigg is a turnpike gate at the top of a hill. We left our car with the man, and turned aside into a field where we looked down upon the Nith, which runs far below in a deep and rocky channel; the banks woody; the view pleasant down the river towards Thornhill; an open country—corn fields, pastures, and scattered trees. Returned to the turnpike house, a cold spot upon a common, black cattle feeding close to the door. Our road led us down the hill to the side of the Nith, and we travelled along its banks for some miles. Here were clay cottages perhaps every half or quarter of a mile. The bed of the stream rough with rocks, banks irregular, now woody, now bare; here a patch of broom, there of corn, then of pasturage; and hills green or heathy above. We were to have given our horse meal and water at a public-house in one of the hamlets we passed through, but missed the house, for, as is common in Scotland, it was without a sign-board. Travelled on, still beside the Nith, till we came to a turnpike house, which stood rather high on the hill-side, and from the door we looked a long way up and down the river. The air coldish, the wind strong.

We asked the turnpike man to let us have some meal and water. He had no meal, but luckily we had part of a feed of corn brought from Keswick, and he procured some hay at a neighbouring house. In the meantime I went into the house, where was an old man with a grey plaid over his shoulders, reading a newspaper. On the shelf lay a volume of the Scotch Encyclopaedia, a History of England, and some other books. The old man was a caller by the way. The man of the house came back, and we began to talk. He was very intelligent; had travelled all over England, Scotland, and Ireland as a gentleman's servant, and now lived alone in that lonesome place. He said he was tired of his bargain, for he feared he should lose by it. And he had indeed a troublesome office, for coal-carts without number were passing by, and the drivers seemed to do their utmost to cheat him. There is always something peculiar in the house of a man living alone. This was but half-furnished, yet nothing seemed wanting for his comfort, though a female who had travelled half as far would have needed fifty other things. He had no other meat or drink in the house but oat bread and cheese—the cheese was made with the addition of seeds—and some skimmed milk. He gave us of his bread and cheese, and milk, which proved to be sour.

We had yet ten or eleven miles to travel and no food with us. William lay under the wind in a corn-field below the house, being not well enough to partake of the milk and bread. Coleridge gave our host a pamphlet, 'The Crisis of the Sugar Colonies;' he was well acquainted with Burns's poems. There was a politeness and a manly freedom in this man's manners which pleased me very much. He told us that he had served a gentleman, a captain in the army—he did not know who he was, for none of his relations had ever come to see him, but he used to receive many letters—that he had lived near Dumfries till they would let him stay no longer. He made such havoc with the game; his whole delight from morning till night, and the long year through, was in field sports; he would be on his feet the worst days in winter, and wade through snow up to the middle after his game. If he had company he was in tortures till they were gone; he would then throw off his coat and put on an old jacket not worth half-a-crown. He drank his bottle of wine every day, and two if he had better sport than usual. Ladies sometimes came to stay with his wife, and he often carried them out in an Irish jaunting-car, and if they vexed him he would choose the dirtiest roads possible, and spoil their clothes by jumping in and out of the car, and treading upon them. 'But for all that'—and so he ended all—'he was a good fellow, and a clever fellow.' And he liked him well. He would have ten or a dozen hares in the larder at once, he half maintained his family with game, and he himself was very fond of eating of the spoil—unusual with true heart-and-soul sportsmen. The man gave us an account of his farm where he had lived, which was so cheap and pleasant that we thought we should have liked to have had it ourselves. Soon after leaving the turnpike house we turned up a hill to the right, the road for a little way very steep;bare hills, with sheep.

After ascending a little while we heard the murmur of a stream far below us, and saw it flowing downwards on our left, towards the Nith, and before us, between steep green hills, coming along a winding valley. The simplicity of the prospect impressed us very much. There was a single cottage by the brook side; the dell was not heathy, but it was impossible not to think of Peter Bell's Highland Girl.

We now felt indeed that we were in Scotland; there was a natural peculiarity in this place. In the scenes of the Nith it had not been the same as England, but yet not simple, naked Scotland. The road led us down the hill, and now there was no room in the vale, but for the river and the road; we had sometimes the stream to the right, sometimes to the left. The hills were pastoral, but we did not see many sheep; green smooth turf on the left, no ferns. On the right the heath-plant grew in abundance, of the most exquisite colour; it covered a whole hillside, or it was in streams and patches. We travelled along the vale without appearing to ascend for some miles; all the reaches were beautiful, in exquisite proportion, the hill seeming very high from being so near to us. It might have seemed a valley which nature had kept to herself for pensive thoughts and tender feelings, but that we were reminded at every turning of the road of something beyond, by the coal-carts which were travelling towards us. Though these carts broke in upon the tranquillity of the glen, they added much to the picturesque effect of the different views, which indeed wanted nothing, though perfectly bare, houseless, and treeless.

After some time our road took us upwards, towards the end of the valley. Now the steeps were heathy all around. Just as we began to climb the hill, we saw three boys who came down the cleft of a brow on our left; one carried a fishing-rod, and the hats of all were braided with honeysuckles; they ran after one another as wanton as the wind. I cannot express what a character of beauty those few honeysuckles in the hats of the three boys gave to the place: what bower could they have come from? We walked up the hill, met two well-dressed travellers, the woman barefoot. Our little lads, before they had gone far, were joined by some half-dozen of their companions, all without shoes and stockings. They told us they lived at Wanlockhead, the village above, pointing to the top of the hill; they went to school and learned Latin, Virgil, and some of them Greek, Homer, but when Coleridge began to inquire further, off they ran, poor things! I suppose afraid of being examined.

When, after a steep ascent, we had reached the top of the hill, we saw a village about half a mile before us, on the side of another hill, which rose up above the spot where we were, after a descent, a sort of valley or hollow. Nothing grew upon this ground, or the hills above or below, but heather, yet round about the village—which consisted of a great number of huts, all alike, and all thatched, with a few larger slated houses among them, and a single modern built one of a considerable size—were a hundred patches of cultivated ground, potatoes, oats, hay, and grass. We were struck with the sight of haycocks fastened down with aprons, sheets, pieces of sacking—as we supposed, to prevent the wind from blowing them away. We afterwards found that this practice was very general in Scotland. Every cottage seemed to have its little plot of ground, fenced by a ridge of earth; this plot contained two or three different divisions, kail, potatoes, oats, hay; the houses all standing in lines, or never far apart;

the cultivated ground was all together also, and made a very strange appearance with its many greens among the dark brown hills, neither tree nor shrub growing; yet the grass and the potatoes looked greener than elsewhere, owing to the bareness of the neighbouring hills; it was indeed a wild and singular spot—to use a woman's illustration, like a collection of patchwork, made of pieces as they might have chanced to have been cut by the mantua-maker, only just smoothed to fit each other, the different sorts of produce being in such a multitude of plots, and those so small and of such irregular shapes. Add to the strangeness of the village itself that we had been climbing upwards, though gently, for many miles, and for the last mile and a half up a steep ascent, and did not know of any village till we saw the boys who had come out to play. The air was very cold, and one could not help thinking what it must be in winter, when those hills, now 'red brown,' should have their three months' covering of snow.

The village, as we guessed, is inhabited by miners; the mines belong to the Duke of Queensberry. The road to the village, down which the lads scampered away, was straight forward. I must mention that we met, just after we had parted from them, another little fellow, about six years old, carrying a bundle over his shoulder; he seemed poor and half-starved, and was scratching his fingers, which were covered with the itch. He was a miner's son, and lived at Wanlockhead; did not go to school, but this was probably en account of his youth. I mention him because he seemed to be a proof that there was poverty and wretchedness among these people, though we saw no other symptom of it; and afterwards we met scores of the inhabitants of this same village. Our road turned to the right, and we saw, it the distance of less than a mile, a tall upright building of grey stone, with several men standing upon the roof, as if they were looking out over battlements. It stood beyond the village, upon higher ground, as if presiding over it,—a kind of enchanter's castle, which it might have been, a place where Don Quixote would have gloried in. When we drew nearer we saw, coming out of the side of the building, a large machine or lever, in appearance like a great forge-hammer, as we supposed for raising water out of the mines. It heaved upwards once in half a minute with a slow motion, and seemed to rest to take breath at the bottom, its motion being accompanied with a sound between a groan and 'jike.'

There would have been something in this object very striking in any place, as it was impossible not to invest the machine with some faculty of intellect; it seemed to have made the first step from brute matter to life and purpose, showing its progress by great power. William made a remark to this effect, and Coleridge observed that it was like a giant with one idea. At all events, the object produced a striking effect in that place, where everything was in unison with it—particularly the building itself, which was turret-shaped, and with the figures upon it resembled much one of the fortresses in the wooden cuts of Bunyan's 'Holy War.' After ascending a considerable way we began to descend again; and now we met a team of horses dragging an immense tree to the lead mines, to repair or add to the building, and presently after we came to a cart, with another large tree, and one horse left in it, right in the middle of the highway. We were a little out of humour, thinking we must wait till the team came back. There were men and boys without number all staring at us. After a little consultation they set their shoulders to the cart, and with a good heave all at once they moved it, and we passed along. These people were decently dressed, and their manners decent; there was no hooting or impudent laughter. Leadhills, another mining village, was the place of our destination for the night; and soon after we had passed the cart we came in sight of it. This village and the mines belong to Lord Hopetoun; it has more stone houses than Wanlockhead, one large old mansion, and a considerable number of old trees—beeches, I believe. The trees told of the coldness of the climate; they were more brown than green—far browner than the ripe grass of the little hay-garths. Here, as at Wanlockhead, were haycocks, hay-stacks, potato-beds, and kail-garths in every possible variety of shape, but, I suppose from the irregularity of the ground, it looked far less artificial—indeed, I should think that a painter might make several beautiful pictures in this village. It straggles down both sides of a mountain glen. As I have said, there is a large mansion. There is also a stone building that looks like a school, and the houses are single, or in clusters, or rows as it may chance.

We passed a decent-looking inn, the Hopetoun Arms; but the house of Mrs. Otto, a widow, had been recommended to us with high encomiums. We did not then understand Scotch inns, and were not quite satisfied at first with our accommodations, but all things were smoothed over by degrees; we had a fire lighted in our dirty parlour, tea came after a reasonable waiting; and the fire with the gentle aid of twilight, burnished up the room into cheerful comfort. Coleridge was weary; but William and I walked out after tea. We talked with one of the miners, who informed us that the building, which we had supposed to be a school, was a library belonging to the village. He said they had got a book into it a few weeks ago, which had cost thirty pounds, and that they had all sorts of books. 'What! Have you Shakespeare?' 'Yes, we have that,' and we found, on further inquiry, that they had a large library,(4) of long standing, that Lord Hopetoun had subscribed liberally to it, and that gentlemen who came with him were in the habit of making larger or smaller donations. Each man who had the benefit of it paid a small sum monthly—I think about fourpence.

The man we talked with spoke much of the comfort and quiet in which they lived one among another; he made use of a noticeable expression, saying that they were 'very peaceable people considering they lived so much underground;'—wages were about thirty pounds a year; they had land for potatoes, warm houses, plenty of coals, and only six hours' work each day, so that they had leisure for reading if they chose. He said the place was healthy, that the inhabitants lived to a great age; and indeed we saw no appearance of ill-health in their countenances; but it is not common for people working in lead mines to be healthy; and I have since heard that it is not a healthy place. However this may be, they are unwilling to allow it; for the landlady the next morning, when I said to her 'You have a cold climate?' replied, 'Ay, but it is *varra halesome.*' We inquired of the man respecting the large mansion; he told us that it was built, as we might see, in the form of an H, and belonged to the Hopetouns, and they took their title from thence, and that part of it was used as a chapel.

We went close to it, and were a good deal amused with the building itself, standing forth in bold contradiction of the story which I daresay *{There is some mistake here. The Hopetoun title was not taken from any place in the Leadhills, much less from the house shaped like an H.—Ed.}* every man of Leadhills tells, and every man believes, that it is in the shape of an

H; it is but half an H, and one must be very accommodating to allow it even so much, for the legs are far too short.

We visited the burying-ground, a plot of land not very small, crowded with graves, and upright grave-stones, overlooking the village and the dell. It was now the closing in of evening. Women and children were gathering in the linen for the night, which was bleaching by the burn-side;—the graves overgrown with grass, such as, by industrious culture, had been raised up about the houses; but there were bunches of heather here and there, and with the blue-bells that grew among the grass the small plot of ground had a beautiful and wild appearance.

William left me, and I went to a shop to purchase some thread; the woman had none that suited me, but she would send a 'wee lad' to the other shop. In the meantime I sat with the mother, and was much pleased with her manner and conversation. She had an excellent fire, and her cottage though very small, looked comfortable and cleanly; but remember I saw it only by firelight. She confirmed what the man had told us of the quiet manner in which they lived; and indeed her house and fireside seemed to need nothing to make it a cheerful happy spot, but health and good humour. There was a bookishness, a certain formality in this woman's language, which was very remarkable. She had a dark complexion, dark eyes, and wore a very white cap, much over her face, which gave her the look of a French woman, and indeed afterwards the women on the roads frequently reminded us of French women, partly from the extremely white caps of the elder women, and still more perhaps from a certain gaiety and party-coloured appearance in their dress in general. White bed-gowns are very common, and you rarely meet a young girl with either hat or cap; they buckle up their hair often in a graceful manner. I returned to the inn, and went into the kitchen to speak with the landlady; she had made a hundred hesitations when I told her we wanted three beds. At last she confessed she had three beds, and showed me into a parlour which looked damp and cold, but she assured me in a tone that showed she was unwilling to be questioned further, that all her beds were well aired. I sat a while by the kitchen fire with the landlady, and began to talk to her; but, much as I had heard in her praise—for the shopkeeper had told me she was a very discreet woman—I cannot say that her

47

manners pleased me much. But her servant made amends, for she was as pleasant and cheerful a lass as was ever seen; and when we asked her to do anything, she answered, 'Oh yes,' with a merry smile, and almost ran to get us what we wanted. She was about sixteen years old: wore shoes and stockings, and had her hair tucked up with a comb. The servant at Brownhill was a coarse-looking wench, barefoot and barelegged. I examined the kitchen round about; it was crowded with furniture, drawers, cupboards, dish-covers, pictures, pans, and pots, arranged without order, except that the plates were on shelves, and the dish-covers hung in rows; these were very clean, but floors, passages, staircase, everything else dirty. There were two beds in recesses in the wall; above one of them I noticed a shelf with some books:—it made me think of Chaucer's Clerke of Oxenforde:—

> *'Liever had he at his bed's head*
> *Twenty books clothed in black and red.'*

They were baking oat-bread, which they cut into quarters, and half-baked over the fire, and half-toasted before it. There was a suspiciousness about Mrs. Otto, almost like ill-nature; she was very jealous of any inquiries that might appear to be made with the faintest idea of a comparison between Leadhills and any other place, except the advantage was evidently on the side of Leadhills. We had nice honey to breakfast. When ready to depart, we learned that we might have seen the library, which we had not thought of till it was too late, and we were very sorry to go away without seeing it.

Saturday, August 20th—Left Leadhills at nine o'clock, regretting much that we could not stay another day, that we might have made more minute inquiries respecting the manner of living of the miners, and been able to form an estimate, from our own observation, of the degree of knowledge, health, and comfort that there was among them. The air was keen and cold; we might have supposed it to be three months later in the season and two hours earlier in the day. The landlady had not lighted us a fire; so I was obliged to get myself toasted in the kitchen, and when we set off I put on both grey cloak and spencer.

Our road carried us down the valley, and we soon lost sight of Leadhills, for the valley made a turn almost immediately, and we saw two miles, perhaps, before us; the glen sloped somewhat rapidly—

heathy, bare, no hut or house. Passed by a shepherd, who was sitting upon the ground, reading, with the book on his knee, screened from the wind by his plaid, while a flock of sheep were feeding near him among the rushes and coarse grass—for, as we descended, we came among lands where grass grew with the heather. Travelled through several reaches of the glen, which somewhat resembled the valley of Menock on the other side of Wanlockhead; but it was not near so beautiful; the forms of the mountains did not melt so exquisitely into each other, and there was a coldness, and, if I may so speak, a want of simplicity in the surface of the earth; the heather was poor, not covering a whole hillside; not in luxuriant streams and beds interveined with rich verdure; but patchy and stunted, with here and there coarse grass and rushes. But we soon came in sight of a spot that impressed us very much. At the lower end of this new reach of the vale was a decayed tree, beside a decayed cottage, the vale spreading out into a level area which was one large field, without fence and without division, of a dull yellow colour; the vale seemed to par-lake of the desolation of the cottage, and to participate in its decay. And yet the spot was, in its nature, so dreary that one would rather have wondered how it ever came to be tenanted by man, than lament that it was left to waste and solitude. Yet the encircling hills were so exquisitely formed that it was impossible to conceive anything more lovely than this place would have been if the valley and hill-sides had been interspersed with trees, cottages, green fields, and hedgerows. But all was desolate; the one large field which filled up the area of the valley appeared, as I have said, in decay, and seemed to retain the memory of its connexion with man in some way analogous to the ruined building; for it was as much of a field as Mr. King's best pasture scattered over with his fattest cattle.

We went on, looking before us, the place losing nothing of its hold upon our minds, when we discovered a woman sitting right in the middle of the field, alone, wrapped up in a grey cloak or plaid. She sat motionless all the time we looked at her, which might be nearly half an hour. We could not conceive why she sat there, for there were neither sheep nor cattle in the field; her appearance was very melancholy. In the meantime our road carried us nearer to the cottage, though we were crossing over the hill to the left, leaving the valley below us, and we perceived that a part of the building was inhabited, and that what we had supposed to be one blasted tree was eight trees, four of which were entirely blasted; the others partly so, and round about the place was a little potato and cabbage garth, fenced with earth. No doubt, that woman had been an inhabitant of the cottage. However this might be, there was so much obscurity and uncertainty about her, and her figure agreed so well with the desolation of the place, that we were indebted to the chance of her being there for some of the most interesting feelings that we had ever had from natural objects connected with man in dreary solitariness.

We had been advised to go along the new road, which would have carried us down the vale; but we met some travellers who recommended us to climb the hill, and go by the village of Crawfordjohn as being much nearer. We had a long hill, and after having reached the top, steep and bad roads, so we continued to walk for a considerable fray. The air was cold and clear—the sky blue. We walked cheerfully along in the sunshine, each of us alone, only William had the charge of the horse and car, so he sometimes took a ride, which did but poorly recompense him for the trouble of driving. I never travelled with more cheerful spirits than this day. Our road was along the side of a high moor: I can always walk over a moor with a light foot; I seem to be drawn more closely to nature in such places than anywhere else; or rather I feel more strongly the power of nature over me, and am better satisfied with myself for being able to find enjoyment in what unfortunately to many persons is either dismal or insipid. This moor, however, was more than commonly interesting; we could see a long way, and on every side of us were larger or smaller tracts of cultivated land. Some were extensive farms, yet in so large a waste they did but look small, with farm-houses, barns, etc., others like little cottages, with enough to feed a cow, and supply the family with vegetables. In looking at these farms we had always one feeling. Why did the plough stop there? Why might not they as well have carried it twice as far? There were no hedgerows near the farms, and very few trees. As we were passing along, we saw an old man, the first we had seen in a Highland bonnet, walking with a staff at a Very slow pace by the edge of one of the moorland cornfields; he wore a grey plaid, and a dog was by his side. There was a scriptural solemnity in this man's figure, a sober simplicity which was most impressive. Scotland is the country above all others that I have seen, in which a man of imagination may carve out his own pleasures. There are so many inhabited solitudes, and the employments of the people are so immediately connected with the places where you find them, and their dresses so simple, so much alike, yet, from their being folding garments, admitting of an endless variety, and falling often so gracefully.

After some time we descended towards a broad vale, passed one farm-house, sheltered by fir trees, with a burn close to it; children playing, linen bleaching. The vale was open pastures and corn-fields unfenced, the land poor. The village of Crawfordjohn on the slope of a hill a long way before us to the left. Asked about our road of a man who was driving a cart; he told us to go through the village, then along some fields, and we should come to a 'herd's house by the burn side.' The highway was right through the vale, unfenced on either side; the people of the village, who were making hay, all stared at us and our carriage. We inquired the road of a middle-aged man, dressed in a shabby black coat, at work in one of the hay fields; he looked like the minister of the place, and when he spoke we felt assured that he was so, for he was not sparing of hard words, which, however, he used with great propriety, and he spoke like one who had been accustomed to dictate. Our car wanted mending in the wheel, and we asked him if there was a blacksmith in the village. 'Yes,' he replied, but when we showed him the wheel he told William that he might mend it himself without a blacksmith, and he would put him in the way; so he fetched hammer and nails and gave his directions, which William obeyed, and repaired the damage entirely to his own satisfaction and the priest's, who did not offer to lend any assistance himself; not as if he would not have been willing in case of need; but as if it were more natural for him to dictate, and because he thought it more fit that William should do it himself. He spoke much about the propriety of every man's lending all the assistance in his power to travellers, and with some ostentation or self-praise. Here I observed a honey-suckle and some flowers growing in a garden, the first I had seen in Scotland. It is a pretty cheerful looking village, but must be very cold in winter; it stands on a hillside, and the vale itself is very high ground, unsheltered by trees.

Left the village behind us, and our road led through arable ground for a considerable way, on which were growing very good crops of corn and potatoes. Our friend accompanied us to show us the way, and Coleridge and he had a scientific conversation concerning the uses and properties of lime and other manures. He seemed to be a well-informed man; somewhat pedantic in his manners; but this might be only the difference between Scotch and English. *{Probably the Rev. John Aird, minister of the parish, 1801-1815-Ed}* Soon after he had parted from us, we came upon a stony, rough road over a black moor; and presently to the 'herd's house by the burn side.' We could hardly cross the burn dry-shod, over which was the only road to the cottage. In England there would have been stepping-stones or a bridge; but the Scotch need not be afraid of wetting their bare feet. The hut had its little kail-garth fenced with earth; there was no other enclosure—but the common, heathy with coarse grass. Travelled along the common for some miles, before we joined the great road from Longtown to Glasgow—saw on the bare hill-sides at a distance, sometimes a solitary farm, now and then a plantation, and one very large wood, with an appearance of richer ground above; but it was so very high we could not think it possible. Having descended considerably, the common was no longer of a peat-mossy brown heath colour, but grass with rushes was its chief produce; there was sometimes a solitary hut, no enclosures except the kail-garth, and sheep pasturing in flocks, with shepherd-boys tending them. I remember one boy in particular; he had no hat on, and only had a grey plaid wrapped about him. It is nothing to describe, but on a bare moor, alone with his sheep, standing, as he did, in utter quietness and silence, there was something uncommonly impressive in his appearance, a solemnity which recalled to our minds the old man in the corn-field. We passed many people who were mowing, or raking the grass of the common; it was little better than rushes; but they did not mow straight forward, only here and there, where it was the best; in such a place hay-cocks had an uncommon appearance to us.

After a long descent we came to some plantations which were not far from Douglas Mill. The country for some time had been growing into cultivation, and now it was a wide vale with large tracts of corn; trees in clumps, no hedgerows, which always make a country look bare and unlovely. For my part, I was better pleased with the desert places we had left behind, though no doubt the inhabitants of this place think it 'a varra bonny spot,' for the Scotch are always pleased with their own abode, be it what it may; and afterwards at Edinburgh, when we were talking with a bookseller of our travels, he observed that it was 'a fine country near Douglas Mill.' Douglas Mill is a single house, a large inn, being one of the regular stages between Longtown and Glasgow, and therefore a fair specimen of the best of the country inns of Scotland. As soon as our car stopped at the door we felt the difference. At an English inn of this size, a waiter, or the master or mistress, would have been at the door immediately, but we remained some time before anybody came; then a barefooted lass made her appearance, but she only looked at us and went away. The mistress, a remarkably handsome woman, showed us into a large parlour; we ordered mutton-chops, and I finished my letter to Mary; writing on the same window-ledge on which William had written to me two years before.

After dinner, William and I sat by a little mill-race in the garden. We had left Leadhills and Wanlockhead far above us, and now were come into a warmer climate; but there was no richness in the face of the country. The shrubs looked cold and poor, and yet there were some very fine trees within a little distance of Douglas Mill, so that the reason, perhaps, why the few low shrubs and trees which were growing in the gardens seemed to be so un-luxuriant, might be, that there being no hedgerows, the general appearance of the country was naked, and I could not help seeing the same coldness where, perhaps, it did not exist in itself to any great degree, for the corn crops are abundant, and I should think the soil is not bad. While we were sitting at the door, two of the landlady's children came out; the elder, a boy about six years old, was running away from his little brother, in petticoats; the ostler called out, 'Sandy, tak' your wee blither wi' you;' another voice from the window, 'Sawny, dinna leave your wee brither;' the mother then came, 'Alexander, tak' your wee brother by the hand;' Alexander obeyed, and the two went off in peace together. We were charged eightpence for hay at this inn, another symptom of our being in Scotland. Left Douglas Mill at about three o'clock; travelled through an open corn country, the tracts of corn large and unenclosed. We often passed women or children who were watching a single cow while it fed upon the slips of grass between the corn. William asked a strong woman, about thirty years of age, who looked like the mistress of a family—I suppose moved by some sentiment of compassion for her being so employed,—if the cow would eat the corn if it were left to itself: she smiled at his simplicity. It is indeed a melancholy thing to see a full-grown woman thus waiting, as it were, body and soul devoted to the poor beast; yet even this is better than working in a manufactory the day through.

We came to a moorish tract; saw before us the hills of Loch Lomond, Ben Lomond and another, distinct each by itself. Not far from the roadside were some benches placed in rows in the middle of a large field, with a sort of covered shed like a sentry-box, but much more like those boxes which the Italian puppet-showmen in London use. We guessed that it was a pulpit or tent for preaching, and were told that a sect met there occasionally, who held that toleration was unscriptural, and would have all religions but their own exterminated. I have forgotten what name the man gave to this sect; we could not learn that it differed in any other respect from the Church of Scotland. Travelled for some miles along the open country, which was all without hedgerows, sometimes arable, sometimes moorish, and often whole tracts covered with grunsel. *{Ragweed}* There was one field, which one might have believed had been sown with grunsel, it was so regularly covered with it—a large square field upon a slope, its boundary marked to our eyes only by the termination of the bright yellow; contiguous to it were other fields of the same size and shape, one of clover, the other of potatoes, all equally regular crops. The oddness of this appearance, the grunsel being uncommonly luxuriant, and the field as yellow as gold, made William laugh. Coleridge was melancholy upon it, observing that there was land enough wasted to rear a healthy child.

We left behind us, considerably to the right, a single high mountain; *{Tinto}* I have forgotten its name; we had had it long in view. Saw before us the river Clyde, its course at right angles to our road, which now made a turn, running parallel with the river; the town of Lanerk in sight long before we came to it. I was somewhat disappointed with the first view of the Clyde (5): the banks, though swelling and varied, had a poverty in their appearance, chiefly from the want of wood and hedgerows. Crossed the river and ascended towards Lanerk, which stands upon a hill. When we were within about a mile of the town, William parted from Coleridge and me, to go to the celebrated waterfalls. Coleridge did not attempt to drive the horse; but led him all the way. We inquired for the best inn, and were told that the New Inn was the best; but that they had very 'genteel apartments' at the Black Bull, and made less charges, and the Black Bull was at the entrance of the town, so we thought we would stop there, as the horse was obstinate and weary. But when we came to the Black Bull we had no wish to enter the apartments; for it seemed the abode of dirt and poverty, yet it was a large building. The town showed a sort of French face, and would have done much more, had it not been for the true British tinge of coal-smoke; the doors and windows dirty, the shops dull, the women too seemed to be very dirty in their dress. The town itself is not ugly; the houses are of grey stone, the streets not very narrow, and the marketplace decent. The New Inn is a handsome old stone building, formerly a gentleman's house. We were conducted into a parlour, where people had been drinking; the tables were unwiped, chairs in disorder, the floor dirty, and the-smell of liquors was most offensive. We were tired, however, and rejoiced in our tea.

The evening sun was now sending a glorious light through the street, which ran from west to east; the houses were of a fire red, and the faces of the people as they walked westward were almost like a blacksmith when he is at work by night. I longed to be out, and meet with William, that we might see the Falls before the day was gone. Poor Coleridge was unwell, and could not go. I inquired my road, and a little girl told me she would go with me to the porter's lodge, where I might be admitted. I was grieved to hear that the Falls of the Clyde were shut up in a gentleman's grounds, and to be viewed only by means of lock and key. Much, however, as the pure feeling with which one would desire to visit such places is disturbed by useless, impertinent, or even unnecessary interference with nature, yet when I was there the next morning I seemed to feel it a less disagreeable

55

thing than in smaller and more delicate spots, if I may use the phrase. My guide, a sensible little girl, answered my inquiries very prettily. She was eight years old, read in the 'Collection,' a book which all the Scotch children whom I have questioned read in. I found it was a collection of hymns; she could repeat several of Dr. Watts'. We passed through a great part of the town, then turned down a steep hill, and came in view of a long range of cotton mills, {*New Lanark, Robert Owen's mills-Ed}* the largest and loftiest I had ever seen; climbed upwards again, our road leading us along the top of the left bank of the river; both banks very steep and richly wooded. The girl left me at the porter's lodge. Having asked after William, I was told that no person had been there, or could enter but by the gate. The night was coming on, therefore I did not venture to go in, as I had no hope of meeting William. I had a delicious walk alone through the wood; the sound of the water was very solemn, and even the cotton mills in the fading light of evening had somewhat of the majesty and stillness of the natural objects. It was nearly dark when I reached the inn. I found Coleridge sitting by a good fire, which always makes an inn room look comfortable. In a few minutes William arrived; he had heard of me at the gate, and followed as quickly as he could, shouting after me. He was pale and exceedingly tired. After he had left us he had taken a wrong road, and while looking about to set himself right had met with a barefooted boy, who said he would go with him. The little fellow carried him by a wild path to the upper of the Falls, the Boniton Linn, and coming down unexpectedly upon it, he was exceedingly affected by the solemn grandeur of the place. This fall is not much admired or spoken of by travellers; you have never a full, breast view of it; it does not make a complete self-satisfying place, an abode of its own, as a perfect waterfall seems to me to do; but the river, down which you look through a long vista of steep and ruin-like rocks, the roaring of the waterfall, and the solemn evening lights, must have been most impressive. One of the rocks on the near bank, even in broad daylight, as we saw it the next morning, is exactly like the fractured arch of an abbey. With the lights and shadows of evening upon it, the resemblance must have been much more striking.

William's guide was a pretty boy, and he was exceedingly pleased with him. Just as they were quitting the waterfall, William's mind being full of the majesty of the scene, the little fellow pointed to the top of a rock, 'There's a fine slae-bush there.' 'Ay,' said William, 'but there are no slaes upon it,' which was true enough; but I suppose the child remembered the slaes of another summer, though, as he said, he was but 'half seven years old,' namely, six and a half. He conducted William to the other fall, and as they were going along a narrow path, they came to a small cavern, where William lost him, and looking about, saw his pretty figure in a sort of natural niche fitted for a statue, from which the boy jumped out laughing, delighted with the success of his trick. William told us a great deal about him, while he sat by the fire, and of the pleasure of his walk, often repeating, 'I wish you had been with me.' Having no change, he gave the boy sixpence, which was certainly, if he had formed any expectations at all, far beyond them; but he received it with the utmost indifference, without any remark of surprise or pleasure; most likely he did not know how many halfpence he could get for it, and twopence would have pleased him more. My little girl was delighted with the sixpence I gave her, and said she would buy a book with it on Monday morning. What a difference between the manner of living and education of boys and of girls among the lower classes of people in towns! She had never seen the Falls of the Clyde, nor had ever been further than the porter's lodge; the boy, I daresay, knew every hiding-place in every accessible rock, as well as the fine 'slae bushes' and the nut trees.

Robert Burns

Ellisland, the home of Burns

Going down the path to Lanark

The River Clyde at Lanark

SECOND WEEK

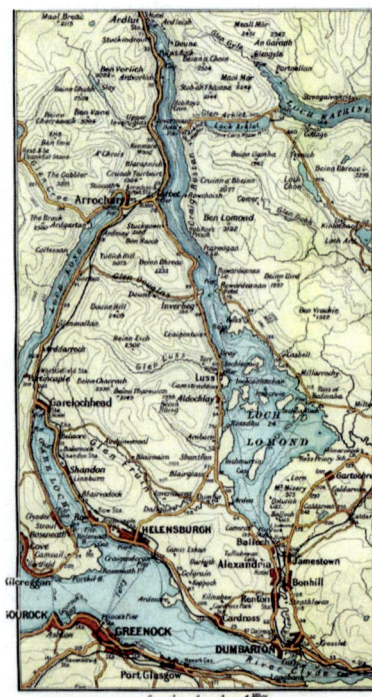

Dorothy followed the route through Glasgow to Loch Lomond,
then Luss, Inversnaid and Tarbet.

Sunday, August 21st—The morning was very hot; a morning to tempt us to linger by the water-side. I wished to have had the day before us, expecting so much from what William had seen; but when we went there, I did not desire to stay longer than till the hour which we had prescribed to ourselves; for it was a rule not to be broken in upon, that the person who conducted us to the Falls was to remain by our side till we chose to depart. We left our inn immediately after breakfast. The lanes were full of people going to church; many of the middle-aged women wore long scarlet cardinals, and were without hats: they brought to my mind the women of Goslar as they used to go to church in their silver or gold caps, with their long cloaks, black or coloured.

The banks of the Clyde, from Lanerk to the Falls, rise immediately from the river; they are lofty and steep, and covered with wood. The road to the Falls is along the top of one of the banks, and to the left you have a prospect of the open country; corn fields and scattered houses. To the right, over the river, the country spreads out, as it were, into a plain covered over with hills, no one hill much higher than another, but hills all over. There were endless pastures overgrown with broom, and scattered trees, without hedges or fences of any kind, and no distinct footpaths. It was delightful to see the lasses in gay dresses running like cattle among the broom, making their way straight forward towards the river, here and there as it might chance. They waded across the stream, and, when they had reached the top of the opposite bank, sat down by the road-side, about half a mile from the town, to put on their shoes and cotton stockings, which they brought tied up in pocket-handkerchiefs. The porter's lodge is about a mile from Lanerk, and the lady's house—for the whole belongs to a lady, whose name I have forgotten *{Lady Mary Ross}*—is upon a hill at a little distance. We walked, after we had entered the private grounds, perhaps two hundred yards along a gravel carriage-road, then came to a little side gate, which opened upon a narrow gravel path under trees, and in a minute and a half, or less, were directly opposite to the great waterfall. I was much affected by the first view of it. The majesty and strength of the water, for I had never before seen so large a cataract, struck me with astonishment, which died away, giving place to more delightful feelings; though there were

59

some buildings that I could have wished had not been there, though at first unnoticed. The chief of them was a neat, white, lady-like house, *{Corehouse}* very near to the waterfall. William and Coleridge however were in a better and perhaps wiser humour, and did not dislike the house; indeed, it was a very nice-looking place, with a moderate-sized garden, leaving the green fields free and open. This house is on the side of the river opposite to the grand house and the pleasure-grounds. The waterfall Cora Linn is composed of two falls, with a sloping space, which appears to be about twenty yards between, but is much more. The basin which receives the fall is enclosed by noble rocks, with trees, chiefly hazels, birch, and ash growing out of their sides whenever there is any hold for them; and a magnificent resting-place it is for such a river; I think more grand than the Falls themselves.

After having stayed some time, we returned by the same footpath into the main carriage-road, and soon came upon what William calls an ell-wide gravel walk, from which we had different views of the Linn. We sat upon a bench, placed for the sake of one of these views, whence we looked down upon the waterfall, and over the open country, and saw a ruined tower, called Wallace's Tower, which stands at a very little distance from the fall, and is an interesting object. A lady and gentleman, more expeditious tourists than ourselves, came to the spot; they left us at the seat, and we found them again at another station above the Falls. Coleridge, who is always good-natured enough to enter into conversation with anybody whom he meets in his way, began to talk with the gentleman, who observed that it was a majestic waterfall. Coleridge was delighted with the accuracy of the epithet, particularly as he had been settling in his own mind the precise meaning of the words grand, majestic, sublime, etc., and had discussed the subject with William at some length the day before. 'Yes, sir,' says Coleridge, 'it is a majestic waterfall.' 'Sublime and beautiful,' replied his friend. Poor Coleridge could make no answer, and, not very desirous to continue the conversation, came to us and related the story, laughing heartily.

The distance from one Linn to the other may be half a mile or more, along the same ell-wide walk. We came to a pleasure-house, of which the little girl had the key; she said it was called the Fog-house, because it was lined with 'fog,' namely moss. On the outside it resembled some of the huts in the prints belonging to Captain Cook's Voyages and within was like a hay-stack scooped out. It was circular, with a dome-like roof, a seat all round fixed to the wall, and a table in the middle,—seat, wall, roof, and table all covered with moss in the neatest manner possible. It was as snug as a bird's nest. I wish we had such a one at the top of our orchard, only a great deal smaller. We afterwards found that huts of the same kind were common in the pleasure-grounds of Scotland; but we never saw any that were so beautifully wrought as this. It had, however, little else to recommend it, the situation being chosen without judgment; there was no prospect from it, nor was it a place of seclusion and retirement, for it stood close to the ell-wide gravel walk. We wished we could have shoved it about a hundred yards further on, when we arrived at a bench which was also close to the walk, for just below the bench, the walk elbowing out into a circle, there was a beautiful spring of clear water, which we could see rise up continually, at the bottom of a round stone basin full to the brim, the water gushing out at a little outlet and passing away under the walk. A reason was wanted for placing the hut where it is; what a good one would this little spring have furnished for bringing it hither! Along the whole of the path were openings at intervals for views of the river, but, as almost always happens in gentlemen's grounds, they were injudiciously managed; you were prepared for a dead stand—by a parapet, a painted seat, or some other device.

We stayed some time at the Boniton Fall, which has one great advantage over the other falls, that it is at the termination of the pleasure-grounds, and we see no traces of the boundary-line; yet, except under some accidental circumstances, such as a sunset like that of the preceding evening, it is greatly inferior to the Cora Linn.

We returned to the inn to dinner. The landlord set the first dish upon the table, as is common in England, and we were well waited upon. This first dish was true Scottish—a boiled sheep's head, with the hair singed off; Coleridge and I ate heartily of it; we had barley broth, in which the sheep's head had been boiled. A party of tourists whom we had met in the pleasure-grounds drove from the door while we were waiting for dinner; I guess they were fresh from England, for they had stuffed the pockets of their carriage with bundles of heather, roots and all, just as if Scotland grew no heather but on the banks of the Clyde. They passed away with their treasure towards Loch Lomond. A party of boys, dressed all alike in blue, very neat, were standing at the chaise-door; we conjectured they were charity scholars; but found on inquiry that they were apprentices to the cotton factory; we were told that they were well instructed in reading and writing. We had seen in the morning a flock of girls dressed in grey coming out of the factory, probably apprentices also.

After dinner set off towards Hamilton, but on foot, for we had to turn aside to the Cartland Rocks, and our car was to meet us on the road. A guide attended us, who might almost in size, and certainly in activity, have been compared with William's companion who hid himself in the niche of the cavern. His method of walking and very quick step soon excited our attention. I could hardly keep up with him; he paddled by our side, just reaching to my shoulder, like a little dog, with his long snout pushed before him—for he had an enormous nose, and walked with his head foremost. I said to him, 'How quick you walk!' he replied, '*That* was *not* quick walking,' and when I asked him what he called so, he said 'Five miles an hour,' and then related in how many hours he had lately walked from Lanerk to Edinburgh, done some errands, and returned to Lanerk—I have forgotten the particulars, but it was a very short time—and added that he had an old father who could walk at the rate of four miles an hour, for twenty-four miles, any day, and had never had an hour's sickness in his life. 'Then,' said I, 'he has not drunk much strong liquor?' 'Yes, enough to drown him.' From his eager manner of uttering this, I inferred that he himself was a drinker; and the man who met us with the car told William that he gained a great deal of money as an errand-goer, but spent it all in tippling. He had been a shoemaker, but could not bear the confinement on account of a weakness in his chest.

The neighbourhood of Lanerk is exceedingly pleasant; we came to a sort of district of glens or little valleys that cleave the hills, leaving a cheerful, open country above them, with no superior hills, but an undulating surface. Our guide pointed to the situation of the Cartland Crags. We were to cross a narrow valley, and walk down on the other side, and then we should be at the spot; but the little fellow made a sharp turn down a footpath to the left, saying, 'We must have some conversation here.' He paddled on with his small pawing feet till we came right opposite to a gentleman's house on the other side of the valley, when he halted, repeating some words, I have forgotten what, which were taken up by the most distinct echo I ever heard—this is saying little: it was the most distinct echo that it is possible to conceive. It shouted the names of our fireside friends in the very tone in which William and Coleridge spoke; but it seemed to make a joke of me, and I could not help laughing at my own voice, it was so shrill and pert, exactly as if someone had been mimicking it very successfully, with an intention of making me ridiculous. I wished Joanna had been there to laugh, (6) for the echo is an excellent laugher, and would have almost made her believe that it was a true story which William has told of her and the mountains. We turned back, crossed the valley, went through the orchard and plantations belonging to the gentleman's house. By the bye, we observed to our guide that the echo must bring many troublesome visitors to disturb the quiet of the owner of that house, 'Oh no,' said he, 'he glories in much company.' He was a native of that neighbourhood, had made a moderate fortune abroad, purchased an estate, built the house, and raised the plantations; and further, had made a convenient walk through his woods to the Cartland Crags. The house was modest and neat, and though not adorned in the best taste, and though the plantations were of fir, we looked at it with great pleasure; there was such true liberality, and kind-heartedness in leaving his orchard path open, and his walks unobstructed by gates. I hope this goodness is not often abused by plunderers of the apple-trees, which were hung with tempting apples close to the path.

At the termination of the little valley, we descended through a wood along a very steep path to a muddy stream running over limestone rocks; turned up to the left along the bed of the stream, and soon we were closed in by rocks on each side. They were very lofty—of limestone, trees starting out of them, high and low, overhanging the stream or shooting up towards the sky. No place of the kind could be more beautiful if the stream had been clear, but it was of a muddy yellow colour; had it been a large river, one might have got the better of the unpleasantness of the muddy water in the grandeur of its

roaring, the boiling up of the foam over the rocks, or the obscurity of
its pools.

We had been told that the Cartland Crags were better worth going to
see than the Falls of the Clyde. I did not think so; but I have seen
rocky dells resembling this before, with clear water instead of that
muddy stream, and never saw anything like the Falls of the Clyde. It
would be a delicious spot to have near one's house; one would linger
out many a day in the cool shade of the caverns, and the stream would
soothe one by its murmuring; still, being an old friend, one would not
love it the less for its homely face. Even we, as we passed along,
could not help stopping for a long while to admire the beauty of the
lazy foam, for ever in motion, and never moved away, in a still place
of the water, covering the whole surface of it with streaks and lines
and ever-varying circles. Wild marjoram grew upon the rocks in great
perfection and beauty; our guide gave me a bunch, and said he should
come hither to collect a store for tea for the winter, and that it was
'varra hale-some:' he drank none else. We walked perhaps half a mile
along the bed of the river; but it might seem to be much further than it
was, owing to the difficulty of the path, and the sharp and many
turnings of the glen. Passed two of Wallace's Caves. There is scarce a
noted glen in Scotland that has not a cave for Wallace or some other
hero. Before we left the river the rocks became less lofty, turned into
a wood through which was a convenient path upwards, met the owner
of the house and the echo-ground, and thanked him for the pleasure
which he had provided for us and other travellers by making such
pretty pathways.

It was four o'clock when we reached the place where the car was
waiting. We were anxious to be off, as we had fifteen miles to go; but
just as we were seating ourselves we found that the cushions were
missing. William was forced to go back to the town, a mile at least,
and Coleridge and I waited with the car. It rained, and we had some
fear that the evening would be wet; but the rain soon ceased, though
the sky continued gloomy—an unfortunate circumstance, for we had
to travel through a beautiful country, and of that sort which is most set
off by sunshine and pleasant weather.

Travelled through the Vale, or Trough of the Clyde, as it is called,
for ten or eleven miles, having the river on our right. We had fine

views both up and down the river for the first three or four miles, our road being not close to it, but above its banks, along the open country, which was here occasionally intersected by hedgerows. Left our car in the road, and turned down a field to the Fall of Stonebyres, another of the falls of the Clyde, which I had not heard spoken of; therefore it gave me the more pleasure. We saw it from the top of the bank of the river at a little distance. It has not the imposing majesty of Cora Linn; but it has the advantage of being left to itself, a grand solitude in the heart of a populous country. We had a prospect above and below it, of cultivated grounds, with hay-stacks, houses, hills; but the river's banks were lonesome, steep, and woody, with rocks near the fall.

A little further on, came more into company with the river; sometimes we were close to it, sometimes above it, but always at no great distance; and now the vale became more interesting and amusing. It is very populous, with villages, hamlets, single cottages, or farm-houses embosomed in orchards, and scattered over with gentlemen's houses, some of them very ugly, tall and obtrusive, others neat and comfortable. We seemed now to have got into a country where poverty and riches were shaking hands together; pears and apples, of which the crop was abundant, hung over the road, often growing in orchards unfenced; or there might be bunches of broom along the road-side in an interrupted line, that looked like a hedge till we came to it and saw the gaps. Bordering on these fruitful orchards perhaps would be a patch, its chief produce being gorse or broom. There was nothing like a moor or common anywhere; but small plots of uncultivated ground were left high and low, among the potatoes, corn and cabbages, which grew intermingled, now among trees, now bare. The Trough of the Clyde is, indeed, a singular and very interesting region; it is somewhat like the upper part of the vale of Nith, but above the Nith is much less cultivated ground—without hedgerows or orchards, or anything that looks like a rich country. We met crowds of people coming from the kirk; the lasses were gaily dressed, often in white gowns, coloured satin bonnets, and coloured silk handkerchiefs, and generally with their shoes and stockings in a bundle hung on their arm. Before we left the river the vale became much less interesting, resembling a poor English country, the fields being large, and unluxuriant hedges.

It had been dark long before we reached Hamilton, and William had some difficulty in driving the tired horse through the town. At the inn they hesitated about being able to give us beds, the house being brim-full—lights at every window. We were rather alarmed for our accommodations during the rest of the tour, supposing the house to be filled with tourists; but they were in general only regular travellers; for out of the main road from town to town we saw scarcely a carriage, and the inns were empty. There was nothing remarkable in the treatment we met with at this inn, except the lazy impertinence of the waiter. It was a townish place, with a great larder set out; the house, throughout, dirty.

Monday, August 22nd—Immediately after breakfast walked to the Duke of Hamilton's house to view the picture-gallery, chiefly the famous picture of Daniel in the Lions' Den, by Rubens. It is a large building, without grandeur, a heavy, lumpish mass, after the fashion of the Hopetoun H, *{The house belonging to the Earls of Hopetoun at Leadhills, not that which bears this name about twelve miles from Edinburgh.}* only five times the size, and with longer legs, which makes it gloomy. We entered the gate, passed the porter's lodge, where we saw nobody, and stopped at the front door, as William had done two years before with Sir William Rush's family. We were met by a little mean-looking man, shabbily dressed, out of livery, who, we found, was the porter. After scanning us over, he told us that we ought not to have come to that door. We said we were sorry for the mistake, but as one of our party had been there two years before, and was admitted by the same entrance, we had supposed it was the regular way. After many hesitations, and having kept us five minutes waiting in the large hall, while he went to consult with the housekeeper, he informed us that we could not be admitted at that time, the housekeeper being unwell; but that we might return in an hour: he then conducted us through long gloomy passages to an obscure door at the corner of the house. We asked if we might be permitted to walk in the park in the meantime; and he told us that this would not be agreeable to the Duke's family. We returned to the inn discontented enough, but resolved not to waste an hour, if there were anything else in the neighbourhood worth seeing. The waiter told us there was a curious place called Baroncleugh, with gardens cut out in rocks, and we determined to go thither. We had to walk through the town, which may be about as large as Penrith, and perhaps a mile further, along a dusty turnpike road. The morning was hot, sunny, and windy, and we were half tired before we reached the place; but were amply repaid for our trouble.

The general face of the country near Hamilton is much in the ordinary English style; not very hilly, with hedgerows, corn fields, and stone houses. The Clyde is here an open river with low banks, and the country spreads out so wide that there is no appearance of a regular vale. Baroncleugh is in a beautiful deep glen through which runs the river Avon, a stream that falls into the Clyde. The house stands very sweetly in complete retirement; it has its gardens and terraces one above another, with flights of steps between, box-trees and yew-trees cut in fantastic shapes, flower-borders and summer-houses; and, still below, apples and pears were hanging in abundance on the branches of large old trees, which grew intermingled with the natural wood, elms, beeches, etc., even to the water's edge. The whole place is in perfect harmony with the taste of our ancestors, and the yews and hollies are shaven as nicely, and the gravel walks and flower-borders kept in as exact order, as if the spirit of the first architect of the terraces still presided over them. The opposite bank of the river is left in its natural wildness, and nothing was to be seen higher up but the deep dell, its steep banks being covered with fine trees, a beautiful relief or contrast to the garden, which is one of the most elaborate old things ever seen, a little hanging garden of Babylon.

I was sorry to hear that the owner of this sweet place did not live there always. He had built a small thatched house to eke out the old one: it was a neat dwelling, with no false ornaments. We were exceedingly sorry to quit this spot, which is left to nature and past times, and should have liked to have pursued the glen further up; we were told that there was a ruined castle; and the walk itself must be very delightful; but we wished to reach Glasgow in good time, and had to go again to Hamilton House. Returned to the town by a much shorter road, and were very angry with the waiter for not having directed us to it; but he was too great a man to speak three words more than he could help.

We stopped at the proper door of the Duke's house, and seated ourselves humbly upon a bench, waiting the pleasure of the porter, who, after a little time, informed us that we could not be admitted, giving no reason whatever. When we got to the inn, we could just gather from the waiter that it was not usual to refuse admittance to strangers; but that was all: he could not, or would not, help us, so we were obliged to give it up, which mortified us, for I had wished much to see the picture. William vowed that he would write that very night to Lord Archibald Hamilton, stating the whole matter, which he did from Glasgow.

I ought to have mentioned the park, though, as we were not allowed to walk there, we saw but little of it. It looked pleasant, as all parks with fine trees must be, but, as it seemed to be only a large, nearly level, plain, it could not be a particularly beautiful park, though it borders upon the Clyde, and the Avon runs, I believe, through it, after leaving the solitude of the glen of Baroncleugh.

Quitted Hamilton at about eleven o'clock. There is nothing interesting between Hamilton and Glasgow till we came to Bothwell Castle, a few miles from Hamilton. The country is cultivated, but not rich, the fields large, a perfect contrast to the huddling together of hills and trees, corn and pasture grounds, hay-stacks, cottages, orchards, broom and gorse, but chiefly broom, that had amused us so much the evening before in passing through the Trough of the Clyde. A native of Scotland would not probably be satisfied with the account I have given of the Trough of the Clyde, for it is one of the most celebrated scenes in Scotland. We certainly received less pleasure from it than we had expected; but it was plain that this was chiefly owing to the unfavourable circumstances under which we saw it—a gloomy sky and a cold blighting wind. It is a very beautiful district, yet there, as in all the other scenes of Scotland celebrated for their fertility; we found something which gave us a notion of barrenness, of what was not altogether genial. The new fir and larch plantations, here as in almost every other part of Scotland, contributed not a little to this effect.

Crossed the Clyde not far from Hamilton, and had the river for some miles at a distance from us, on our left; but after having gone, it might be, three miles, we came to a porter's lodge on the left side of the road, where we were to turn to Bothwell Castle, which is in Lord Douglas's grounds. The woman who keeps the gate brought us a book, in which we wrote down our names. Went about half a mile before we came to the pleasure-grounds. Came to a large range of stables, where we were to leave the car; but there was no one to unyoke the horse, so William was obliged to do it himself, a task which he performed very awkwardly, being then new to it. We saw the ruined castle embosomed in trees, passed the house, and soon found ourselves on the edge of a steep brow immediately above and overlooking the course of the river Clyde through a deep hollow between woods and green steeps. We had approached at right angles from the main road to the place over a flat, and had seen nothing before us but a nearly level country terminated by distant slopes, the Clyde hiding himself in his deep bed. It was exceedingly delightful to come thus unexpectedly upon such a beautiful region.

The Castle stands nobly, overlooking the Clyde. When we came up to it I was hurt to see that flower-borders had taken place of the natural overgrowings of the ruin, the scattered stones and wild plants. It is a large and grand pile, of red freestone, harmonizing perfectly with the rocks of the river, from which, no doubt, it has been hewn. When I was a little accustomed to the unnatural-ness of a modern garden, I could not help admiring the excessive beauty and luxuriance of some of the plants, particularly the purple-flowered clematis, and a broad-leaved creeping plant without flowers, which scrambled up the castle wall along with the ivy, and spread its vine-like branches so lavishly that it seemed to be in its natural situation, and one could not help thinking that, though not self-planted among the ruins of this country, it must somewhere have its natural abode in such places. If Both-well Castle had not been close to the Douglas mansion we should have been disgusted with the possessor's miserable conception of 'adorning' such a venerable ruin; but it is so very near to the house that, of necessity, the pleasure-grounds must have extended beyond it, and perhaps the neatness of a shaven lawn and the complete desolation natural to a ruin might have made an unpleasing contrast; and besides, being within the precincts of the pleasure-grounds, and so very near to the modern mansion of a noble family, it has forfeited in some degree its independent majesty, and becomes a tributary to the mansion; its solitude being interrupted, it has no longer the same command over the mind in sending it back into past times, or excluding the ordinary feelings which we bear about us in daily life. We had then only to regret that the castle and house were so near to each other; and it was impossible *not* to regret it; for the ruin presides in state over the river, far from city or town, as if it might have had a peculiar privilege to preserve its memorials of past ages and maintain its own character and independence for centuries to come.

We sat upon a bench under the high trees, and had beautiful views of the different reaches of the river above and below. On the opposite bank, which is finely wooded with elms and other trees, are the remains of an ancient priory, built upon a rock: and rock and ruin are so blended together that it is impossible to separate the one from the other. Nothing can be more beautiful than the little remnants of this holy place; elm trees—for we were near enough to distinguish them by their branches—grow out of the walls, and overshadow a small but very elegant window. It can scarcely be conceived what a grace the castle and priory impart to each other; and the river Clyde flows on smooth and unruffled below, seeming to my thoughts more in harmony with the sober and stately images of former times, than if it had roared over a rocky channel, forcing its sound upon the ear. It blended gently with the warbling of the smaller birds and chattering of the larger ones that had made their nests in the ruins. In this fortress the chief of the English nobility were confined after the battle of Bannockburn. If a man is to be a prisoner, he scarcely could have a more pleasant place to solace his captivity; but I thought that for close confinement I should prefer the banks of a lake or the sea-side. The greatest charm of a brook or river is in the liberty to pursue it through its windings; you can then take it in whatever mood you like; silent or noisy, sportive or quiet. The beauties of a brook or river must be sought; and the pleasure is in going in search of them; those of a lake or of the sea come to you of themselves. These rude warriors cared little perhaps about either; and yet if one may judge from the writings of Chaucer and from the old romances, more interesting passions were connected with natural objects in the days of chivalry than now, though going in search of scenery, as it is called, had not then been thought of. I had heard nothing of Bothwell Castle, at least nothing that I remembered; therefore, perhaps, my pleasure was greater, compared with what I received elsewhere, than others might feel.

At our return to the stables we found an inferior groom, who helped William to yoke the horse, and was very civil. We grew hungry before we had travelled many miles, and seeing a large public-house—it was in a walled court some yards from the road—Coleridge got off the car to inquire if we could dine there, and was told we could have nothing but eggs. It was a miserable place, very like a French house; indeed we observed, in almost every part of Scotland, except Edinburgh, that we were reminded ten times of France and Germany for once of England.

Saw nothing remarkable after leaving Bothwell, except the first view of Glasgow, at some miles distance, terminated by the mountains of Loch Lomond. The suburbs of Glasgow extend very far; houses on each side of the highway—all ugly, and the inhabitants dirty. The roads are very wide; and everything seems to tell of the neighbourhood of a large town. We were annoyed by carts and dirt, and the road was full of people, who all noticed our car in one way or other; the children often sent a hooting after us.

Wearied completely, we at last reached the town, and were glad to walk, leading the car to the first decent inn, which was luckily not far from the end of the town. William, who gained most of his road-knowledge from ostlers, had been informed of this house by the ostler at Hamilton; it proved quiet and tolerably cheap, a new building—the Saracen's Head. I shall never forget how glad I was to be landed in a little quiet back-parlour, for my head was beating with the noise of carts which we had left, and the wearisomeness of the disagreeable objects near the highway; but with my first pleasant sensations also came the feeling that we were not in an English inn—partly from its half-unfurnished appearance, which is common in Scotland, for in general the deal wainscots and doors are unpainted, and partly from the dirtiness of the floors. Having dined, William and I walked to the post-office and, after much seeking, found out a quiet timber-yard wherein to sit down and read our letter. We then walked a considerable time in the streets, which are perhaps as handsome as streets can be, which derive no particular effect from their situation in connexion with natural advantages, such as rivers, sea, or hills. The

Trongate, an old street, is very picturesque—high houses, with an intermixture of gable fronts towards the street. The New Town is built of fine stone, in the best style of the very best London streets at the west end of the town, but, not being of brick, they are greatly superior. One thing must strike every stranger in his first walk through Glasgow—an appearance of business and bustle, but no coaches or gentlemen's carriages; during all the time we walked in the streets I only saw three carriages, and these were travelling chaises. I also could not but observe a want of cleanliness in the appearance of the lower orders of the people, and a dullness in the dress and outside of the whole mass, as they moved along. We returned to the inn before it was dark. I had a bad headache, and was tired, and we all went to bed soon.

Tuesday, August 23rd—A cold morning. Walked to the bleaching-ground, *{Glasgow Green}* a large field bordering on the Clyde, the banks of which are perfectly flat, and the general face of the country is nearly so in the neighbourhood of Glasgow. This field, the whole summer through, is covered with women of all ages, children, and young girls spreading out their linen, and watching it while it bleaches. The scene must be very cheerful on a fine day, but it rained when we were there, and though there was linen spread out in all parts, and great numbers of women and girls were at work, yet there would have been many more on a fine day, and they would have appeared happy, instead of stupid and cheerless. In the middle of the field is a wash-house, whither the in-habitants of this large town, rich and poor, send or carry their linen to be washed. There are two very large rooms, with each a cistern in the middle for hot water; and all-round the rooms are benches for the women to set their tubs upon. Both the rooms were crowded with washers; there might be a hundred, or two, or even three; for it is not easy to form an accurate notion of so great a number; however, the rooms were large, and they were both full. It was amusing to see so many women, arms, head, and face all in motion, all busy in an ordinary household employment, in which we are accustomed to see, at the most, only three or four women employed in one place. The women were very civil. I learnt from them the regulations of the house; but I have forgotten the particulars. The substance of them is, that 'so much' is to be paid for each tub of water, 'so much' for a tub, and the privilege of washing for a day, and, 'so much' to the general overlookers of the linen, when it is left to be bleached. An old man and woman have this office, who were walking about; two melancholy figures.

The shops at Glasgow are large, and like London shops, and we passed by the largest coffee-room I ever saw. You look across the piazza of the Exchange, and see to the end of the coffee-room, where there is a circular window, the width of the room Perhaps there might be thirty gentlemen sitting on the circular bench of the window, each reading a newspaper. They had the appearance of figures in a fantoccini, or men seen at the extremity of the opera-house, diminished into puppets.

I am sorry I did not see the High Church: both William and I were tired, and it rained very hard after we had left the bleaching-ground; besides, I am less eager to walk in a large town than anywhere else; so we put it off, and I have since repented of my irresolution.

Dined, and left Glasgow at about three o'clock, in a heavy rain. We were obliged to ride through the streets to keep our feet dry, and, in spite of the rain, every person as we went along stayed his steps to look at us; indeed, we had the pleasure of spreading smiles from one end of Glasgow to the other—for we travelled the whole length of the town. A set of schoolboys, perhaps there might be eight, with satchels over their shoulders, and, except one or two, without shoes and stockings, yet very well dressed in jackets and trousers, like gentlemen's children, followed us in great delight, admiring the car and longing to jump up. At last, though we were seated, they made several attempts to get on behind; and they looked so pretty and wild, and at the same time so modest, that we wished to give them a ride, and there being a little hill near the end of the town, we got off, and four of them who still remained, the rest having dropped into their homes by the way, took our places; and indeed I would have walked two miles willingly, to have had the pleasure of seeing them so happy. When they were to ride no longer, they scampered away, laughing and rejoicing. New houses are rising up in great numbers round Glasgow; citizen-like houses, and new plantations, chiefly of fir. The fields are frequently enclosed by hedgerows, but there is no richness, nor any particular beauty for some miles.

The first object that interested us was a gentleman's house upon a green plain or holm, almost close to the Clyde, sheltered by tall trees, a quiet modest mansion, and, though white-washed, being an old building, and no other house near it, or in connexion with it, and standing upon the level field, which belonged to it, its own domain, the whole scene together brought to our minds an image of the retiredness and sober elegance of a nunnery; but this might be owing to the greyness of the afternoon, and our having come immediately from Glasgow, and through a country which, till now, had either had a townish taint, or at best little of rural beauty. While we were looking at the house we overtook a foot-traveller, who, like many others, began to talk about our car. We alighted to walk up a hill, and, continuing the conversation, the man told us, with something like a national pride that it belonged to a Scotch Lord, Lord Semple; he added that a little further on we should see a much finer prospect, as fine a one as ever we had seen in our lives. Accordingly, when we came to the top of the hill, it opened upon us most magnificently. We saw the Clyde, now a stately sea-river, winding away mile after mile, spotted with boats and ships, each side of the river hilly, the right populous with single houses and villages—Dunglass Castle upon a promontory, the whole view terminated by the rock of Dumbarton, at five or six miles distance, which stands by itself, without any hills near it, like a sea-rock.

We travelled for some time near the river, passing through clusters of houses which seemed to owe their existence rather to the wealth of the river than the land, for the banks were mostly bare, and the soil appeared poor, even near the water. The left side of the river was generally uninhabited and moorish, yet there are some beautiful spots: for instance, a nobleman's house, *{No doubt Erskine House, the seat of Lord Blantyre.}* where the fields and trees were rich and, in combination with the river, looked very lovely. As we went along William and I were reminded of the views upon the Thames in Kent, which, though greatly superior in richness and softness, are much inferior in grandeur. Not far from Dumbarton, we passed under some rocky, copse-covered hills, which were so like some of the hills near Grasmere that we could have half believed they were the same. Arrived at Dumbarton before it was dark, having pushed on briskly that we might have start of a traveller at the inn, who was following us as fast as he could in a gig. Every front room was full, and we were afraid we should not have been admitted. They put us into a little parlour, dirty, and smelling of liquors, the table uncleaned, and not a chair in its place; we were glad, however, of our sorry accommodations.

While tea was preparing we lolled at our ease, and though the room-window overlooked the stable-yard, and at our entrance there appeared to be nothing but gloom and unloveliness, yet while I lay stretched upon the carriage cushions on three chairs, I discovered a little side peep which was enough to set the mind at work. It was no more than a smoky vessel lying at anchor, with its bare masts, a clay hut and the shelving bank of the river, with a green pasture above. Perhaps you will think that there is not much in this, as I describe it: it is true; but the effect produced by these simple objects, as they happened to be combined, together with the gloom of the evening, was exceedingly wild. Our room was parted by a slender partition from a large dining-room, in which were a number of officers and their wives, who, after the first hour, never ceased singing, dancing, laughing, or loud talking. The ladies sang some pretty songs, a great relief to us. We went early to bed; but poor Coleridge could not sleep for the noise at the street door; he lay in the parlour below stairs. It is no uncommon thing in the best inns of Scotland to have shutting-up beds in the sitting-rooms.

Wednesday, August 24th—As soon as breakfast was over, William and I walked towards the Castle, a short mile from the town. We overtook two young men, who, on our asking the road, offered to conduct us, though it might seem it was not easy to miss our way, for the rock rises singly by itself from the plain on which the town stands. The rock of Dumbarton is very grand when you are close to it, but at a little distance, under an ordinary sky, and in open day, it is not grand, but curiously wild. The castle and fortifications add little effect to the general view of the rock, especially since the building of a modern house, which is white-washed, and consequently jars, wherever it is seen, with the natural character of the place. There is a path up to the house, but it being low water we could walk round the rock, which we resolved to do. On that side next the town green grass grows to a considerable height up the rock, but wherever the river borders upon it, it is naked stone. I never saw rock in nobler masses, or more deeply stained by time and weather; nor is this to be wondered at, for it is in the very eye of sea-storms and land-storms, of mountain winds and water winds. It is of all colours, but a rusty yellow predominates. As we walked along, we could not but look up continually, and the mass above being on every side so huge, it appeared more wonderful than when we saw the whole together.

We sat down on one of the large stones which lie scattered near the base of the rock, with sea-weed growing amongst them. Above our heads the rock was perpendicular for a considerable height, nay, as it seemed, to the very top, and on the brink of the precipice a few sheep, two of them rams with twisted horns, stood, as if on the look-out over the wide country. At the same time we saw a sentinel in his red coat, walking backwards and forwards between us and the sky, with his firelock over his shoulder. The sheep, I suppose owing to our being accustomed to see them in similar situations, appeared to retain their real size, while, on the contrary, the soldier seemed to be diminished by the distance, till he almost looked like a puppet moved with wires for the pleasure of children, or an eight years old drummer in his stiff, manly dress beside a company of grenadiers. I had never before, perhaps, thought of sheep and men in soldiers' dresses at the same time, and here they were brought together in a strange fantastic way. As will be easily conceived, the fearlessness and stillness of those quiet creatures, on the brow of the rock, pursuing their natural occupations, contrasted with the restless and apparently unmeaning motions of the dwarf soldier, added not a little to the general effect of this place, which is that of wild singularity, and the whole was aided by a blustering wind and a gloomy sky. Coleridge joined us, and we went up to the top of the rock.

The road to a considerable height is through a narrow cleft, in which a flight of steps is hewn; the steps nearly fill the cleft, and on each side the rocks form a high and irregular wall; it is almost like a long sloping cavern, only that it is roofed by the sky. We came to the barracks; soldiers' wives were hanging out linen upon the rails, while the wind beat about them furiously—there was nothing which it could set in motion but the garments of the women and the linen upon the rails; the grass—for we had now come to green grass—was close and smooth, and not one pile an inch above another, and neither tree nor shrub. The standard pole stood erect without a flag. The rock has two summits, one much broader and higher than the other. When we were near to the top of the lower eminence we had the pleasure of finding a little garden of flowers and vegetables belonging to the soldiers. There are three distinct and very noble prospects—the first up the Clyde towards Glasgow—Dunglass Castle, seen on its promontory— boats, sloops, hills, and many buildings; the second, down the river to the sea—Greenock and Port-Glasgow, and the distant mountains at the entrance of Loch Long; and the third extensive and distant view is up the Leven, which here falls into the Clyde, to the mountains of Loch Lomond. The distant mountains in all these views were obscured by mists and dingy clouds, but if the grand outline of any one of the views can be seen, it is sufficient recompense for the trouble of climbing the rock of Dumbarton.

The soldier who was our guide told us that an old ruin, which we came to at the top of the higher eminence, had been a wind-mill—an inconvenient station, though certainly a glorious place for wind; perhaps if it really had been a wind-mill it was only for the use of the garrison. We looked over cannons on the battery-walls, and saw in an open field below the yeomanry cavalry exercising, while we could hear from the town, which was full of soldiers, 'Dumbarton's drums beat bonny, o!' Yet while we stood upon this eminence, rising up so far as it does—inland, and having the habitual old English feeling of our own security as islanders—we could not help looking upon the fortress, in spite of its cannon and soldiers, and the rumours of invasion, as set up against the hostilities of wind and weather rather than for any other warfare. On our return we were invited into the guard-room, about half-way down the rock, where we were shown a large rusty sword, which they called Wallace's Sword, and a trout boxed up in a well close by, where they said he had been confined for upwards of thirty years. For the pleasure of the soldiers, who were anxious that we should see him, we took some pains to spy him out in his black den, and at last succeeded. It was pleasing to observe how much interest the poor soldiers—though themselves probably new to the place—seemed to attach to this antiquated inhabitant of their garrison.

When we had reached the bottom of the rock along the same road by which we had ascended, we made our way over the rough stones left bare by the tide, round the bottom of the rock, to the point where we had set off. This is a wild and melancholy walk on a blustering cloudy day: the naked bed of the river scattered over with sea-weed; grey swampy fields on the other shore; sea-birds flying overhead; the high rock perpendicular and bare. We came to two very large fragments, which had fallen from the main rock; Coleridge thought that one of them was as large as Bowder-Stone, *{A huge isolated rock in Borrowdale, Cumberland, which bears that name.}* impossible to judge accurately; we probably, without knowing it, compared them with the whole mass from which they had fallen, which, from its situation, we consider as one rock or stone, and there is no object of the kind for comparison with the Bowder-Stone. When we leave the shore of the Clyde grass begins to show itself on the rock; go a considerable way—still under the rock—along a flat field, and pass immediately below the white house, which, where-ever seen, looks so ugly.

Left Dumbarton at about eleven o'clock. The sky was cheerless and the air ungenial, which we regretted, as we were going to Loch Lomond, and wished to greet the first of the Scottish lakes with our cheerfullest and best feelings. Crossed the Leven at the end of Dumbarton, and, when we looked behind, had a pleasing view of the town, bridge, and rock; but when we took in a reach of the river at the distance of perhaps half a mile, the swamp ground, being so near a town, and not in its natural wildness, but seemingly half cultivated, with houses here and there, gave us an idea of extreme poverty of soil, or that the inhabitants were either indolent or miserable. We had to travel four miles on the banks of the 'Water of Leven' before we should come to Loch Lomond. Having expected a grand river from so grand a lake, we were disappointed; for it appeared to me not to be very much larger than the Emont, and is not near so beautiful; but we must not forget that the day was cold and gloomy. Near Dumbarton it is like a river in a flat country, or under the influence of tides; but a little higher up it resembles one of our rivers, flowing through a vale of no extreme beauty, though prettily wooded; the hills on each side not very high, sloping backwards from the bed of the vale, which is neither very narrow nor very wide; the prospect terminated by Ben Lomond and other mountains. The vale is populous, but looks as if it were not inhabited by cultivators of the earth; the houses are chiefly of stone; often in rows by the river-side; they stand pleasantly, but have a tradish look, as if they might have been off-sets from Glasgow. We saw many bleach-yards, but no other symptom of a manufactory, except something in the houses that was not rural, and a want of independent comforts. Perhaps if the river had been glittering in the sun, and the smoke of the cottages rising in distinct volumes towards the sky, as I have seen in the vale or basin below Pillsden in Dorsetshire, when every cottage, hidden from the eye, pointed out its lurking-place by an upright wreath of white smoke, the whole scene might have excited ideas of perfect cheerfulness.

Here, as on the Nith, and much more than in the Trough of the Clyde, a great portion of the ground was uncultivated, but the hills being less wild, the river more stately, and the ground not heaved up so irregularly and tossed about, the imperfect cultivation was the more to be lamented, particularly as there were so many houses near the river. In a small enclosure by the wayside is a pillar erected to the memory of Dr. Smollett, who was born in a village at a little distance, which we could see at the same time, and where, I believe, some of the family still reside. There is a long Latin inscription, which Coleridge translated for my benefit. The Latin is miserably bad—as Coleridge said, such as poor Smollett, who was an excellent scholar, would have been ashamed of. *{The inscription on the pillar was written by Professor George Stuart of Edinburgh, John Ramsay of Ochtertyre, and Dr. Samuel Johnson; for Dr. Johnson's share in the work see Croker's Boswell, p.392.}*

Before we came to Loch Lomond the vale widened, and became less populous. We climbed over a wall into a large field to have a better front view of the lake than from the road. This view is very much like that from Mr. Clark-son's windows: the mountain in front resembles Hallan; indeed, is almost the same; but Ben Lomond is not seen standing in such majestic company as Helvellyn, and the meadows are less beautiful than Ulswater. The reach of the lake is. very magnificent; you see it, as Ulswater is seen beyond the promontory of Old Church, winding away behind a large woody island that looks like a promontory. The outlet of the lake—we had a distinct view of it in the field—is very insignificant. The bulk of the river is frittered away by small alder bushes, as I recollect. I do not remember that it was reedy, but the ground had a swampy appearance; and here the vale spreads out wide and shapeless, as if the river were born to no inheritance, had no sheltering cradle, no hills of its own. As we have seen, this does not continue long; it flows through a distinct, though not a magnificent vale. But, having lost the pastoral character, which it had in the youthful days of Smollett—if the description in his ode to his native stream be a faithful one— it is less interesting than it was then.

The road carried us sometimes close to the lake, sometimes at a considerable distance from it, over moorish grounds, or through half-cultivated enclosures; we had the lake on our right, which is here so wide that the opposite hills, not being high, are cast into insignificance, and we could not distinguish any buildings near the water, if any there were. It is however always delightful to travel by a lake of clear waters, if you see nothing else but a very ordinary country; but we had some beautiful distant views, one in particular, down the high road, through a vista of over-arching trees; and the near shore was frequently very pleasing, with its gravel banks, bendings, and small bays. In one part it was bordered for a considerable way by irregular groups of forest trees or single stragglers, which, not large, seemed old; their branches were stunted and knotty, as if they had been striving with storms, and had half yielded to them. Under these trees we had a variety of pleasing views across the lake, and the very rolling over the road and looking at its smooth and beautiful surface was itself a pleasure. It was as smooth as a gravel walk, and of the bluish colour of some of the roads among the lakes of the north of England.

Passed no very remarkable place till we came to Sir James Colquhoun's house, which stands upon a large, flat, woody peninsula, looking towards Ben Lomond. There must be many beautiful walks among the copses of the peninsula, and delicious views over the water; but the general surface of the country is poor, and looks as if it ought to be rich and well peopled, for it is not mountainous; nor had we passed any hills which a Cumbrian would dignify with the name of mountains. There was many a little plain or gently-sloping hill covered with poor heath or broom without trees, where one should have liked to see a cottage in a bower of wood, with its patch of corn and potatoes, and a green field with a hedge to keep it warm. As we advanced we perceived less of the coldness of poverty, the hills not having so large a space between them and the lake. The surface of the hills being in its natural state, is always beautiful; but where there is only a half cultivated and half peopled soil near the banks of a lake or river, the idea is forced upon one that they who do live there have not much of cheerful enjoyment.

But soon we came to just such a place as we had wanted to see. The road was close to the water, and a hill, bare, rocky, or with scattered copses rose above it. A deep shade hung over the road, where some little boys were at play; we expected a dwelling-house of some sort; and when we came nearer, saw three or four thatched huts under the trees, and at the same moment felt that it was a paradise. We had before seen the lake only as one wide plain of water; but here the portion of it which we saw was bounded by a high and steep, heathy and woody island opposite, which did not appear like an island, but the main shore, and framed out a little oblong lake apparently not so broad as Rydale-water, with one small island covered with trees, resembling some of the most beautiful of the holms of Windermere, and only a narrow river's breadth from the shore. This was a place where we should have liked to have lived, and the only one we had seen near Loch Lomond. How delightful to have a little shed concealed under the branches of the fairy island! The cottages and the island might have been made for the pleasure of each other. It was but like a natural garden, the distance was so small; nay, one could not have forgiven anyone living there, not compelled to daily labour, if he did not connect it with his dwelling by some feeling of domestic attachment, like what he has for the orchard where his children play. I thought what a place for William! He might row himself over with twenty strokes of the oars, escaping from the business of the house, and as safe from intruders, with his boat anchored beside him, as if he had locked himself up in the strong tower of a castle. We were unwilling to leave this sweet spot; but it was so simple, and therefore so rememberable, that it seemed almost as if we could have carried it away with us. It was nothing more than a small lake enclosed by trees at the ends and by the way-side, and opposite, by the island, a steep bank on which the purple heath was seen under low oak coppice-wood, a group of houses over shadowed by trees, and a bending road. There was one remarkable tree, an old larch with hairy branches, which sent out its main stem horizontally across the road, an object that seemed to have been singled out for injury where everything else was lovely and thriving, tortured into that shape by storms, which one might have thought could not have reached it in that sheltered place.

We were now entering into the Highlands. I believe Luss is the place where we were told that country begins; but at these cottages I would have gladly believed that we were there, for it was like a new region. The huts were after the Highland fashion, and the boys who were playing wore the Highland dress and philabeg. On going into a new country I seem to myself to waken up, and afterwards it surprises me to remember how much alive I have been to the distinctions of dress, household arrangements, etc. etc., and what a spirit these little things give to wild, barren, or ordinary places. The cottages are within about two miles of Luss. Came in view of several islands; but the lake being so very wide, we could see little of their peculiar beauties, and they, being large, hardly looked like islands. Passed another gentleman's house, which stands prettily in a bay, *{Camstraddan House and bay.}* and soon after reached Luss, where we intended to lodge. On seeing the outside of the inn, we were glad that we were to have such pleasant quarters. It is a nice-looking white house, by the road-side; but there was not much promise of hospitality when we stopped at the door: no person came out till we had shouted a considerable time. A barefooted lass showed me up-stairs, and again my hopes revived; the house was clean for a Scotch inn, and the view very pleasant to the lake, over the top of the village—a cluster of thatched houses among trees, with a large chapel in the midst of them. Like most of the Scotch kirks which we had seen, this building resembles a big house; but it is a much more pleasing building than they generally are, and has one of our rustic belfries, not unlike that at Ambleside, with two bells hanging in the open air. (7) We chose one of the back rooms to sit in, being more snug, and they looked upon a very sweet prospect—

a stream tumbling down a cleft or glen on the hill-side, rocky coppice ground, a rural lane, such as we have from house to house at Grasmere, and a few out-houses. We had a poor dinner, and sour ale; but as long as the people were civil we were contented.

Coleridge was not well, so he did not stir out, but William and I walked through the village to the shore of the lake. When I came close to the houses, I could not but regret a want of loveliness correspondent with the beauty of the situation and the appearance of the village at a little distance; not a single ornamented garden. We saw potatoes and cabbages, but never a honeysuckle. Yet there were wild gardens, as beautiful as any that ever man cultivated, overgrowing the roofs of some of the cottages, flowers and creeping plants. How elegant were the wreaths of the bramble that had 'built its own bower' upon the riggins in several parts of the village; therefore we had chiefly to regret the want of gardens, as they are symptoms of leisure and comfort, or at least of no painful industry. Here we first saw houses without windows, the smoke coming out of the open window-places; the chimneys were like stools with four legs, a hole being left in the roof for the smoke, and over that a slate placed upon four sticks—sometimes the whole leaned as if it were going to fall. The fields close to Luss lie flat to the lake, and a river, as large as our stream near the church at Grasmere, flows by the end of the village, being the same which comes down the glen behind the inn; it is very much like our stream—beds of blue pebbles upon the shores.

We walked towards the head of the lake, and from a large pasture field near Luss, a gentle eminence, had a very interesting view back upon the village and the lake and islands beyond. We then perceived that Luss stood in the centre of a spacious bay, and that close to it lay another small one, within the larger, where the boats of the inhabitants were lying at anchor, a beautiful natural harbour. The islands, as we look down the water, are seen in great beauty. Inch-ta-vanach, the same that framed out the little peaceful lake which we had passed in the morning, towers above the rest. The lake is very wide here, and the opposite shores not being lofty the chief part of the permanent beauty of this view is among the islands, and on the near shore, including the low promontories of the bay of Luss, and the village; and we saw it under its dullest aspect—the air cold, the sky gloomy, without a glimpse of sunshine. On a splendid evening, with the light of the sun diffused over the whole islands, distant hills, and the broad expanse of the lake, with its creeks, bays, and little slips of water among the islands, it must be a glorious sight.

Up the lake there are no islands; Ben Lomond terminates the view, without any other large mountains; no clouds were upon it, therefore we saw the whole size and form of the mountain, yet it did not appear to me so large as Skiddaw does from Derwent-water. Continued our walk a considerable way towards the head of the lake, and went up a high hill, but saw no other reach of the water. The hills on the Luss side become much steeper, and the lake, having narrowed a little above Luss, was no longer a very wide lake where we lost sight of it.

Came to a bark hut by the shores, and sate for some time under the shelter of it. While we were here a poor woman with a little child by her side begged a penny of me, and asked where she could 'find quarters in the village.' She was a travelling beggar, a native of Scotland, had often 'heard of that water,' but was never there before. This woman's appearance, while the wind was rustling about us, and the waves breaking at our feet, was very melancholy: the waters looked wide, the hills many, and dark, and far off—no house but at Luss. I thought what a dreary waste must this lake be to such poor creatures, struggling with fatigue and poverty and unknown ways!

We ordered tea when we reached the inn, and desired the girl to light us a fire; she replied, 'I dinna ken whether she'll gie fire,' meaning her mistress. We told her we did not wish her mistress to give fire, we only desired her to let her make it and we would pay for it. The girl brought in the tea-things, but no fire, and when I asked if she was coming to light it, she said 'her mistress was not varra willing to gie fire.' At last, however, on our insisting upon it, the fire was lighted: we got tea by candlelight, and spent a comfortable evening. I had seen the landlady before we went out, for, as had been usual in all the country inns, there was a demur respecting beds, notwithstanding the house was empty, and there were at least half-a-dozen spare beds. Her countenance corresponded with the unkindness of denying us a fire on a cold night, (8) for she was the most cruel and hateful-looking woman I ever saw. She was overgrown with fat, and was sitting with her feet and legs in a tub of water for the dropsy,— probably brought on by whisky-drinking. The sympathy which I felt and expressed for her, on seeing her in this wretched condition—for her legs were swollen as thick as mill-posts—seemed to produce no effect; and I was obliged, after five minutes' conversation, to leave the affair of the beds undecided. Coleridge had some talk with her daughter, a smart lass in a cotton gown, with a bandeau round her head, without shoes and stockings. She told Coleridge with some pride that she had not spent all her time at Luss, but was then fresh from Glasgow.

It came on a very stormy night; the wind rattled every window in the house, and it rained heavily. William and Coleridge had bad beds, in a two-bedded room in the garrets, though there were empty rooms on the first floor, and they were disturbed by a drunken man, who had come to the inn when we were gone to sleep.

Thursday, August 25th—We were glad when we awoke to see that it was a fine morning—the sky was bright blue, with quick-moving clouds, the hills cheerful, lights and shadows vivid and distinct. The village looked exceedingly beautiful this morning from the garret windows —the stream glittering near it, while it flowed under trees through the level fields to the lake. After breakfast, William and I went down to the water-side. The roads were as dry as if no drop of rain had fallen, which added to the pure cheerfulness of the appearance of the village, and even of the distant prospect, an effect which I always seem to perceive from clearly bright roads, for they are always brightened by rain, after a storm; but when we came among the houses I regretted even more than last night, because the contrast was greater, the slovenliness and dirt near the doors; and could not but remember, with pain from the contrast, the cottages of Somersetshire, covered with roses and myrtle, and their small gardens of herbs and flowers. While lingering by the shore we began to talk with a man who offered to row us to Inch-ta-vanach; but the sky began to darken; and the wind being high, we doubted whether we should venture, therefore made no engagement; he offered to sell me some thread, pointing to his cottage, and added that many English ladies carried thread away from Luss.

Presently after, Coleridge joined us, and we determined to go to the island. I was sorry that the man who had been talking with us was not our boatman; William by some chance had engaged another. We had two rowers and a strong boat; so I felt myself bold, though there was a great chance of a high wind. The nearest point of Inch-ta-vanach is not perhaps more than a mile and a quarter from Luss; we did not land there, but rowed round the end, and landed on that side which looks towards our favourite cottages, and their own island, which, wherever seen, is still their own. It rained a little when we landed, and I took my cloak, which afterwards served us to sit down upon in our road up the hill, when the day grew much finer, with gleams of sunshine. This island belongs to Sir James Colquhoun, who has made a convenient road that winds gently to the top of it.

We had not climbed far before we were stopped by A sudden burst of prospect, so singular and beautiful that it was like a flash of images from another world. We stood with our backs to the hill of the island, which we were ascending, and which shut out Ben Lomond entirely, and all the upper part of the lake, and we looked towards the foot of the lake, scattered over with islands without beginning and without end. The sun shone, and the distant hills were visible, some through sunny mists, others in gloom with patches of sunshine; the lake was lost under the low and distant hills, and the islands lost in the lake, which was all in motion with travelling fields of light or dark shadows under rainy clouds. There are many hills, but no commanding eminence at a distance to confine the prospect, so that the land seemed endless as the water.

What I had heard of Loch Lomond, or any other place in Great Britain, had given me no idea of anything like what we beheld: it was an outlandish scene—we might have believed ourselves in North America. The islands were of every possible variety of shape and surface—hilly and level, large and small, bare, rocky, pastoral, or covered with wood. Immediately under my eyes lay one large flat island, bare and green, so flat and low that it scarcely appeared to rise above the water, with straggling peat-stacks and a single hut upon one of its out-shooting promontories—for it was of a very irregular shape, though perfectly flat. Another, its next neighbour, and still nearer to us, was covered over with heath and coppice-wood, the surface undulating, with flat or sloping banks towards the water, and hollow places, cradle-like valleys, behind. These two islands, with Inch-ta-vanach, where we were standing, were intermingled with the water, I might say interbedded and interveined with it, in a manner that was exquisitely pleasing. There were bays innumerable, straits or passages like calm rivers, landlocked lakes, and, to the main water, stormy promontories. The solitary hut on the flat green island seemed unsheltered and desolate, and yet not wholly so, for it was but a broad river's breadth from the covert of the wood of the other island. Near to these is a miniature, an islet covered with trees, on which stands a small ruin that looks like the remains of a religious house; it is overgrown with ivy, and were it not that the arch of a window or gateway may be distinctly seen, it would be difficult to believe that it was not a tuft of trees growing in the shape of a ruin, rather than a ruin overshadowed by trees. When we had walked a little further we saw below us, on the nearest large island, where some of the wood had been cut down, a hut, which we conjectured to be a bark hut. It appeared to be on the shore of a little forest lake, enclosed by Inch-ta-vanach, where we were, and the woody island on which the hut stands.

Beyond we had the same intricate view as before, and could discover Dumbarton rock with its double head. There being a mist over it, it had a ghost-like appearance—as I observed to William and Coleridge, something like the Tor of Glastonbury from the Dorsetshire hills. Right before us, on the flat island mentioned before, were several small single trees or shrubs, growing at different distances from each other, close to the shore, but some optical delusion had detached them from the land on which they stood, and they had the appearance of so many little vessels sailing along the coast of it. I mention the circumstance, because, with the ghostly image of Dumbarton Castle, and the ambiguous ruin on the small island, it was much in the character of the scene, which was throughout magical and enchanting—a new world in its great permanent outline and composition, and changing at every moment in every part of it by the effect of sun and wind, and mist and shower and cloud, and the blending lights and deep shades which took place of each other, traversing the lake in every direction. The whole was indeed a strange mixture of soothing and restless images, of images inviting to rest, and others hurrying the fancy away into an activity still more pleasing than repose. Yet, intricate and homeless, that is, without lasting abiding-place for the mind, as the prospect was, there was no perplexity; we had still a guide to lead us forward.

Wherever we looked, it was a delightful feeling that there was something beyond. Meanwhile, the sense of quiet was never lost sight of; the little peaceful lakes among the islands might make you forget that the great water, Loch Lomond, was so near; and yet are more beautiful, because you know that it is so: they have their own bays and creeks sheltered within a shelter. When we had ascended to the top of the island we had a view up to Ben Lomond, over the long, broad water without spot or rock; and, looking backwards, saw the islands below us as on a map. This view, as may be supposed, was not nearly so interesting as those we had seen before. We hunted out all the houses on the shore, which were very few: there was the village of Luss, the two gentlemen's houses, our favourite cottages, and here and there a hut; but I do not recollect any comfortable-looking farm-houses, and on the opposite shore not a single dwelling. The whole scene was a combination of natural wildness, loveliness, beauty, and barrenness, or rather bareness, yet not comfortless or cold; but the whole was beautiful. We were too far off the more distant shore to distinguish any particular spots which we might have regretted were not better cultivated, and near Luss there was no want of houses.

After we had left the island, having been so much taken with the beauty of the bark hut and the little lake by which it appeared to stand, we desired the boatman to row us through it, and we landed at the hut. Walked upon the island for some time, and found out sheltered places for cottages. There were several woodman's huts, which, with some scattered fir-trees, and others in irregular knots, that made a delicious murmuring in the wind, added greatly to the romantic effect of the scene. They were built in the form of a cone from the ground, like savages' huts, the door being just large enough for a man to enter with stooping. Straw beds were raised on logs of wood, tools lying about, and a forked bough of a tree was generally suspended from the roof in the middle to hang a kettle upon. It was a place that might have been just visited by new settlers. I thought of Ruth and her dreams of romantic love:

> 'And then he said how sweet it were,
> A fisher or a hunter there,

> *A gardener in the shade,*
> *Still wandering with an easy mind,*
> *To build a household fire,*
> *and find A home in every glade.'*

We found the main lake very stormy when we had left the shelter of the islands, and there was again a threatening of rain, but it did not come on. I wanted much to go to the old ruin, but the boatmen were in a hurry to be at home. They told us it had been a stronghold built by a man who lived there alone, and was used to swim over and make depredations on the shore,—that nobody could ever lay hands on him, he was such a good swimmer, but at last they caught him in a net. The men pointed out to us an island belonging to Sir James Colquhoun, on which were a great quantity of deer.

Arrived at the inn at about twelve o'clock, and prepared to depart immediately: we should have gone with great regret if the weather had been warmer and the inn more comfortable. When we were leaving the door, a party with smart carriage and servants drove up, and I observed that the people of the house were just as slow in their attendance upon them as on us, with one single horse and outlandish Hibernian vehicle.

When we had travelled about two miles the lake became considerably narrower, the hills rocky, covered with copses, or bare, rising more immediately from the bed of the water, and therefore we had not so often to regret the want of inhabitants. Passed by, or saw at a distance, sometimes a single cottage, or two or three together, but the whole space between Luss and Tarbet is a solitude to the eye. We were reminded of Ulswater, but missed the pleasant farms, and the mountains were not so interesting: we had not seen them in companies or brotherhoods rising one above another at a long distance. Ben Lomond stood alone, opposite to us, majestically overlooking the lake; yet there was something in this mountain which disappointed me,—a want of massiveness and simplicity, perhaps from the top being broken into three distinct stages. The road carried us over a bold promontory by a steep and high ascent, and we had a long view of the lake pushing itself up in a narrow line through an avenue of mountains, terminated by the mountains at the head of the lake, of which Ben Lui, if I do not mistake, is the most considerable.

The afternoon was showery and misty, therefore we did not see this prospect so distinctly as we could have wished, but there was a grand obscurity over it which might make the mountains appear more numerous.

I have said so much of this lake that I am tired myself, and I fear I must have tired my friends. We had a pleasant journey to Tarbet; more than half of it on foot, for the road was hilly, and after we had climbed one small hill we were not desirous to get into the car again, seeing another before us, and our path was always delightful, near the lake, and frequently through woods. When we were within about half a mile of Tarbet, at a sudden turning looking to the left, we saw a very craggy-topped mountain amongst other smooth ones; the rocks on the summit distinct in shape as if they were buildings raised up by man, or uncouth images of some strange creature. We called out with one voice, 'That's what we wanted!' alluding to the frame-like uniformity of the side-screens of the lake for the last five or six miles. As we conjectured, this singular mountain was the famous Cobbler, near Arrochar. Tarbet was before us in the recess of a deep, large bay, under the shelter of a hill. When we came up to the village we had to inquire for the inn, there being no signboard. It was a well-sized white house, the best in the place. We were conducted up-stairs into a sitting-room that might make any good-humoured travellers happy—a square room, with windows on each side, looking, one way, towards the mountains, and across the lake to Ben Lomond, the other.

There was a pretty stone house before (i.e. towards the lake) some huts, scattered trees, two or three green fields with hedgerows, and a little brook making its way towards the lake; the fields are almost flat, and screened on that side nearest the head of the lake by a hill, which, pushing itself out, forms the bay of Tarbet, and, towards the foot, by a gentle slope and trees. The lake is narrow, and Ben Lomond shuts up the prospect, rising directly from the water. We could have believed ourselves to be by the side of Ulswater, at Glenridden, or in some other of the inhabited retirements of that lake. We were in a sheltered place among mountains; it was not an open joyous bay, with a cheerful populous village, like Luss; but a pastoral and retired spot, with a few single dwellings. The people of the inn stared at us when we spoke, without giving us an answer immediately, which we were at first disposed to attribute to coarseness of manners, but found afterwards that they did not understand us at once, Erse being the language spoken in the family. Nothing but salt meat and eggs for dinner—no potatoes; the house smelt strongly of herrings, which were hung to dry over the kitchen fire.

Walked in the evening towards the head of the lake; the road was steep over the hill, and when we had reached the top of it we had long views up and down the water. Passed a troop of women who were resting themselves by the roadside, as if returning from their day's labour. Amongst them was a man, who had walked with us a considerable way in the morning, and told us he was just come from America, where he had been for some years,— was going to his own home, and should return to America. He spoke of emigration as a glorious thing for them who had money. Poor fellow! I do not think that he had brought much back with him, for he had worked his passage over. I much suspected that a bundle, which he carried upon a stick, tied in a pocket-handkerchief, contained his all. He was almost blind, he said, as were many of the crew. He intended crossing the lake at the ferry; but it was stormy, and he thought he should not be able to get over that day. I could not help smiling when I saw him lying by the roadside (9) with such a company about him, not like a wayfaring man, but seeming as much at home and at his ease as if he had just stepped out of his hut among them, and they had been neighbours all their lives. Passed one pretty house, a large thatched dwelling with out-houses, but the prospect above and below was solitary.

The sun had long been set before we returned to the inn. As travellers, we were glad to see the moon over the top of one of the hills, but it was a cloudy night, without any peculiar beauty or solemnity. After tea we made inquiries respecting the best way to go to Loch Ketterine; the landlord could give but little information, and nobody seemed to know anything distinctly of the place, though it was but ten miles off. We applied to the maid-servant who waited on us: she was a fine-looking young woman, dressed in a white bed-gown, her hair fastened up by a comb, and without shoes and stockings. When we asked her about the Trossachs she could give us no information, but on our saying, 'Do you know Loch Ketterine?'

she answered with a smile, 'I should know that loch, for I was bred and born there.' After much difficulty we learned from her that the Trossachs were at the foot of the lake, and that by the way we were to go we should come upon them at the head, should have to travel ten miles to the foot of the water, *{This distinction between the foot and head is not very clear. What is meant is this: They would have to travel the whole length of the lake, from the west to the east end of it, before they came to the Trossachs, the pass leading away from the east end of the lake.}* and that there was no inn by the way. The girl spoke English very distinctly; but she had few words, and found it difficult to understand us. She did not much encourage us to go, because the roads were bad, and it was a long way, 'and there was no putting-up for the like of us.' We determined, however, to venture, and throw ourselves upon the hospitality of some cottager or gentleman. We desired the landlady to roast us a couple of fowls to carry with us. There are always plenty of fowls at the doors of a Scotch inn, and eggs are as regularly brought to table at breakfast as bread and butter.

Friday, August 26th—We did not set off till between ten and eleven o'clock, much too late for a long day's journey. Our boatman lived at the pretty white house which we saw from the windows: we called at his door by the way, and, even when we were near the house, the outside looked comfortable; but within I never saw anything so miserable from dirt, and dirt alone: it reminded one of the house of a decayed weaver in the suburbs of a large town, with a sickly wife and a large family; but William says it was far worse; that it was quite Hottentotish.

After long waiting, and many clumsy preparations, we got ourselves seated in the boat; but we had not floated five yards before we perceived that if any of the party—and there was a little Highland woman who was going over the water with us, the boatman, his helper, and ourselves—should stir but a few inches, leaning to one side or the other, the boat would be full in an instant, and we at the bottom; besides, it was very leaky, and the woman was employed to lade out the water continually. It appeared that this crazy vessel was not the man's own, and that his was lying in a bay at a little distance. He said he would take us to it as fast as possible, but I was so much frightened I would gladly have given up the whole day's journey;

indeed, not one of us would have attempted to cross the lake in that boat for a thousand pounds. We reached the larger boat in safety after coasting a considerable way near the shore, but just as we were landing, William dropped the bundle which contained our food into the water. The fowls were no worse, but some sugar, ground coffee, and pepper-cake seemed to be entirely spoiled. We gathered together as much of the coffee and sugar as we could and tied it up and again trusted ourselves to the lake. The sun shone, and the air was calm— luckily it had been so, while we were in the crazy boat—we had rocks and woods on each side of us, or bare hills; seldom a single cottage, and there was no rememberable place till we came opposite to a waterfall of no inconsiderable size, that appeared to drop directly into the lake. Close to it was a hut, which we were told was the ferry-house. On the other side of the lake was a pretty farm under the mountains, beside a river, the cultivated grounds lying all together, and sloping towards the lake from the mountain hollow down which the river came. It is not easy to conceive how beautiful these spots appeared after moving on so long between the solitary steeps.

We went a considerable way further, and landed at Rob Roy's Caves, which are in fact no caves, but some fine rocks on the brink of the lake, in the crevices of which a man might bide himself cunningly enough; the water is very deep below them, and the hills above steep and covered with wood. The little Highland woman, who was in size about a match for our guide at Lanerk, accompanied us hither. There was something very gracious in the manners of this woman; she could scarcely speak five English words, yet she gave me, whenever I spoke to her, as many intelligible smiles as I had needed English words to answer me, and helped me over the rocks in the most obliging manner. She had left the boat out of good-will to us, or for her own amusement. She had never seen these caves before, but no doubt had heard of them, the tales of Rob Roy's exploits being told familiarly round the 'ingles' hereabouts, for this neighbourhood was his home. We landed at Inversneyde, the ferry-house by the waterfall, and were not sorry to part with our boatman, who was a coarse hard-featured man, and, speaking of the French, uttered the basest and most cowardly sentiments. His helper, a youth fresh from the Isle of Skye, was innocent of this fault, and though but a bad rower, was a far better companion; he could not speak a word of English, and sang a plaintive Gaelic air in a low tone while he plied his oar.

The ferry-house stood on the bank a few yards above the landing-place where the boat lies. It is a small hut under a steep wood, and a few yards to the right, looking towards the hut, is the waterfall The fall is not very high, but the stream is considerable, as we could see by the large black stones that were lying bare, but the rains, if they had reached this place, had had little effect upon the waterfall; its noise was not so great as to form a contrast with the stillness of the bay into which it falls, where the boat, and house, and waterfall itself seemed all sheltered and protected. The Highland woman was to go with us the two first miles of our journey. She led us along a bye foot-path a shorter way up the hill from the ferry-house. There is a considerable settling in the hills that border Loch Lomond, at the passage by which we were to cross to Loch Ketterine; Ben Lomond, terminating near the ferry-house, is on the same side of the water with it, and about three miles above Tarbet.

We had to climb right up the hill, which is very steep, and, when close under it, seemed to be high, but we soon reached the top, and when we were there had lost sight of the lake; and now our road was over a moor, or rather through a wide moorland hollow. Having gone a little way, we saw before us, at the distance of about half a mile, a very large stone building, a singular structure, with a high wall round it, naked hill above, and neither field nor tree near; but the moor was not overgrown with heath merely, but grey grass, such as cattle might pasture upon. We could not conjecture what this building was; it appeared as if it had been built strong to defend it from storms; but for what purpose? William called out to us that we should observe that place well, for it was exactly like one of the spittals of the Alps, built for the reception of travellers, and indeed I had thought it must be so before he spoke. This building, from its singular structure and appearance, made the place, which is itself in a country like Scotland nowise remarkable, take a character of unusual wildness and desolation—this when we first came in view of it; and afterwards, when we had passed it and looked back, three pyramidal mountains on the opposite side of Loch Lomond terminated the view, which under certain accidents of weather must be very grand. Our Highland companion had not English enough to give us any information concerning this strange building; we could only get from her that it was a 'large house,' which was plain enough.

We walked about a mile and a half over the moor without seeing any other dwelling but one hut by the burn-side, with a peat-stack and a ten-yards'-square enclosure for potatoes; then we came to several clusters of houses, even hamlets they might be called, but where there is any land belonging to the Highland huts there are so many outbuildings near, which differ in no respect from the dwelling-houses except that they send out no smoke, that one house looks like two or three. Near these houses was a considerable quantity of cultivated ground, potatoes and corn, and the people were busy making hay in the hollow places of the open vale, and all along the sides of the becks. It was a pretty sight altogether—men and women, dogs, the little running streams, with linen bleaching near them, and cheerful sunny hills and rocks on every side. We passed by one patch of potatoes that a florist might have been proud of; no carnation-bed ever looked more gay than this square plot of ground on the waste common. The flowers were in very large bunches, and of an extraordinary size, and of every conceivable shade of colouring from snow-white to deep purple. It was pleasing in that place, where perhaps was never yet a flower cultivated by man for his own pleasure, to see these blossoms grow more gladly than elsewhere, making a summer garden near the mountain dwellings.

At one of the clusters of houses we parted with our companion, who had insisted on bearing my bundle while she stayed with us. I often tried to enter into conversation with her, and seeing a small tarn before us, was reminded of the pleasure of fishing and the manner of living there, and asked her what sort of food was eaten in that place, if they lived much upon fish, or had mutton from the hills; she looked earnestly at me, and shaking her head, replied, 'Oh yes! eat fish—no papistes, eat everything.' The tarn had one small island covered with wood; the stream that runs from it falls into Loch Ketterine, which, after we had gone a little beyond the tarn, we saw at some distance before us.

Pursued the road, a mountain horse-track, till we came to a corner of what seemed the head of the lake, and there sate down completely tired, and hopeless as to the rest of our journey. The road ended at the shore, and no houses were to be seen on the opposite side except a few widely parted huts, and on the near side was a trackless heath. The land at the head of the lake was but a continuation of the common we had come along, and was covered with heather, intersected by a few straggling foot-paths.

Coleridge and I were faint with hunger, and could go no further till we had refreshed ourselves, so we ate up one of our fowls, and drank of the water of Loch Ketterine; but William could not be easy till he had examined the coast, so he left us, and made his way along the moor across the head of the lake. Coleridge and I, as we sate, had what seemed to us but a dreary prospect—a waste of unknown ground which we guessed we must travel over before it was possible for us to find a shelter. We saw a long way down the lake; it was all moor on the near side; on the other the hills were steep from the water, and there were large coppice-woods, but no cheerful green fields, and no road that we could see; we knew, however, that there must be a road from house to house; but the whole lake appeared a solitude—neither boats, islands, nor houses, no grandeur in the hills, nor any loveliness in the shores. When we first came in view of it we had said it was like a barren Ulswater—Ulswater dismantled of its grandeur, and cropped of its lesser beauties. When I had swallowed my dinner I hastened after William, and Coleridge followed me. Walked through the heather with some labour for perhaps half a mile, and found William sitting on the top of a small eminence, whence we saw the real head of the lake, which was pushed up into the vale a considerable way beyond the promontory where we now sate. The view up the lake was very pleasing, resembling Thirlemere below Armath. There were rocky promontories and woody islands, and, what was most cheering to us, a neat white house on the opposite shore; but we could see no boats, so, in order to get to it we should be obliged to go round the head of the lake, a long and weary way.

After Coleridge came up to us, while we were debating whether we should turn back or go forward, we espied a man on horseback at a little distance, with a boy following him on foot, no doubt a welcome sight, and we hailed him. We should have been glad to have seen either man, woman, or child at this time, but there was something uncommon and interesting in this man's appearance, which would have fixed our attention wherever we had met him. He was a complete Highlander in dress, figure, and face, and a very fine-looking man, hardy and vigorous, though past his prime. While he stood waiting for us in his bonnet and plaid, which never look more graceful than on horseback, I forgot our errand, and only felt glad that we were in the Highlands. William accosted him with, 'Sir, do you speak English?' He replied, 'A little.' He spoke however, sufficiently well for our purpose, and very distinctly, as all the Highlanders do who learn English as a foreign language; but in a long conversation they want words; he informed us that he himself was going beyond the Trossachs, to Callander, that no boats were kept to 'let;' but there were two gentlemen's houses at this end of the lake, one of which we could not yet see, it being hidden from us by a part of the hill on which we stood. The other house was that which we saw opposite to us; both the gentlemen kept boats, and probably might be able to spare one of their servants to go with us. After we had asked many questions, which the Highlander answered with patience and courtesy, he parted from us, going along a sort of horse-track, which a foot-passenger, if he once get into it, need not lose if he be careful.

When he was gone we again debated whether we should go back to Tarbet, or throw ourselves upon the mercy of one of the two gentlemen for a night's lodging. What we had seen of the main body of the lake made us little desire to see more of it; the Highlander upon the naked heath, in his Highland dress, upon his careful-going horse, with the boy following him, was worth it all; but after a little while we resolved to go on, ashamed to shrink from an adventure. Pursued the horse-track, and soon came in sight of the other gentleman's house, which stood on the opposite side of the vale, a little above the lake. It was a white house; no trees near it except a new plantation of firs; but the fields were green, sprinkled over with haycocks, and the brook which comes down the valley and falls into the lake ran through them. It was like a new-made farm in a mountain vale, and yet very pleasing after the depressing prospect which had been before us.

Our road was rough, and not easy to be kept. It was between five and six o'clock when we reached the brook side, where Coleridge and I stopped, and William went up towards the house, which was in a field, where about half a dozen people were at work. He addressed himself to one who appeared like the master, and all drew near him, staring at William as nobody could have stared but out of sheer rudeness, except in such a lonely place. He told his tale, and inquired about boats; there were no boats, and no lodging nearer than Callander, ten miles beyond the foot of the lake. A laugh was on every face when William said we were come to see the Trossachs; no doubt they thought we had better have stayed at our own homes. William endeavoured to make it appear not so very foolish, by in-forming them that it was a place much celebrated in England, though perhaps little thought of by them, and that we only differed from many of our countrymen in having come the wrong way in consequence of an erroneous direction.

After a little time the gentleman said we should be accommodated with such beds as they had, and should be welcome to rest in their house if we pleased. William came back for Coleridge and me; the men all stood at the door to receive us, and now their behaviour was perfectly courteous. We were conducted into the house by the same man who had directed us hither on the other side of the lake, and afterwards we learned that he was the father of our hostess. He showed us into a room up-stairs, begged we would sit at our ease, walk out, or do just as we pleased. It was a large square deal wainscoted room, the wainscot black with age, yet had never been painted : it did not look like an English room, and yet I do not know in what it differed, except that in England it is not common to see so large and well-built a room so ill-furnished: there were two or three large tables, and a few old chairs of different sorts, as if they had been picked up one did not know how, at sales, or had belonged to different rooms of the house ever since it was built. We sat perhaps three quarters of an hour, and I was about to carry down our wet coffee and sugar and ask leave to boil it, when the mistress of the house entered, a tall fine-looking woman, neatly dressed in a dark-coloured gown, with a white handkerchief tied round her head; she spoke to us in a very pleasing manner, begging permission to make tea for us, an offer which we thankfully accepted. Encouraged by the sweetness of her manners, I went down-stairs to dry my feet by the kitchen fire; she lent me a pair of stockings, and behaved to me with the utmost attention and kindness. She carried the tea-things into the room herself, leaving me to make tea, and set before us cheese and butter and barley cakes. These cakes are as thin as our oat-bread, but, instead of being crisp, are soft and leathery, yet we, being hungry, and the butter delicious, ate them with great pleasure, but when the same bread was set before us afterwards we did not like it.

After tea William and I walked out; we amused ourselves with watching the Highlanders at work: they went leisurely about everything, and whatever was to be done, all followed, old men, and young, and little children. We were driven into the house by a shower, which came on with the evening darkness, and the people leaving their work paused at the same time. I was pleased to see them a while after sitting round a blazing fire in the kitchen, father and son-in-law, master and man, and the mother with her little child on her knee. When I had been there before tea I had observed what a contrast there was between the mistress and her kitchen; she did not differ in appearance from an English country lady; but her kitchen, roof, Avails, and floor of mud, was all black alike; yet now, with the light of a bright fire upon so many happy countenances, the whole room made a pretty sight.

We heard the company laughing and talking long after we were in bed; indeed I believe they never work till they are tired. The children could not speak a word of English. They were very shy at first; but after I had caressed the eldest, and given her a red leather purse, with which she was delighted, she took hold of my hand and hung about me, changing her side-long looks for pretty smiles. Her mother lamented they were so far from school, they should be obliged to send the children down into the Lowlands to be taught reading and English. Callander, the nearest town, was twenty miles from them, and it was only a small place: they had their groceries from Glasgow. She said that at Callander was their nearest church, but sometimes 'got a preaching at the Garrison.' In explaining herself she informed us that the large building which had puzzled us in the morning had been built by Government, at the request of one of the Dukes of Montrose, for the defence of his domains against the attacks of Rob Roy. I will not answer for the truth of this; perhaps it might have been built for this purpose, and as a check on the Highlands in general; certain it is, however, that it was a garrison; soldiers used to be constantly stationed there, and have only been withdrawn within the last thirteen or fourteen years. Mrs. Macfarlane attended me to my room; she said she hoped I should be able to sleep upon blankets, and said they were 'fresh from the fauld.'

Saturday, August 27th—Before I rose, Mrs. Macfarlane came into my room to see if I wanted anything, and told me she should send the servant up with a basin of whey, saying, "We make very good whey in this country, indeed." I thought it the best I had ever tasted, but I cannot tell how this should be, for they only make skimmed-milk cheeses. I asked her for a little bread and milk for our breakfast, but she said it would be no trouble to make tea, as she must make it for the family; so we all breakfasted together. The cheese was set out, as before, with plenty of butter and barley-cakes, and fresh baked oaten cakes, which, no doubt, were made for us: they had been kneaded with cream, and were excellent. All the party pressed us to eat, and were very jocose about the necessity of helping out their coarse bread with butter, and they themselves ate almost as much butter as bread. In talking of the French and the present times, their language was what most people would call Jacobinical. They spoke much of the oppressions endured by the Highlanders further up, of the absolute impossibility of their living in any comfort, and of the cruelty of laying so many restraints on emigration. Then they spoke with animation of the attachment of the clans to their lairds: 'The laird of this place, Glengyle, where we live, could have commanded so many men who would have followed him to the death; and now there are none left.' It appeared that Mr. Macfarlane, and his wife's brother, Mr. Macalpine, farmed the place, inclusive of the whole vale upwards to the mountains, and the mountains themselves, under the lady of Glengyle, the mother of the young laird, a minor. It was a sheep-farm.

Speaking of another neighbouring laird, they said he had gone, like the rest of them, to Edinburgh, left his lands and his own people, spending his money where it brought him not any esteem, so that he was of no value either at home or abroad. We mentioned Rob Roy, and the eyes of all glistened; even the lady of the house, who was very diffident, and no great talker, exclaimed, 'He was a good man, Rob Roy! He had been dead only about eighty years, had lived in the next farm, which belonged to him, and there his bones were laid.' *{There is a mistake here. His bones were laid about fifteen or twenty miles from thence, in Balquhidder kirkyard. But it was under the belief that his grave is near the head of Loch Ketterine, in one of those pinfold-like burial grounds, of neglected and desolate appearance, which the traveller meets with in the Highlands of Scotland,' that the well-known poem on' Rob Roy's Grave' was composed. See Note 15 at the end of volume.}*

He was a famous swordsman. Having an arm much longer than other men, he had a greater command with his sword. As a proof of the length of his arm, they told us that he could garter his tartan stockings below the knee without stooping, and added a dozen different stories of single combats, which he had fought, all in perfect good-humour, merely to prove his prowess. I daresay they had stories of this kind which would hardly have been exhausted in the long evenings of a whole December week, Rob Roy being as famous here as ever Robin Hood was in the Forest of Sherwood; he also robbed from the rich, giving to the poor, and defending them from oppression. They tell of his confining the factor of the Duke of Montrose in one of the islands of Loch Ketterine, after having taken his money from him—the Duke's rents—in open day, while they were sitting at table. He was a formidable enemy of the Duke, but being a small laird against a greater, was overcome at last, and forced to resign all his lands on the Braes of Loch Lomond, including the caves which we visited, on account of the money he had taken from the Duke and could not repay.

When breakfast was ended the mistress desired the person whom we took to be her husband to 'return thanks.' He said a short grace, and in a few minutes they all went off to their work. We saw them about the door following one another like a flock of sheep, with the children after, whatever job they were engaged in. Mrs. Macfarlane told me she would show me the burying-place of the lairds of Glengyle, and took me to a square enclosure like a pinfold, with a stone ball at every corner; we had noticed it the evening before, and wondered what it could be. It was in the middle of a 'planting,' as they call plantations, which was enclosed for the preservation of the trees, therefore we had to climb over a high wall: it was a dismal spot, containing four or five graves overgrown with long grass, nettles, and brambles. Against the wall was a marble monument to the memory of one of the lairds, of whom they spoke with veneration: some English verses were inscribed upon the marble, purporting that he had been the father of his clan, a brave and good man. When we returned to the house she said she would show me what curious feathers they had in their country, and brought out a bunch carefully wrapped up in paper. On my asking her what bird they came from, 'Oh!' she replied, 'it is a great beast.' We conjectured it was an eagle, and from her description of its ways, and the manner of destroying it, we knew it was so. She begged me to accept of some of the feathers, telling me that some ladies wore them in their heads. I was much pleased with the gift, which I shall preserve in memory of her kindness and simplicity of manners, and the Highland solitude where she lived.

We took leave of the family with regret: they were handsome, healthy, and happy-looking people. It was ten o'clock when we departed. We had learned that there was a ferry-boat kept at three miles' distance, and if the man was at home he would row us down the lake to the Trossachs. Our walk was mostly through coppice-woods, along a horse-road, upon which narrow carts might travel. Passed that white house which had looked at us with such a friendly face when we were on the other side; it stood on the slope of a hill, with green pastures below it, plots of corn and coppice-wood, and behind, a rocky steep covered with wood. It was a very pretty place, but the morning being cold and dull, the opposite shore appeared dreary. Near to the white house we passed by another of those little pinfold squares, which we knew to be a burying-place; it was in a sloping green field among woods, and within sound of the beating of the water against the shore, if there were but a gentle breeze to stir it: I thought if I lived in that house, and my ancestors and kindred were buried there, I should sit many an hour under the walls of this plot of earth, where all the household would be gathered together.

We found the ferryman at work in the field above his hut, and he was at liberty to go with us, but, being wet and hungry, we begged that he would let us sit by his fire till we had refreshed ourselves. This was the first genuine Highland hut we had been in. We entered by the cowhouse, the house-door being within, at right angles to the outer door. The woman was distressed that she had a bad fire, but she heaped up some dry peats and heather, and, blowing it with her breath, in a short time raised a blaze that scorched us into comfortable feelings. A small part of the smoke found its way out of the hole of the chimney, the rest through the open window-places, one of which was within the recess of the fireplace, and made a frame to a little picture of the restless lake and the opposite shore, seen when the outer door was open. The woman of the house was very kind: whenever we asked her for anything it seemed a fresh pleasure to her that she had it for us; she always answered with a sort of softening down of the Scotch exclamation, 'Hoot!' 'Ho! yes, ye'll get that,' and hied to her cupboard in the spence. We were amused with the phrase 'Ye'll get that' in the Highlands, which appeared to us as if it came from a perpetual feeling of the difficulty with which most things are procured. We got oatmeal, butter, bread and milk, made some porridge, and then departed. It was rainy and cold, with a strong wind.

Coleridge was afraid of the cold in the boat, so he determined to walk down the lake, pursuing the same road we had come along. There was nothing very interesting for the first three or four miles on either side of the water; to the right, uncultivated heath or poor coppice-wood, and to the left, a scattering of meadow ground, patches of corn, coppice-woods, and here and there a cottage. The wind fell, and it began to rain heavily. On this William wrapped himself in the boatman's plaid, and lay at the bottom of the boat till we came to a place where I could not help rousing him.

We were rowing down that side of the lake which had hitherto been little else than a moorish ridge. After turning a rocky point we came to a bay closed in by rocks and steep woods, chiefly of full-grown birch. The lake was elsewhere ruffled, but at the entrance of this bay the breezes sunk, and it was calm: a small island was near, and the opposite shore, covered with wood, looked soft through the misty rain. William, rubbing his eyes, for he had been asleep, called out that he hoped I had not let him pass by anything that was so beautiful as this; and I was glad to tell him that it was but the beginning of a new land. After we had left this bay we saw before us a long reach of woods and rocks and rocky points that promised other bays more beautiful than what we had passed. The ferryman was a good-natured fellow, and rowed very industriously, following the ins and outs of the shore; he was delighted with the pleasure we expressed, continually repeating how pleasant it would have been on a fine day. I believe he was attached to the lake by some sentiment of pride, as his own domain—his being almost the only boat upon it—which made him, seeing we were willing gazers, take far more pains than an ordinary boatman; he would often say, after he had compassed the turning of a point, 'This is a bonny part,' and he always chose the bonniest, with greater skill than our prospect-hunters and 'picturesque travellers;' places screened from the winds—that was the first point; the rest followed of course,—richer growing trees, rocks and banks, and curves which the eye delights in. The second bay we came to differed from the rest; the hills retired a short space from the lake, leaving a few level fields between, on which was a cottage embosomed in trees: the bay was defended by rocks at each end, and the hills behind made a shelter for the cottage, the only dwelling, I believe, except one, on this side of Loch Ketterine. We now came to steeps that rose directly from the lake, and passed by a place called in the Gaelic the Den of the Ghosts, *{Goblins' Cave}* which reminded us of Lodore; it is a rock, or mass of rock, with a stream of large black stones like the naked or dried-up bed of a torrent down the side of it; birch-trees start out of the rock in every direction, and cover the hill above, further than we could see. The water of the lake below was very deep, black and calm. Our delight increased as we advanced, till we came in view of the termination of the lake, seeing where the river issues out of it through a narrow chasm between the hills.

Here I ought to rest, as we rested, and attempt to give utterance to our pleasure; but indeed I can impart but little of what we felt. We were still on the same side of the water, and, being immediately under the hill, within a considerable bending of the shore, we were enclosed by hills all round, as if we had been upon a smaller lake of which the whole was visible. It was an entire solitude; and all that we beheld was the perfection of loveliness and beauty.

We had been through many solitary places since we came into Scotland, but this place differed as much from any we had seen before as if there had been nothing in common between them: no thought of dreariness or desolation found entrance here; yet nothing was to be seen but water, wood, rocks, and heather, and bare mountains above. We saw the mountains by glimpses as the clouds passed by them, and were not disposed to regret, with our boatman, that it was not a fine day, for the near objects were not concealed from us, but softened by being seen through the mists. The lake is not very wide here, but appeared to be much narrower than it really is, owing to the many promontories, which are pushed so far into it that they are much more like islands than promontories. We had a longing desire to row to the outlet and look up into the narrow passage through which the river went; but the point where we were to land was on the other side, so we bent our course right across, and just as we came in sight of two huts, which have been built by Lady Perth as a shelter for those who visit the Trossachs, Coleridge hailed us with a shout of triumph from the door of one of them, exulting in the glory of Scotland. The huts stand at a small distance from each other, on a high and perpendicular rock that rises from the bed of the lake. A road, which has a very wild appearance, has been cut through the rock; yet even here, among these bold precipices, the feeling of excessive beautifulness overcomes every other. While we were upon the lake, on every side of us were bays within bays, often more like tiny lakes or pools than bays, and these not in long succession only, but all round, some almost on the broad breast of the water, the promontories shot out so far.

After we had landed we walked along the road to the uppermost of the huts, where Coleridge was standing. From the door of this hut we saw Benvenue opposite to us—a high mountain, but clouds concealed its top; its side, rising directly from the lake, is covered with birch-trees to a great height, and seamed with innumerable channels of torrents; but now there was no water in them, nothing to break in upon the stillness and repose of the scene; nor do I recollect hearing the sound of water from any side, the wind being fallen and the lake perfectly still; the place was all eye, and completely satisfied the sense and the heart. Above and below us, to the right and to the left, were rocks, knolls, and hills, which, wherever anything could grow—and that was everywhere between the rocks—were covered with trees and heather; the trees did not in any place grow so thick as an ordinary wood; yet I think there was never a bare space of twenty yards: it was more like a natural forest, where the trees grow in groups or singly, not hiding the surface of the ground, which, instead of being green and mossy, was of the richest-purple. The heather was indeed the most luxuriant I ever saw; it was so tall that a child of ten years old struggling through it would often have been buried head and shoulders, and the exquisite beauty of the colour, near or at a distance, seen under the trees, is not to be conceived. But if I were to go on describing for evermore, I should give but a faint, and very often a false, idea of the different objects and the various combinations of them in this most intricate and delicious place; besides, I tired myself out with describing at Loch Lomond, so I will hasten to the end of my tale. This reminds me of a sentence in a little pamphlet written by the minister of Callander, descriptive of the environs of that place. After having taken up at least six closely-printed pages with the Trossachs, he concludes thus, 'In a word, the Trossachs beggar all description,' (10) — a conclusion in which everybody who has been there will agree with him. I believe the word Trossachs signifies 'many hills': it is a name given to all the eminences at the foot of Loch Ketterine, and about half a mile beyond.

We left the hut, retracing the few yards of road which we had climbed; our boat lay at anchor under the rock in the last of all the compartments of the lake, a small oblong pool, almost shut up within itself, as several others had appeared to be, by jutting points of rock. The termination of a long out-shooting of the water, pushed up between the steps of the main shore, where the huts stand, and a broad promontory, which, with its hillocks and points and lesser promontories, occupies the centre of the foot of the lake. A person sailing through the lake up the middle of it, would just as naturally suppose that the outlet was here as on the other side; and so it might have been, with the most trifling change in the disposition of the ground, for at the end of this slip of water the lake is confined only by a gentle rising of a few yards towards an opening between the hills, a narrow pass or valley through which the river might have flowed. The road is carried through this valley, which only differs from the lower part of the vale of the lake in being excessively narrow, and without water; it is enclosed by mountains, rocky mounds, hills and hillocks, scattered over with birch-trees, and covered with Dutch myrtle (11) and heather, even surpassing what we had seen before. Our mother

Eve had no fairer, though a more diversified garden, to tend, than we found within this little close valley. It rained all the time, but the mists and calm air made us ample amends for a wetting.

At the opening of the pass we climbed up a low eminence, and had an unexpected prospect suddenly before us—another lake, small compared with Loch Ketterine, though perhaps four miles long, but the misty air concealed the end of it. The transition from the solitary wildness of Loch Ketterine and the narrow valley or pass to this scene was very delightful: it was a gentle place, with lovely open bays, one small island, corn fields, woods, and a group of cottages. This vale seemed to have been made to be tributary to the comforts of man, Loch Ketterine for the lonely delight of Nature, and kind spirits delighting in beauty. The sky was grey and heavy,—floating mists on the hill-sides, which softened the objects, and where we lost sight of the lake it appeared so near to the sky that they almost touched one another, giving a visionary beauty to the prospect. While we overlooked this quiet scene we could hear the stream rumbling among the rocks between the lakes, but the mists concealed any glimpse of it which we might have had. This small lake is called Loch Achray.

We returned, of course, by the same road. Our guide repeated over and over again his lamentations that the day was so bad, though we had often told him—not indeed with much hope that he would believe us—that we were glad of it. As we walked along he pulled a leafy twig from a birch-tree, and, after smelling it, gave it to me, saying, how 'sweet and halesome' it was, and that it was pleasant and very halesome on a fine summer's morning to sail under the banks where the birks are growing. This reminded me of the old Scotch songs, in which you continually hear of the 'pu'ing the birks.' Common as birches are in the north of England, I believe their sweet smell is a thing unnoticed among the peasants. We returned again to the huts to take a farewell look. We had shared our food with the ferryman and a traveller whom we had met here, who was going up the lake, and wished to lodge at the ferry-house, so we offered him a place in the boat. Coleridge chose to walk. We took the same side of the lake as before, and had much delight in visiting the bays over again; but the evening began to darken, and it rained so heavily before we had gone two miles that we were completely wet. It was dark when we landed, and on entering the house I was sick with cold.

The good woman had provided, according to her promise, a better fire than we had found in the morning; and indeed when I sate down in the chimney-corner of her smoky biggin' I thought I had never been more comfortable in my life. Coleridge had been there long enough to have a pan of coffee boiling for us, and having put our clothes in the way of drying, we all sate down, thankful for a shelter. We could not prevail upon the man of the house to draw near the fire, though he was cold and wet, or to suffer his wife to get him dry clothes till she had served us, which she did, though most willingly, not very expeditiously. A Cumberland man of the same rank would not have had such a notion of what was fit and right in his own house, or if he had, one would have accused him of servility; but in the Highlander it only seemed like politeness, however erroneous and painful to us, naturally growing out of the dependence of the inferiors of the clan upon their laird; he did not, however, refuse to let his wife bring out the whisky-bottle at our request: 'She keeps a dram,' as the phrase is; indeed, I believe there is scarcely a lonely house by the wayside in Scotland where travellers may not be accommodated with a dram. We asked for sugar, butter, barley-bread, and milk, and with a smile and a stare more of kindness than wonder, she replied, 'Ye'll get that,' bringing each article separately.

We caroused our cups of coffee, laughing like children at the strange atmosphere in which we were: the smoke came in gusts, and spread along the walls and above our heads in the chimney, where the hens were roosting like light clouds in the sky. We laughed and laughed again, in spite of the smarting of our eyes, yet had a quieter pleasure in observing the beauty of the beams and rafters gleaming between the clouds of smoke. They had been crusted over and varnished by many winters, till, where the firelight fell upon them; they were as glossy as black rocks on a sunny day cased in ice. When we had eaten our supper we sat about half an hour, and I think, I had never felt so deeply the blessing of a hospitable welcome and a warm fire. The man of the house repeated from time to time that we should often tell of this night when we got to our homes, and interposed praises of this, his own lake, which he had more than once, when we were returning in the boat, ventured to say was 'bonnier than Loch Lomond.' (12)

Our companion from the Trossachs, who it appeared was an Edinburgh drawing-master going during the vacation on a pedestrian tour to John o' Groat's House, was to sleep in the barn with William and Coleridge, where the man said he had plenty of dry hay. I do not believe that the hay of the Highlands is often very dry, but this year it had a better chance than usual: wet or dry, however, the next morning they said they had slept comfortably. When I went to bed, the mistress, desiring me to 'go ben' attended me with a candle, and assured me that the bed was dry, though not 'sic as I had been used to.' It was of chaff; there were two others in the room, a cupboard, and two chests, on one of which stood the milk in wooden vessels covered over; I should have thought that milk so kept could not have been sweet, but the cheese and butter were good. The walls of the whole house were of stone unplastered. It consisted of three apartments,—the cow-house at one end, the kitchen or house in the middle, and the spence at the other end. The rooms were divided, not up to the rigging, but only to the beginning of the roof, so that there was a free passage for light and smoke from one end of the house to the other.

I went to bed some time before the family. The door was shut between us, and they had a bright fire, which I could not see; but the light it sent up among the varnished rafters and beams, which crossed each other in almost as intricate and fantastic a manner as I have seen the under-boughs of a large beech-tree withered by the depth of the shade above, produced the most beautiful effect that can be conceived. It was like what I should suppose an underground cave or temple to be, with a dripping or moist roof, and the moonlight entering in upon it by some means or other, and yet the colours were more like melted gems. I lay looking up till the light of the fire faded away, and the man and his wife and child had crept into their bed at the other end of the room. I did not sleep much, but passed a comfortable night, for my bed, though hard, was warm and clean: the unusualness of my situation prevented me from sleeping. I could hear the waves beat against the shore of the lake; a little 'syke' close to the door made a much louder noise; and when I sate up in my bed I could see the lake through an open window-place at the bed's head. Add to this, it rained all night. I was less occupied by remembrance of the Trossachs, beautiful as they were, than the vision of the Highland hut, which I could not get out of my head. I thought of the Fairyland of Spenser, and what I had read in romance at other times, and then, what a feast would it be for a London pantomime-maker, could he but transplant it to Drury Lane, with all its beautiful colours!

The Tontine, on the right, where she saw the coffee drinkers

Dumbarton Castle on the Firth of Clyde

North Loch Lomond and Luss to the bottom left

Ben Lomond

Tarbet to Arrochar

Arrochar and the hotel

The Cobbler

Looking across Loch Lomond
from Inversnaid harbour

In the Trossachs towards
Loch Katrine

The large building Dorothy saw was Inversnaid Barracks. These were destroyed
in the '45 by the Mac Gregors.

THIRD WEEK

Sunday, August 28th—We were desirous to have crossed the mountains above Glengyle to Glenfalloch, at the head of Loch Lomond, but it rained so heavily that it was impossible, so the ferryman engaged to row us to the point where Coleridge and I had rested, while William was going on our doubtful adventure. The hostess provided us with tea and sugar for our breakfast; the water was boiled in an iron pan, and dealt out to us in a jug, a proof that she does not often drink tea, though she said she had always tea and sugar in the house. She and the rest of the family breakfasted on curds and whey, as taken out of the pot in which she was making cheese; she insisted upon my taking some also; and her husband joined in with the old story, that it was 'varra halesome.' I thought it exceedingly good, and said to myself that they lived nicely with their cow: she was meat, drink, and company. Before breakfast the housewife was milking behind the chimney, and I thought I had seldom heard a sweeter fire-side sound. In an evening, sitting over a sleepy, low-burnt fire, it would lull one like the purring of a cat.

When we departed, the good woman shook me cordially by the hand, saying she hoped that, if ever we came into Scotland again, we would come and see her. The lake was calm, but it rained so heavily that we could see little. Landed at about ten o'clock, almost wet to the skin, and, with no prospect but of streaming rains, faced the mountain-road to Loch Lomond. We recognised the same objects passed before,—the tarn, the potato-bed, and the cottages with their burnies, which were no longer, as one might say, household streams, but made us only think of the mountains and rocks they came from. Indeed, it is not easy to imagine how different everything appeared; the mountains with mists and torrents alive and always changing; but the low grounds where the inhabitants had been at work the day before were melancholy, with here and there a few haycocks and hay scattered about.

Wet as we were, William and I turned out of our path to the Garrison house. A few rooms of it seemed to be inhabited by some wretchedly poor families, and it had all the desolation of a large, decayed mansion in the suburbs of a town, abandoned of its proper inhabitants, and become the abode of paupers. In spite of its outside bravery, it was but a poor protection against 'the sword of winter, keen and cold.' We looked at the building through the arch of a broken gateway of the courtyard, in the middle of which it stands. Upon that stormy day it appeared more than desolate; there was something about it even frightful.

When beginning to descend the hill towards Loch Lomond, we overtook two girls, who told us we could not cross the ferry till evening, for the boat was gone with a number of people to church. One of the girls was exceedingly beautiful; and the figures of both of them, in grey plaids falling to their feet, their faces only being uncovered, excited our attention before we spoke to them; but they answered us so sweetly that we were quite delighted, at the same time that they stared at us with an innocent look of wonder. I think I never heard the English language sound more sweetly than from the mouth of the elder of these girls, while she stood at the gate answering our inquiries, her face flushed with the rain; her pronunciation was clear and distinct: without difficulty, yet slow, like that of a foreign speech. They told us we might sit in the ferry-house till the return of the boat, went in with us, and made a good fire as fast as possible to dry our wet clothes. We learnt that the taller was the sister of the ferryman, and had been left in charge with the house for the day, that the other was his wife's sister, and was come with her mother on a visit,—an old woman, who sate in a corner beside the cradle, nursing her little grandchild. We were glad to be housed, with our feet upon a warm hearth-stone; and our attendants were so active and good-humoured that it was pleasant to have to desire them to do anything. The younger was a delicate and unhealthy-looking girl; but there was an uncommon meekness in her countenance, with an air of premature intelligence, which is often seen in sickly young persons. The other made me think of Peter Bell's 'Highland Girl:'

'As light and beauteous as a squirrel,
As beauteous and as wild.'

She moved with unusual activity, which was chastened very delicately by a certain hesitation in her looks when she spoke, being able to understand us but imperfectly. They were both exceedingly desirous to get me what I wanted to make me comfortable. I was to have a gown and petticoat of the mistress's; so they turned out her whole wardrobe upon the parlour floor, talking Erse to one another, and laughing all the time. It was long before they could decide which of the gowns I was to have; they chose at last, no doubt thinking that it was the best, a light-coloured sprigged cotton, with long sleeves, and they both laughed while I was putting it on, with the blue linsey petticoat, and one or the other, or both together, helped me to dress, repeating at least half a dozen times, 'You never had on the like of that before.' They held a consultation of several minutes over a pair of coarse woollen stockings, gabbling Erse as fast as their tongues could move, and looked as if uncertain what to do. At last, with great diffidence, they offered them to me, adding, as before, that I had never worn 'the like of them.' When we entered the house we had been not a little glad to see a fowl stewing in barley-broth; and now, when the wettest of our clothes were stripped off, began again to recollect that we were hungry, and asked if we could have dinner. 'Oh yes, ye may get that,' the elder replied, pointing to the pan on the fire.

Conceive what a busy house it was—all our wet clothes to be dried, dinner prepared and set out for us four strangers, and a second cooking for the family. Add to this, two rough 'callans' as they called them, boys about eight years old, were playing beside us; the poor baby was fretful all the while; the old woman sang doleful Erse songs, rocking it in its cradle the more violently the more it cried; then there were a dozen cookings of porridge, and it could never be fed without the assistance of all three. The hut was after the Highland fashion, but without anything beautiful, except its situation. The floor was rough, and wet with the rain that came in at the door, so that the lasses' bare feet were as wet as if they had been walking through street puddles, in passing from one room to another. The windows were open, as at the other hut, but the kitchen had a bed in it, and was much smaller, and the shape of the house was like that of a common English cottage, without its comfort; yet there was no appearance of poverty— indeed, quite the contrary. The peep out of the open door-place across the lake made some amends for the want of the long roof and elegant rafters of our boatman's cottage, and all the while the waterfall, which we could not see, was roaring at the end of the hut, which seemed to serve as a sounding-board for its noise, so that it was not unlike sitting in a house where a mill is going. The dashing of the waves against the shore could not be distinguished; yet in spite of my knowledge of this I could not help fancying that the tumult and storm came from the lake, and went out several times to see if it was possible to row over in safety.

After long waiting we grew impatient for our dinner; at last the pan was taken off, and carried into the other room; but we had to wait at least another half hour before the ceremony of dishing up was completed; yet, with all this bustle and difficulty, the manner in which they, and particularly the elder of the girls, performed everything, was perfectly graceful. We ate a hearty dinner, and had time to get our clothes quite dry before the arrival of the boat. The girls could not say at what time it would be at home; on our asking them if the church was far off they replied, 'Not very far;' and when we asked how far, they said, 'Perhaps about four or five miles.' I believe a Church of England congregation would hold themselves excused for non-attendance three parts of the year, having but half as far to go; but in the lonely parts of Scotland they make little of a journey of nine or ten miles to a preaching. They have not perhaps an opportunity of going more than once in a quarter of a year, and, setting piety aside, have other motives to attend; they hear the news, public and private, and see their friends and neighbours; for, though the people who meet at these times may be gathered together from a circle of twenty miles' diameter, a sort of neighbourly connexion must be so brought about. There is something exceedingly pleasing to my imagination in this gathering together of the inhabitants of these secluded districts—for instance, the borderers of these two large lakes meeting at the deserted garrison which I have described. The manner of their travelling is on foot, on horseback, and in boats across the waters,—young and old, rich and poor, all in their best dress.

If it were not for these Sabbath-day meetings one summer month would be like another summer month, one winter month like another—detached from the goings-on of the world, and solitary throughout. From the time of earliest childhood they will be like landing-places in the memory of a person who has passed his life in these thinly-peopled regions. They must generally leave distinct impressions, differing from each other so much as they do in circumstances, in time and place, etc.,—some in the open fields, upon hills, in houses, under large rocks, in storms, and in fine weather.

After long waiting, the girls, who had been on the look-out, informed us that the boat was coming. I went to the water-side, and saw a cluster of people on the opposite shore; but, being yet at a distance, they looked more like soldiers surrounding a carriage than a group of men and women; red and green were the distinguishable colours.

We hastened to get ourselves ready as soon as we saw the party approach, but had longer to wait than we expected, the lake being wider than it appears to be. As they drew near we could distinguish men in tartan plaids, women in scarlet cloaks, and green umbrellas by the half-dozen. The landing was as pretty a sight as ever I saw. The bay, which had been so quiet two days before, was all in motion with small waves, while the swoln waterfall roared in our ears. The boat came steadily up, being pressed almost to the water's edge by the weight of its cargo; perhaps twenty people landed, one after another. It did not rain much, but the women held up their umbrellas; they were dressed in all the colours of the rainbow, and with their scarlet cardinals, the tartan plaids of the men, and Scotch bonnets, made a gay appearance. There was a joyous bustle surrounding the boat, which even imparted something of the same character to the waterfall in its tumult, and the restless grey waves; the young men laughed and shouted, the lasses laughed, and the elder folks seemed to be in a bustle to be away. I remember well with what haste the mistress of the house, where we were, ran up to seek after her child, and seeing us, how anxiously and kindly she inquired how we had fared, if we had had a good fire, had been well waited upon, etc. etc. All this in three minutes—for the boatman had another party to bring from the other side, and hurried us off.

The hospitality we had met with at the two cottages and Mr. Macfarlane's gave us very favourable impressions on this our first entrance into the Highlands, and at this day the innocent merriment of the girls, with their kindness to us, and the beautiful figure and face of the elder, come to my mind whenever I think of the ferry-house and waterfall of Loch Lomond, and I never think of the two girls but the whole image of that romantic spot is before me, a living image, as it will be to my dying day. The following poem *{To a Highland Girl. At Inversneyde upon Loch Lomond}* was written by William not long after our return from Scotland:—

Sweet Highland Girl, a very shower
Of beauty is thy earthly dower!
Twice seven consenting years have shed
This fall of water, that doth make
A murmur near the silent Lake;
This little Bay, a quiet road
That holds in shelter thy abode;
In truth together ye do seem
Like something fashion'd in a dream;
Such forms as from their covert peep
When earthly cares are laid asleep!
Yet, dream and vision as thou art,
I bless thee with a human heart:
God shield thee to thy latest years!
I neither know thee nor thy peers;
And yet my eyes are filled with tears.
With earnest feeling I shall pray
For thee when I am far away:
For never saw I mien or face,
In which more plainly I could trace
Benignity and home-bred sense
Ripening in perfect innocence.
Here, scattered like a random seed,
Remote from men, thou dost not need
Th' embarrass'd look of shy distress
And maidenly shamefacedness;
Thou wear'st upon thy forehead clear
The freedom of a mountaineer:
A face with gladness overspread!
Sweet smiles, by human-kindness bred!
And seemliness complete,that sways
Thy courtesies, about thee plays;
With no restraint but such as springs
From quick and eager visitings
Of thoughts that lie beyond the reach
Of thy few words of English speech:
A bondage sweetly brook'd, a strife
That gives thy gestures grace and life!

Their utmost bounty on thy head:
And these grey rocks; this household lawn;
These trees, a veil just half withdrawn;
So have I, not unmoved in mind,
Seen birds of tempest-loving kind,
Thus beating up against the wind.
What hand but would a garland cull
For thee, who art so beautifull?
0 happy pleasure! here to dwell
Beside thee in some heathy dell;
Adopt your homely ways and dress,
A Shepherd, thou a Shepherdess!
But I could frame a wish for thee
More like a grave reality:
Thou art to me but as a wave
Of the wild sea: and I would have
Some claim upon thee, if I could,
Though but of common neighbourhood.
What joy to hear thee and to see!
Thy elder brother I would be,
Thy father anything to thee.
Now thanks to Heaven! that of its grace
Hath led me to this lonely place!
Joy have I had; and going hence
I bear away my recompence.
In spots like these it is we prize
Our memory, feel that she hath eyes:
Then why should I be loth to stir 1
I feel this place is made for her;
To give new pleasure like the past
Continued long as life shall last.
Nor am I loth, though pleased at heart,
Sweet Highland Girl, from thee to part;
For I, methinks, till I grow old,
As fair before me shall behold
As I do now, the Cabin small,
The Lake, the Bay, the Waterfall,
And thee, the Spirit of them all.

We were rowed over speedily by the assistance of two youths, who went backwards and forwards for their own amusement, helping at the oars, and pulled as if they had strength and spirits to spare for a year to come. We noticed that they had uncommonly fine teeth, and that they and the boatmen were very handsome people. Another merry crew took our place in the boat.

We had three miles to walk to Tarbet. It rained, but not heavily; the mountains were not concealed from us by the mists, but appeared larger and more grand; twilight was coming on, and the obscurity under which we saw the objects, with the sounding of the torrents, kept our minds alive and wakeful; all was solitary and huge—sky, water, and mountains mingled together. While we were walking forward, the road leading us over the top of a brow, we stopped suddenly at the sound of a half-articulate Gaelic hooting from the field close to us. It came from a little boy, whom we could see on the hill between us and the lake, wrapped up in a grey plaid. He was probably calling home the cattle for the night. His appearance was in the highest degree moving to the imagination: mists were on the hillsides, darkness shutting in upon the huge avenue of mountains, torrents roaring, no house in sight to which the child might belong; his dress, cry, and appearance all different from anything we had been accustomed to. It was a text, as William has since observed to me, containing in itself the whole history of the Highlander's life—his melancholy, his simplicity, his poverty, his superstition, and above all, that visionariness which results from a communion with the unworldliness of nature.

When we reached Tarbet the people of the house were anxious to know how we had fared, particularly the girl who had waited upon us. Our praises of Loch Ketterine made her exceedingly happy, and she ventured to say, of which we had heard not a word before, that it was 'bonnier to her fancy than Loch Lomond.' The landlord, who was not at home when we had set off, told us that if he had known of our going he would have recommended us to Mr. Macfarlane's or the other farm-house, adding that they were hospitable people in that vale. Coleridge and I got tea, and William and the drawing-master chose supper; they asked to have a broiled fowl, a dish very common in Scotland, to which the mistress replied, 'Would not a "boiled" one do as well' They consented, supposing that it would be more easily cooked; but when the fowl made its appearance, to their great disappointment it proved a cold one that had been stewed in the broth at dinner.

Monday, August 29^{*th*}—It rained heavily this morning and, having heard so much of the long rains since we came into Scotland, as well as before, we had no hope that it would be over in less than three weeks at the least, so poor Coleridge, being very unwell, determined to send his clothes to Edinburgh and make the best of his way thither, being afraid to face much wet weather in an open carriage. William and I were unwilling to be confined at Tarbet, so we resolved to go to Arrochar, a mile and a half on the road to Inverary, where there is an inn celebrated as a place of good accommodation for travellers. Coleridge and I set off on foot, and William was to follow with the car, but a heavy shower coming on, Coleridge left me to shelter in a hut and wait for William while he went on before. This hut was unplastered, and without windows, crowded with beds, uncomfortable, and not in the simplicity of the ferryman's house. A number of good clothes were hanging against the walls, and a green silk umbrella was set up in a corner. I should have been surprised to see an umbrella in such a place before we came into the Highlands; but umbrellas are not so common anywhere as there—a plain proof of the wetness of the climate; even five minutes after this a girl passed us without shoes and stockings, whose gown and petticoat were not worth half a crown, holding an umbrella over her bare head.

 We turned at a guide-post, 'To the New Inn,' and, after descending a little, and winding round the bottom of a hill, saw, at a small distance, a white house half hidden by tall trees upon a lawn that slopes down to the side of Loch Long, a sea-loch, which is here very narrow. Right before us, across the lake, was The Cobbler, which appeared to rise directly from the water; but, in fact, it overtopped another hill, being a considerable way behind. The inn looked so much like a gentleman's house that we could hardly believe it was an inn. We drove down the broad gravel walk, and, making a sweep, stopped at the front door, were shown into a large parlour with a fire, and my first thought was, 'How comfortable we should be!' But Coleridge, who had arrived before us, checked my pleasure: the waiter had shown himself disposed to look coolly upon us, and there had been a hint that we could not have beds. A party was expected, who had engaged all the beds. We conjectured this might be but a pretence, and ordered dinner in the hope that matters would clear up a little, and we thought they could not have the heart to turn us out in so heavy a rain if it were possible to lodge us. We had a nice dinner, yet would have gladly changed our roasted lamb and pickles, and the gentleman-waiter with his napkin in his pocket, for the more homely fare of the smoky hut at Loch Ketterine, and the good woman's busy attentions, with the certainty of a hospitable shelter at night. After dinner I spoke to the landlord himself, but he was not to be moved; he could not even provide one bed for me, so nothing was to be done, but either to return to Tarbet with Coleridge, or that William and I should push on the next stage, to Cairndow. We had an interesting close view from the windows of the room where we sate, looking across the lake, which did not differ in appearance, as we saw it here, from a fresh-water lake. The sloping lawn on which the house stood was prettily scattered over with trees; but we had seen the place to great advantage at our first approach, owing to the mists upon the mountains, which had made them seem exceedingly high, while the strange figures on The Cobbler appeared and disappeared, like living things; but, as the day cleared, we were disappointed in what was more like the permanent effect of the scene. The mountains were not so lofty as we had supposed, and the low grounds not so fertile; yet still it is a very interesting, I may say beautiful, place.

The rain ceased entirely, so we resolved to go on to Cairndow, and had the satisfaction of seeing that our landlord had not told us an untruth concerning the expected company; for just before our departure we saw, on the opposite side of the vale, a coach with four horses, another carriage, and two or three men on horseback—a striking procession, as it moved along between the bare mountain and the lake. Twenty years ago, perhaps, such a sight had not been seen here except when the Duke of Argyle, or some other Highland chieftain, might chance to be going with his family to London or Edinburgh. They had to cross a bridge at the head of the lake, which we could not see, so, after disappearing about ten minutes, they drove up to the door—three old ladies, two waiting-women, and store of men-servants. The old ladies were as gaily dressed as bullfinches in spring-time. We heard the next day that they were the renowned Miss Waughs of Carlisle, and that they enjoyed themselves over a game at cards in the evening.

Left Arrochar at about four o'clock in the afternoon. Coleridge accompanied us a little way; we portioned out the contents of our purse before our parting and, after we had lost sight of him, drove heavily along. Crossed the bridge, and looked to the right, up the vale, which is soon terminated by mountains: it was of a yellow green, with but few trees and few houses; sea-gulls were flying above it. Our road—the same along which the carriages had come—was directly under the mountains on our right hand, and the lake was close to us on our left, the waves breaking among stones overgrown with yellow sea-weed; fishermen's boats, and other larger vessels than are seen on fresh-water lakes were lying at anchor near the opposite shore; sea-birds flying overhead; the noise of torrents mingled with the beating of the waves, and misty mountains enclosed the vale;—a melancholy but not a dreary scene. Often have I, in looking over a map of Scotland, followed the intricate windings of one of these sea-lochs, till, pleasing myself with my own imaginations, I have felt a longing, almost painful, to travel among them by land or by water.

This was the first sea-loch we had seen. We came prepared for a new and great delight, and the first impression which William and I received, as we drove rapidly through the rain down the lawn of Arrochar, the objects dancing before us, was even more delightful than we had expected. But, as I have said, when we looked through the window, as the mists disappeared and the objects were seen more distinctly, there was less of sheltered valley-comfort than we had fancied to ourselves, and the mountains were not so grand; and now that we were near to the shore of the lake, and could see that it was not of fresh water, the wreck, the broken sea-shells, and scattered sea-weed gave somewhat of a dull and uncleanly look to the whole lake, and yet the water was clear, and might have appeared as beautiful as that of Loch Lomond, if with the same pure, pebbly shore. Perhaps, had we been in a more cheerful mood of mind we might have seen everything with a different eye. The stillness of the mountains, the motion of the waves, the streaming torrents, the sea-birds, the fishing-boats were all melancholy; yet still, occupied as my mind was with other things, I thought of the long windings through which the waters of the sea had come to this inland retreat, visiting the inner solitudes of the mountains, and I could have wished to have mused out a summer's day on the shores of the lake. From the foot of these mountains whither might not a little barque carry one away. Though so far inland, it is but a slip of the great ocean: seamen, fishermen, and shepherds here find a natural home. We did not travel far down the lake, but, turning to the right through an opening of the mountains, entered a glen called Glen Croe.

Our thoughts were full of Coleridge, and when we were enclosed in the narrow dale, with a length of winding road before us, a road that seemed to have insinuated itself into the very heart of the mountains—the brook, the road, bare hills, floating mists, scattered stones, rocks, and herds of black cattle being all that we could see,—I shivered at the thought of his being sickly and alone, travelling from place to place.

The Cobbler, on our right, was pre-eminent above the other hills; the singular rocks on its summit, seen so near, were like ruins—castles or watch-towers. After we had passed one reach of the glen, another opened out, long, narrow, deep, and houseless, with herds of cattle and large stones; but the third reach was softer and more beautiful, as if the mountains had there made a warmer shelter, and there were a more gentle climate. The rocks by the riverside had dwindled away, the mountains were smooth and green, and towards the end, where the glen sloped upwards, it was a cradle-like hollow, and at that point where the slope became a hill, at the very bottom of the curve of the cradle, stood one cottage, with a few fields and beds of potatoes. There was also another house near the roadside, which appeared to be a herdsman's hut. The dwelling in the middle of the vale was a very pleasing object. I said within myself, 'How quietly might a family live in this pensive solitude, cultivating and loving their own fields!' But the herdsman's hut, being the only one in the vale, had a melancholy face; not being attached to any particular plot of land, one could not help considering it as just kept alive and above ground by some dreary connexion with the long barren tract we had travelled through.

The afternoon had been exceedingly pleasant after we had left the vale of Arrochar; the sky was often threatening, but the rain blew off, and the evening was uncommonly fine. The sun had set a short time before we had dismounted from the car to walk up the steep hill at the end of the glen. Clouds were moving all over the sky—some of a brilliant yellow hue, which shed a light like bright moonlight upon the mountains. We could not have seen the head of the valley under more favourable circumstances.

The passing away of a storm is always a time of life and cheerfulness, especially in a mountainous country; but, that afternoon and evening, the sky was in an extraordinary degree vivid and beautiful. We often stopped in ascending the hill to look down the long reach of the glen. The road, following the course of the river as far as we could see, the farm and cottage, hills, smooth towards the base and rocky higher up, were the sole objects before us. This part of Glen Croe reminded us of some of the dales of the north of England— Grisdale above. Ulswater, for instance; but the length of it, and the broad highway, which is always to be seen at a great distance, a sort of centre of the vale, a point of reference, gives to the whole of the glen, and each division of it, a very different character.

At the top of the hill we came to a seat with the well-known inscription, 'Rest and be thankful.' On the same stone it was recorded that the road had been made by Col. Wade's regiment. The seat is placed so as to command a full view of the valley, and the long, long road, which, with the fact recorded, and the exhortation, makes it an affecting resting-place. We called to mind with pleasure a seat under the braes of Loch Lomond on which I had rested, where the traveller is informed by an inscription upon a stone that the road was made by Col. Lascelles' regiment. There, the spot had not been chosen merely as a resting-place, for there was no steep ascent in the highway, but it might be for the sake of a spring of water and a beautiful rock, or, more probably, because at that point the labour had been more than usually toilsome in hewing through the rock. Soon after we had climbed the hill we began to descend into another glen, called Glen Kinglas. We now saw the western sky, which had hitherto been hidden from us by the hill—a glorious mass of clouds uprising from a sea of distant mountains, stretched out in length before us, towards the west—and close by us was a small lake or tarn. From the reflection of the crimson clouds the water appeared of a deep red, like melted rubies, yet with a mixture of a grey or blackish hue; the gorgeous light of the sky, with the singular colour of the lake, made the scene exceedingly romantic; yet it was more melancholy than cheerful. With all the power of light from the clouds, there was an overcasting of the gloom of evening, a twilight upon the hills.

We descended rapidly into the glen, which resembles-the lower part of Glen Croe, though it seemed to be inferior in beauty; but before we had passed through one reach it was quite dark, and I only know that the steeps were high, and that we had the company of a foaming stream; and many a vagrant torrent crossed us, dashing down the hills. The road was bad, and, uncertain how we should fare, we were eager and somewhat uneasy to get forward; but when we were out of the close glen, and near to Cairndow, as a traveller had told us, the moon showed her clear face in the sky, revealing a spacious vale, with a broad loch and sloping corn fields; the hills not very high. This cheerful sight put us into spirits, and we thought it was at least no dismal place to sit up all night in, if they had no beds, and they could not refuse us a shelter. We were, however, well received, and sate down in a neat parlour with a good fire.

Tuesday, August 30th—Breakfasted before our departure, and ate a herring, fresh from the water, at our landlord's earnest recommendation—much superior to the herrings we get in the north of England. {*I should rather think so!—Ed.*} Though we rose at seven, could not set off before nine o'clock; the servants were in bed; the kettle did not boil—indeed, we were completely out of patience; but it had always been so, and we resolved to go off in future without breakfast. Cairndow is a single house by the side of the loch, I believe resorted to by gentlemen in the fishing season; it is a pleasant place for such a purpose;—but the vale did not look so beautiful as by moonlight—it had a sort of sea-coldness without mountain grandeur. There is a ferry for foot-passengers from Cairndow to the other side of the water, and the road, along which all carriages go, is carried round the head of the lake, perhaps a distance of three miles.

After we had passed the landing-place of the ferry opposite to Cairndow we saw the lake spread out to a great width, more like an arm of the sea or a great river than one of our lakes; it reminded us of the Severn at the Chepstow passage, but the shores were less rich and the hills higher. The sun shone, which made the morning cheerful, though there was a cold wind. Our road never carried us far from the lake, and with the beating of the waves, the sparkling sunshiny water, boats, the opposite hills, and, on the side on which we travelled, the chance cottages, the coppice woods, and common business of the fields, the ride could not but be amusing. But what most excited our attention was, at one particular place, a cluster of fishing-boats at anchor in a still corner of the lake, a small bay or harbour by the wayside. They were overshadowed by fishermen's nets hung out to dry, which formed a dark awning that covered them like a tent, overhanging the water on each side, and falling in the most exquisitely graceful folds. There was a monastic pensiveness, a funereal gloom in the appearance of this little company of vessels, which was the more interesting from the general liveliness and glancing motions of the water, they being perfectly still and silent in their sheltered nook.

When we had travelled about seven miles from Cairndow, winding round the bottom of a hill, we came in view of a great basin or elbow of the lake. Completely out of sight of the long track of water we had coasted, we seemed now to be on the edge of a very large, almost circular, lake, the town of Inverary before us, a line of white buildings on a low promontory right opposite, and close to the water's edge; the whole landscape a showy scene, and bursting upon us at once. A traveller who was riding by our side called out, 'Can that be the Castle?' Recollecting the prints which we had seen, we knew it could not; but the mistake is a natural one at that distance: it is so little like an ordinary town, from the mixture of regularity and irregularity in the buildings. With the expanse of water and pleasant mountains, the scattered boats and sloops, and those gathered together, it had a truly-festive appearance. A few steps more brought us in view of the Castle, a stately turreted mansion, but with a modern air, standing on a lawn, retired from the water, and screened behind by woods covering the sides of high hills to the top, and still beyond, by bare mountains. Our road wound round the semi-circular shore, crossing two bridges of lordly architecture. The town looked pretty when we drew near to it in connexion with its situation, different from any place I had ever seen, yet exceedingly like what I imaged to myself from representations in raree-shows, or pictures of foreign places— Venice, for example—painted on the scene of a play-house, which one is apt to fancy are as cleanly and gay as they look through the magnifying-glass of the raree-show or in the candle-light dazzle of a theatre. At the door of the inn, though certainly the buildings had not that delightful outside which they appeared to have at a distance, yet they looked very pleasant. The range bordering on the water consisted of little else than the inn, being a large house, with very large stables, the county gaol, the opening into the main street into the town, and an arched gateway, the entrance into the Duke of Argyle's private domain.

We were decently well received at the inn, but it was over-rich in waiters and large rooms, to be exactly to our taste, though quite in harmony with the neighbourhood. Before dinner we went into the Duke's pleasure-grounds, which are extensive, and of course command a variety of lively and interesting views. Walked through avenues of tall beech-trees, and observed some that we thought even the tallest we had ever seen; but they were all scantily covered with leaves, and the leaves exceedingly small—indeed, some of them, in the most exposed situations, were almost bare as if it had been winter. Travellers who wish to view the inside of the castle send in their names, and the Duke appoints the time of their going; but we did not think that what we should see could repay us for the trouble, there being no pictures, and the house, which I believe has not been built above half a century, is fitted up in the modern style. If there had been any reliques of the ancient costume of the castle of a Highland chieftain, we should have been sorry to have passed it.

Sate after dinner by the fireside till near sunset, for it was very cold, though the sun shone all day. At the beginning of this, our second walk, we passed through the town, which is but a doleful example of Scotch filth. The houses are plastered or rough-cast, and washed yellow—well built, well sized, and sash-windowed, bespeaking a connexion with the Duke, such a dependence as may be expected in a small town so near to his mansion; and indeed he seems to have done his utmost to make them comfortable, according to our English notions of comfort. They are fit for the houses of people living decently upon a decent trade; but the windows and door-steads were as dirty as in a dirty by-street of a large town, making a most unpleasant contrast with the comely face of the buildings towards the water, and the ducal grandeur and natural festivity of the scene. Smoke and blackness are the wild growth of a Highland hut: the mud floors cannot be washed, the door-steads are trampled by cattle, and if the inhabitants be not very cleanly it gives one little pain; but dirty people living in two-storied stone houses, with dirty sash windows, are a melancholy spectacle anywhere, giving the notion either of vice or the extreme of wretchedness.

Returning through the town, we went towards the Castle, and entered the Duke's grounds by a porter's lodge, following the carriage-road through the park, which is prettily scattered over with trees, and slopes gently towards the lake. A great number of lime-trees were growing singly, not beautiful in their shape, but I mention them for their resemblance to one of the same kind we had seen in the morning, which formed a shade as impenetrable as the roof of any house. The branches did not spread far, nor any one branch much further than another; on the outside it was like a green bush shorn with shears, but when we sate upon a bench under it, looking upwards, in the middle of the tree we could not perceive any green at all; it was like a hundred thousand magpies' nests clustered and matted together, the twigs and boughs being so intertwined that neither the light of the mid-day sun nor showers of hail or rain could pierce through them. The lime-trees on the lawn resembled this tree both in shape and in the manner of intertwisting their twigs, but they were much smaller, and not an impenetrable shade.

The views from the Castle are delightful. Opposite is the lake, girt with mountains, or rather smooth high hills; to the left appears a very steep rocky hill, called Duniquoich Hill, on the top of which is a building like a watch-tower; it rises boldly and almost perpendicular from the plain, at a little distance from the river Arey, that runs through the grounds. To the right is the town, overtopped by a sort of spire or pinnacle of the church, a thing unusual in Scotland, except in the large towns, and which would often give an elegant appearance to the villages, which, from the uniformity of the huts, and the frequent want of tall trees, they seldom exhibit.

In looking at an extensive prospect, or travelling through a large vale, the Trough of the Clyde for instance, I could not help thinking that in England there would have been somewhere a tower or spire to warn us of a village lurking under the covert of a wood or bank, or to point out some particular spot on the distant hills which we might look at with kindly feelings. I well remember how we used to love the little nest of trees out of which Ganton spire rose on the distant Wolds opposite to the windows at Gallow Hill. The spire of Inverary is not of so beautiful a shape as those of the English churches, and, not being one of a class of buildings which is understood at once, seen near or at a distance, is a less interesting object; but it suits well with the outlandish trimness of the buildings bordering on the water; indeed, there is no one thing of the many gathered together in the extensive circuit of the basin or vale of Inverary, that is not in harmony with the effect of the whole place. The Castle is built of a beautiful hewn stone, in colour resembling our blue slates. The author-tourists have quarrelled with the architecture of it, but we did not find much that we were disposed to blame. A castle in a deep glen, overlooking a roaring stream, and defended by precipitous rocks, is, no doubt, an object far more interesting; but, dropping all ideas of danger or insecurity, the natural retinue in our minds of an ancient Highland chieftain,—take a Duke of Argyle at the end of the eighteenth century, let him have his house in Grosvenor Square, his London liveries, and daughters glittering at St James's, and I think you will be satisfied with his present mansion in the Highlands, which seems to suit with the present times and its situation, and that is indeed a noble one for a modern Duke of the mountainous district of Argyleshire, with its bare valleys, its rocky coasts, and sea lochs.

There is, in the natural endowments of Inverary, something akin to every feature of the general character of the county; yet even the very mountains and the lake itself have a kind of princely festivity in their appearance. I do not know how to communicate the feeling, but it seemed as if it were no insult to the hills to look on them as the shield and enclosure of the ducal domain, to which the water might delight in bearing its tribute. The hills near the lake are smooth, so smooth that they might have been shaven or swept; the shores, too, had somewhat of the same effect, being bare, and having no roughness, no woody points; yet the whole circuit being very large, and the hills so extensive, the scene was not the less cheerful and festive, rejoicing in the light of heaven. Behind the Castle the hills are planted to a great height, and the pleasure-ground extend far up the valley of Arey. We continued our walk a short way along the river, and were sorry to see it stripped of its natural ornaments, after the fashion of Mr. Brown, *{'Capability' Brown}* and left to tell its tale—for it would not be silent like the river at Blenheim—to naked fields and the planted trees on the hills. We were disgusted with the stables, outhouses, or farm-houses in different parts of the grounds behind the Castle: they were broad, out-spreading, fantastic, and unintelligible buildings.

Sate in the park till the moonlight was perceived more than the light of day. We then walked near the town by the water-side. I observed that the children who were playing did not speak Erse, but a much worse English than is spoken by those Highlanders whose common language is the Erse. I went into the town to purchase tea and sugar to carry with us on our journey. We were tired when we returned to the inn, and went to bed directly after tea. My room was at the very top of the house—one flight of steps after another!—but when I drew back the curtains of my window I was repaid for the trouble of panting up-stairs by one of the most splendid moonlight prospects that can be conceived: the whole circuit of the hills, the Castle, the two bridges, the tower on Duniquoich Hill, and the lake with many boats—fit scene for summer midnight festivities! I should have liked to have seen a bevy of Scottish ladies sailing, with music, in a gay barge. William, to whom I have read this, tells me that I have used the very words of Browne of Ottery, Coleridge's fellow-townsman:—

> 'As I have seen when on the breast of Thames
> A heavenly bevy of sweet English dames,
> In some calm evening of delightful May,
> With music give a farewell to the day,
> Or as they would (with an admired tone)
> Greet night's ascension to her ebon throne.'
> BROWNE'S Britannia's Pastorals.

Wednesday, August 31ˢᵗ—We had a long day's journey before us, without a regular baiting-place on the road, so we breakfasted at Inverary, and did not set off till nine o'clock, having, as usual, to complain of the laziness of the servants. Our road was up the valley behind the Castle, the same we had gone along the evening before. Further up, though the plantations on the hills are noble, the valley was cold and naked, wanting hedgerows and comfortable houses. We travelled several miles under the plantations, the vale all along seeming to belong almost exclusively to the Castle. It might have been better distinguished and adorned, as we thought, by neater farm-houses and cottages than are common in Scotland, and snugger fields with warm hedgerows, at the same time testifying as boldly its adherence to the chief.

At that point of the valley, where the pleasure-grounds appear to end, we left our horse at a cottage door, and turned a few steps out of the road to see a waterfall, which roared so loud that we could not have gone by without looking about for it, even if we had not known that there was one near Inverary. The waterfall is not remarkable for anything but the good taste with which it has been left to itself, though there is a pleasure-road from the Castle to it. As we went further up the valley the roads died away, and it became an ordinary Scotch glen, the poor pasturage of the hills creeping down into the valley, where it was little better for the shelter; I mean little greener than on the hill-sides. But a man must be of a churlish nature if, with a mind free to look about, he should not find such a glen a pleasing place to travel through, though seeing little but the busy brook, with here and there a bush or tree, and cattle pasturing near the thinly-scattered dwellings. But we came to one spot which I cannot forget, a single green field at the junction of another brook with the Arey, a peninsula surrounded with a close row of trees, which overhung the streams and, under their branches, we could just see a neat white house that stood in the middle of the field enclosed by the trees. Before us was nothing but bare hills, and the road through the bare glen. A person who has not travelled in Scotland can scarcely imagine the pleasure we have had from a stone house, though fresh from the workmen's hands, square and sharp; there is generally such an appearance of equality in poverty through the long glens of Scotland, giving the notion of savage ignorance—no house better than another, and barns and houses all alike. This house had, however, other recommendations of its own; even in the fertile parts of Somersetshire it would have been a delicious spot. Here, 'Mid mountain wild set like a little nest,' it was a resting-place for the fancy, and to this day I often think of it, the cottage and its green covert, as an image of romance, a place of which I have the same sort of knowledge as of some of the retirements, the little valleys, described so livelily by Spenser in his Fairy Queen.

We travelled on, the glen now becoming entirely bare. Passed a miserable hut on a naked hill-side, not far from the road, where we were told by a man who came out of it that we might refresh ourselves with a dram of whisky. Went over the hill, and saw nothing remarkable till we came in view of Loch Awe, a large lake far below us, among high mountains—one very large mountain right opposite, which we afterwards found was called Cruachan. The day was pleasant—sunny gleams and a fresh breeze; the lake—we looked across it—as bright as silver, which made the islands, three or four in number, appear very green. We descended gladly, invited by the prospect before us, travelling downwards, along the side of the hill, above a deep glen, woody towards the lower part near the brook. The hills on all sides were high and bare, and not very stony: it made us think of the descent from Newlands into Buttermere, though on a wider scale, and much inferior in simple majesty. After walking down the hill a long way we came to a bridge, under which the water dashed through a dark channel of rocks among trees, the lake being at a considerable distance below, with cultivated lands between. Close upon the bridge was a small hamlet, *{Quaere, Cladich.— Ed}*a few houses near together, and huddled up in trees—a very sweet spot, the only retired village we had yet seen which was characterized by 'beautiful' wildness with sheltering warmth. We had been told at Inverary that we should come to a place where we might give our horse a feed of corn, and found on inquiry that there was a little public-house here, or rather a hut 'where they kept a dram.' It was a cottage, like all the rest, without a signboard. The woman of the house helped to take the horse out of harness and, being hungry, we asked her if she could make us some porridge, to which she replied that 'we should get that,' and I followed her into the house, and sate over her hearth while she was making it. As to fire, there was little sign of it, save the smoke, for a long time, she having no fuel but green wood, and no bellows but her breath. My eyes smarted exceedingly, but the woman seemed so kind and cheerful that I was willing to endure it for the sake of warming my feet in the ashes and talking to her. The fire was in the middle of the room, a crook being suspended from a cross-beam, and a hole left at the top for the smoke to find its way out by: it was a rude Highland hut, unadulterated by Lowland fashions, but it had not the elegant shape of the ferry-house at Loch Ketterine, and the fire, being in the middle of the room, could not be such a snug place to draw to on a winter's night.

We had a long afternoon before us, with only eight miles to travel to Dalmally, and, having been told that a ferry-boat was kept at one of the islands, we resolved to call for it, and row to the island, so we went to the top of an eminence, and the man who was with us set some children to work to gather sticks and withered leaves to make a smoky fire—a signal for the boatman, whose hut is on a flat green island, like a sheep pasture, without trees, and of a considerable size: the man told us it was a rabbit-warren. There were other small islands, on one of which was a ruined house, fortification, or small castle: we could not learn anything of its history, only a girl told us that formerly gentlemen lived in such places. Immediately from the water's edge rose the mountain Cruachan on the opposite side of the lake; it is weedy near the water and craggy above, with deep hollows on the surface. We thought it the grandest mountain we had seen and on saying to the man who was with us that it was a fine mountain, 'Yes,' he replied, 'it is an excellent mountain,' adding that it was higher than Ben Lomond, and then told us some wild stories of the enormous profits it brought to Lord Breadalbane, its lawful owner. The shape of Loch Awe is very remarkable, its outlet being at one side, and only about eight miles from the head, and the whole lake twenty-four miles in length. We looked with longing after that, branch of it opposite to us out of which the water issues: it seemed almost like a river gliding under steep precipices. What we saw of the larger branch, or what might be called the body of the lake, was less promising, the banks being merely gentle slopes, with not very high mountains behind, and the ground moorish and cold.

The children, after having collected fuel for our fire, began to play on the green hill where we stood, as heedless as if we had been trees or stones, and amused us exceedingly with their activity. They wrestled, rolled down the hill, pushing one another over and over again, laughing, screaming, and chattering Erse. They were all without shoes and stockings which, making them fearless of hurting or being hurt, gave a freedom to the action of their limbs which I never saw in English children. They stood upon one another, body, breast, or face, or any other part; sometimes one was uppermost, sometimes another, and sometimes they rolled all together, so that we could not know to which body this leg or that arm belonged. We waited, watching them, till we were assured that the boatman had noticed our signal.—By the bye, if we had received proper directions at Loch Lomond, on our journey to Loch Ketterine, we should have made our way down the lake till we had come opposite to the ferryman's house, where there is a hut, and the people who live there are accustomed to call him by the same signal as here. Luckily for us we were not so well instructed, for we should have missed the pleasure of receiving the kindness of Mr. and Mrs. Macfarlane and their family.

A young woman who wanted to go to the island accompanied us to the water-side. The walk was pleasant, through fields with hedgerows, the greenest fields we had seen in Scotland; but we were obliged to return without going to the island. The poor man had taken his boat to another place, and the waters were swollen so that we could not go close to the shore, and show ourselves to him, nor could we make him hear by shouting. On our return to the public-house we asked the woman what we should pay her, and were not a little surprised when she answered, 'Three shillings.' Our horse had had a sixpenny feed of miserable corn, not worth threepence; the rest of the charge was for skimmed milk, oat-bread, porridge, and blue milk cheese: we told her it was far too much and, giving her half-a-crown, departed. I was sorry she had made this unreasonable demand, because we had liked the woman, and we had before been so well treated in the Highland cottages; but, on thinking more about it, I satisfied myself that it was no scheme to impose upon us, for she was contented with the half-crown, and would, I daresay, have been so with two shillings, if we had offered it her at first. Not being accustomed to fix a price upon porridge and milk, too such as we, at least, when we asked her she did not know what to say; but, seeing that we were travelling for pleasure, no doubt she concluded we were rich, and that what was a small gain to her could be no great loss to us.

When we had gone a little way we saw before us a young man with a bundle over his shoulder, hung on a stick, bearing a great boy on his back: seeing that they were travellers, we offered to take the boy on the car, to which the man replied that he should be more than thankful, and set him up beside me. They had walked from Glasgow, and that morning from Inverary; the boy was only six years old, 'But,' said his father, 'he is a stout walker,' and a fine fellow he was, smartly dressed in tight clean clothes and a nice round hat. He was going to stay with his grandmother at Dalmally. I found him good company; though I could not draw a single word out of him, it was a pleasure to see his happiness gleaming through the shy glances of his healthy countenance. Passed a pretty chapel by the lake-side, and an island with a farm-house upon it, and corn and pasture fields; but, as we went along, we had frequent reason to regret the want of English hedgerows and English culture; for the ground was often swampy or moorish near the lake where comfortable dwellings among green fields might have been. When we came near to the end of the lake we had a steep hill to climb, so William and I walked; and we had such confidence in our horse that we were not afraid to leave the car to his guidance with the child in it; we were soon, however, alarmed at seeing him trot up the hill a long way before us; the child, having raised himself up upon the seat, was beating him as hard as he could with a little stick which he carried in his hand; and when he saw our eyes were on him he sate down, I believe very sorry to resign his office. The horse slackened his pace, and no accident happened.

When we had ascended half-way up the hill, directed by the man, I took a nearer footpath, and at the top came in view of a most impressive scene, a ruined castle on an island almost in the middle of the last compartment of the lake, backed by a mountain cove, down which came a roaring stream. The castle occupied every foot of the island that was visible to us, appearing to rise out of the water; mists rested upon the mountain side, with spots of sunshine between; there was a mild desolation in the low grounds, a solemn grandeur in the mountains, and the castle was wild, yet stately, not dismantled of its turrets, nor the walls broken down, though completely in ruin. After having stood some minutes I joined William on the high road and, both wishing to stay longer near this place, we requested the man to drive his little boy on to Dalmally, about two miles further, and leave the car at the inn. He told us that the ruin was called Kilchurn Castle, that it belonged to Lord Breadalbane, and had been built by one of the ladies of that family for her defence during her Lord's absence at the Crusades, for which purpose she levied a tax of seven years' rent upon her tenants. *{Not very probable}* He said that from that side of the lake it did not appear, in very dry weather, to stand upon an island, but that it was possible to go over to it without being wet-shod. We were very lucky in seeing it after a great flood; for its enchanting effect was chiefly owing to its situation in the lake, a decayed palace rising out of the plain of waters! I have called it a palace, for such feeling it gave to me, though having been built as a place of defence, a castle or fortress. We turned again and reascended the hill, and sate a long time in the middle of it, looking on the castle and the huge mountain cove opposite, and William, addressing himself to the ruin, poured out these verses:—

> *Child of loud-throated War! the mountain stream*
> *Roars in thy hearing; but thy hour of rest*
> *Is come, and thou art silent in thy age.*

We walked up the hill again, and, looking down the vale, had a fine view of the lake and islands, resembling the views down Windermere, though much less rich. Our walk to Dalmally was pleasant. The vale makes a turn to the right, beyond the head of the lake, and the village of Dalmally which is, in fact, only a few huts, the manse or minister's house, the chapel, and the inn, stands near the river, which flows into the head of the lake. The whole vale is very pleasing, the lower part of the hill-sides being sprinkled with thatched cottages, cultivated ground in small patches near them, which evidently belonged to the cottages.

We were overtaken by a gentleman who rode on a beautiful white pony, like Lilly, and was followed by his servant, a Highland boy, on another pony, a little creature, not much bigger than a large mastiff, on which were slung a pair of crutches and a tartan plaid. The gentleman entered into conversation with us, and on our telling him that we were going to Glen Coe, he advised us, instead of proceeding directly to Tyndrum, the next stage, to go round by the outlet of Loch Awe to Loch Etive, and thence to Glen Coe. We were glad to change our plan, for we wanted much to see more of Loch Awe, and he told us that the whole of the way by Loch Etive was pleasant, and the road to Tyndrum as dreary as possible; indeed, we could see it at that time several miles before us upon the side of a bleak mountain; and he said that there was nothing but moors and mountains all the way. We reached the inn a little before sunset, ordered supper, and I walked out. Crossed a bridge to look more nearly at the parsonage-house and the chapel which stands upon a bank close to the river, a pretty stream overhung in some parts by trees. The vale is very pleasing but, like all the other Scotch vales we had yet seen, it told of its kinship with the mountains and of poverty or some neglect on the part of man.

Thursday, September 1st—We had been attended at supper by a civil boy, whom we engaged to rouse us at six o'clock, and to provide us each a basin of milk and bread, and have the car ready, all which he did punctually, and we were off in good time. The morning was not unpleasant, though rather cold, and we had some fear of rain. Crossed the bridge, and passed by the manse and chapel, our road carrying us back again in the direction we had come; but on the opposite side of the river. Passed close to many of the houses we had seen on the hillappinside, which the lame gentleman had told us belonged to Lord Breadalbane, and were attached to little farms, or 'crofts,' as he called them. Lord Breadalbane had lately laid out a part of his estates in this way as an experiment, in the hope of preventing discontent and emigration. We were sorry we had not an opportunity of seeing into these cottages, and of learning how far the people were happy or otherwise. The dwellings certainly did not look so comfortable when we were near to them, as from a distance; but this might be chiefly owing to what the inhabitants did not feel as an evil—the dirt about the doors. We saw, however—a sight always painful to me—two or

137

three women, each creeping after her single cow, while it was feeding on the slips of grass between the corn-grounds. Went round the head of the lake, and onwards close to the lake-side. Kilchurn Castle was always interesting, though not so grand as seen from the other side, with its own mountain cove and roaring stream. It combined with the vale of Dalmally and the distant hills—a beautiful scene, yet overspread with a gentle desolation. As we went further down we lost sight of the vale of Dalmally. The castle, which we often stopped to look back upon, was very beautiful seen in combination with the opposite shore of the lake—perhaps a little bay, a tuft of trees, or a slope of the hill. Travelled under the foot of the mountain Cruachan, along an excellent road, having the lake close to us on our left, woods overhead, and frequent torrents tumbling down the hills. The distant views across the lake were not peculiarly interesting after we were out of sight of Kilchurn Castle, the lake being wide, and the opposite shore not rich, and those mountains which we could see were not high. Came opposite to the village where we had dined the day before, and, losing sight of the body of the lake, pursued the narrow channel or pass, *{The Pass of Awe.—Ed}* which is, I believe, three miles long, out of which issues the river that flows into Loch Etive. We were now enclosed between steep hills, on the opposite side entirely bare, on our side bare or woody; the branch of the lake generally filling the whole area of the vale. It was a pleasing, solitary scene; the long reach of naked precipices on the other side rose directly out of the water, exceedingly steep, not rugged or rocky, but with scanty sheep pasturage and large beds of small stones, purple, dove-coloured, or red, such as are called Screes in Cumberland and Westmoreland. These beds, or rather streams of stones, appeared as smooth as the turf itself, nay, I might say, as soft as the feathers of birds which they resembled in colour. There was no building on either side of the water; in many parts only just room for the road, and on the other shore no footing, as it might seem, for any creature larger than the mountain sheep, and they, in treading amongst the shelving stones, must often send them down into the lake below.

After we had wound for some time through the valley, having met neither foot-traveller, horse, nor cart, we started at the sight of a single vessel, just as it turned round the point of a hill, coming into the reach of the valley where we were. She floated steadily through the middle of the water, with one large sail spread out, full swollen by the breeze that blew her right towards us. I cannot express what romantic images this vessel brought along with her—how much more beautiful the mountains appeared, the lake how much more graceful. There was one man on board, who sate at the helm, and he, having no companion, made the boat look more silent than if we could not have seen him. I had almost said the ship, for on that narrow water it appeared as large as the ships which I have watched sailing out of a harbour of the sea. A little further on we passed a stone hut by the lake-side, near which were many charcoal sacks, and we conjectured that the vessel had been depositing charcoal brought from other parts of Loch Awe to be carried to the iron-works at Loch Etive. A little further on we came to the end of the lake, but where exactly it ended was not easy to determine, for the river was as broad as the lake, and we could only say when it became positively a river by the rushing of the water. It is, indeed, a grand stream, the quantity of water being very large, frequently forming rapids, and always flowing very quickly; but its greatness is short-lived, for, after a course of three miles, it is lost in the great waters of Loch Etive, a sea loch. Crossed a bridge, and climbing a hill towards Taynuilt, our baiting-place, we saw a hollow to the right below us, through which the river continued its course between rocks and steep banks of wood. William turned aside to look into the dell, but I was too much tired. We had left it, two or three hundred yards behind, an open river, the hills, enclosing the branch of the lake, having settled down into irregular slopes. We were glad when we reached Taynuilt, a village of huts, with a chapel and one stone house, which was the inn. It had begun to rain, and I was almost benumbed with the cold, besides having a bad headache; so it rejoiced me to see kind looks on the landlady's face, and that she was willing to put herself in a bustle for our comfort; we had a good fire presently, and breakfast was set out—eggs, preserved gooseberries, excellent cream, cheese, and butter, but no wheat bread, and the oaten cakes were so hard I could not chew them. We wished to go upon Loch Etive; so, having desired the landlady to prepare a fowl for supper, and engaged beds, which she promised us willingly—a proof that we were not in the great road—we determined to find our way to the lake and endeavour to procure a boat. It rained heavily, but we went on, hoping the sky would clear up. Walked through unenclosed fields, a sort of half-desolate country; but when we came to the mouth of the river which issues out of Loch Awe, and which we had to cross by a ferry, looking up that river we saw that the vale down which it flowed was richly wooded and beautiful.

We were now among familiar fireside names. We could see the town of Bunawe, a place of which the old woman with whom William lodged ten years at Hawkshead used to tell tales half as long as an ancient romance. It is a small village or port on the same side of Loch Etive on which we stood, and at a little distance is a house built by a Mr. Knott of Coniston Water-head, a partner in the iron-foundry at Bunawe, in the service of whose family the old woman had spent her youth. It was an ugly, yellow-daubed building, staring this way and that, but William looked at it with pleasure for poor Ann Tyson's sake. (13) We hailed the ferry-boat, and a little boy came to fetch us; he rowed up against the stream with all his might for a considerable way, and then yielding to it, the boat was shot towards the shore almost like an arrow from a bow. It was pleasing to observe the dexterity with which the lad managed his oars, glorying in the appearance of danger—for he observed us watching him, and afterwards, while he conveyed us over, his pride redoubled; for my part, I was completely dizzy with the swiftness of the motion.

We could not have a boat from the ferry, but were told that if we would walk to a house half a mile up the river, we had a chance of getting one. I went a part of the way with William, and then sate down under the umbrella near some houses. A woman came out to talk with me, and pressed me to take shelter in her house, which I refused, afraid of missing William. She eyed me with extreme curiosity, asking fifty questions respecting the object of our journey. She told me that it rained most parts of the year there, and that there was no chance of fine weather that day; and I believe, when William came to tell me that we could have a boat, she thought I was half crazed. We went down to the shore of the lake, and, after having sate some time under a wall, the boatman came to us, and we went upon the water. At first it did not rain heavily, and the air was not cold, and before we had gone far we rejoiced that we had not been fainthearted. The loch is of a considerable width, but the mountains are so very high that, whether we were close under them or looked from one shore to the other, they maintained their dignity. I speak of the higher part of the loch, above the town of Bunawe and the large river, for downwards they are but hills, and the water spreads out wide towards undetermined shores. On our right was the mountain Cruachan, rising directly from the lake, and on the opposite side another mountain, called Ben Durinish, craggy, and exceedingly steep, with wild wood growing among the rocks and stones.

We crossed the water, which was very rough in the middle, but calmer near the shores, and some of the rocky basins and little creeks among the rocks were as still as a mirror, and they were so beautiful with the reflection of the orange-coloured seaweed growing on the stones or rocks, that a child, with a child's delight in gay colours, might have danced with joy at the sight of them. It never ceased raining, and the tops of the mountains were concealed by mists, but as long as we could see across the water we were contented; for though little could be seen of the true shapes and permanent appearances of the mountains, we saw enough to give us the most exquisite delight: the powerful lake which filled the large vale, roaring torrents, clouds floating on the mountain sides, sheep that pastured there, sea-birds and land-birds. We sailed a considerable way without coming to any houses or cultivated fields. There was no horse-road on either side of the loch, but a person on foot, as the boatman told us, might make his way at the foot of Ben Durinish, namely on that side of the loch on which we were; there was, however, not the least track to be seen, and it must be very difficult and laborious.

We happened to say that we were going to Glen Coe, which would be the journey of a long day and a half, when one of the men, pointing to the head of the loch, replied that if we were there we should be but an hour's walk from Glen Coe. Though it continued raining, and there was no hope that the rain would cease, we could not help wishing to go by that way: it was an adventure; we were not afraid of trusting ourselves to the hospitality of the Highlanders, and we wanted to give our horse a day's rest, his back having been galled by the saddle. The owner of the boat, who understood English much better than the other man, his helper, said he would make inquiries about the road at a farm-house a little further on. He was very ready to talk with us, and was rather an interesting companion; he spoke after a slow and solemn manner, in book and sermon language and phrases:

'A stately speech, such as grave livers do in Scotland use.'

When we came to the farm-house of which the man had spoken, William and he landed to make the necessary inquiries. It was a thatched house at the foot of the high mountain Ben Durinish—a few patches or little beds of corn belonging to it; but the spot was pastoral, the green grass growing to the walls of the house. The dwelling-house was distinguished from the outer buildings, which were numerous, making it look like two or three houses, as is common in Scotland, by a chimney and one small window with sash-panes; on one side was a little woody glen, with a precipitous stream that fell into the bay, which was perfectly still, and bordered with the rich orange-colour reflected from the sea-weed. Cruachan, on the other side of the lake, was exceedingly grand, and appeared of an enormous height, spreading out two large arms that made a cove down which fell many streams swoln by the rain, and in the hollow of the cove were some huts which looked like a village. The top of the mountain was concealed from us by clouds, and the mists floated high and low upon the sides of it.

William came back to the boat highly pleased with the cheerful hospitality and kindness of the woman of the house, who would scarcely permit him and his guide to go away without taking some refreshment. She was the only person at home, so they could not obtain the desired information; but William had been well repaid for the trouble of landing; indeed, rainy as it was, I regretted that I had not landed also, for I should have wished to bear away in my memory a perfect image of this place,—the view from the doors, as well as the simple Highland comforts and contrivances which were near it. I think I never saw a retirement that would have so completely satisfied me, if I had wanted to be altogether shut out from the world, and at the same time among the grandest of the works of God; but it must be remembered that mountains are often so much dignified by clouds, mists, and other accidents of weather, that one could not know them again in the full sunshine of a summer's noon. But, whatever the mountains may be in their own shapes, the farm-house, with its pastoral grounds and corn fields won from the mountain, its warm out-houses in irregular stages one above another on the side of the hill, the rocks, the stream, and sheltering bay, must at all times be interesting objects. The household boat lay at anchor, chained to a rock, which, like the whole border of the lake, was edged with sea-weed, and some fishing-nets were hung upon poles,—affecting images, which led our thoughts out to the wide ocean, yet made these solitudes of the mountains hear the impression of greater safety and more deep seclusion.

The rain became so heavy that we should certainly have turned back if we had not felt more than usual courage from the pleasure we had enjoyed, which raised hope where none was. There were some houses a little higher up and we determined to go thither and make further inquiries. We could now hardly see to the other side of the lake, yet continued to go on, and presently heard some people pushing through a thicket close to us, on which the boatman called out, 'There's one that can tell us something about the road to Glen Coe, for he was born there.' We looked up and saw a ragged, lame fellow, followed by some others, with a fishing-rod over his shoulder; and he was making such good speed through the boughs that one might have half believed he was the better for his lame leg. He was the head of a company of tinkers, who, as the men told us, travel with their fishing-rods as duly as their hammers. On being hailed by us the whole company stopped; and their lame leader and our boatmen shouted to each other in Erse—a savage cry to our ears, in that lonely and romantic place. We could not learn from the tinker all we wished to know, therefore when we came near to the houses William landed again with the owner of the boat. The rain was now so heavy that we could see nothing at all—not even the houses whither William was going.

We had given up all thought of proceeding further at that time, but were desirous to know how far that road to Glen Coe was practicable for us. They met with an intelligent man, who was at work with others in a hay field, though it rained so heavily; he gave them the information they desired, and said that there was an acquaintance of his between that place and Glen Coe, who, he had no doubt, would gladly accommodate us with lodging and anything else we might need. When William returned to the boat we shaped our course back again down the water, leaving the head of Loch Etive not only un-visited, but unseen—to our great regret. The rain was very heavy; the wind had risen, and both wind and tide were against us, so that it was hard labour for the boatmen to push us on. They kept as close to the shore as they could, to be under the wind; but at the doubling of many of the rocky points the tide was so strong that it was difficult to get on at all, and I was sometimes afraid that we should be dashed against the rocks, though I believe, indeed, there was not much danger.

Came down the same side of the lake under Ben Durinish, and landed at a ferry-house opposite to Bunawe, where we gave the men a glass of whisky; but our chief motive for landing was to look about the place, which had a most wild aspect at that time. It was a low promontory, pushed far into the water, narrowing the lake exceedingly; in the obscurity occasioned by the mist and rain it appeared to be an island; it was stained and weather beaten, a rocky place, seeming to bear no produce but such as might be cherished by cold and storms, lichens or the incrustation of sea rocks. We rowed right across the water to the mouth of the river of Loch Awe, our boat following the ferry-boat which was conveying the tinker crew to the other side, whither they were going to lodge, as the men told us, in some kiln, which they considered as their right and privilege—a lodging always to be found where there was any arable land—for every farm has its kiln to dry the corn in: another proof of the wetness of the climate. The kilns are built of stone, covered in, and probably as good a shelter as the huts in which these Highland vagrants were born. They gather sticks or heather for their fire, and, as they are obstinate beggars, for the men said they would not be denied, they probably have plenty of food with little other trouble than that of wandering in search of it, for their smutty faces and tinker equipage serve chiefly for a passport to a free and careless life. It rained very heavily, and the wind blew when we crossed the lake, and their boat and ours went tilting over the high waves. They made a romantic appearance; three women were of the party; two men rowed them over; the lame fellow sate at one end of the boat, and his companion at the other, each with an enormous fishing-rod, which looked very graceful, something like masts to the boat. When we had landed at the other side we saw them after having begged at the ferry-house, strike merrily through the fields, no doubt betaking themselves to their shelter for the night.

We were completely wet when we reached the inn; the landlady wanted to make a fire for me up-stairs, but I went into her own parlour to undress, and her daughter, a pretty little girl, who could speak a few words of English, waited on me; I rewarded her with one of the penny books bought at Dumfries for Johnny, with which she was greatly delighted. We had an excellent supper—fresh salmon, a fowl, gooseberries and cream, and potatoes; good beds; and the next morning boiled milk and bread, and were only charged seven shillings and sixpence for the whole—horse, liquor, supper, and the two breakfasts. We thought they had made a mistake, and told them so—for it was only just half as much as we had paid the day before at Dalmally, the case being that Dalmally is in the main road of the tourists. The landlady insisted on my bringing away a little cup instead of our tin can, which she told me had been taken from the car by some children: we set no little value on this cup as a memorial of the good woman's honesty and kindness, and hoped to have brought it home. . . .

*Friday, September 2nd*—Departed at about seven o'clock this morning, having to travel eight miles down Loch Etive, and then to cross a ferry. Our road was at first at a considerable distance from the lake, and out of sight of it, among undulating hills covered with coppice woods, resembling the country between Coniston and Windermere, but it afterwards carried us close to the water's edge; and in this part of our ride we were disappointed. We knew that the high mountains were all at the head of the lake, therefore had not expected the same awful grandeur which we beheld the day before, and perceived by glimpses; but the gentleman whom we met with at Dalmally had told us that there were many fine situations for gentlemen's seats on this part of the lake, which had made us expect greater loveliness near the shores, and better cultivation. It is true there are pleasant bays, with grounds prettily sloping to the water, and coppice woods, where houses would stand in shelter and sun, looking on the lake; but much is yet wanting—waste lands to be ploughed, peat-mosses drained, hedgerows reared, and the woods demand a grant of longer life than is now their privilege.

But after we had journeyed about six miles a beautiful scene opened upon us. The morning had been gloomy, and at this time the sun shone out, scattering the clouds. We looked right down the lake that was covered with streams of dazzling sunshine, which revealed the indentings of the dark shores. On a bold promontory, on the same side of the loch where we were, stood an old castle, an irregular tall building, not without majesty; and beyond, with leagues of water between, our eyes settled upon the island of Mull, a high mountain, green in the sunshine, and overcast with clouds,—an object as inviting to the fancy as the evening sky in the west, and, though of a terrestrial green, almost as visionary. We saw that it was an island of the sea, but were unacquainted with its name; it was of a gem-like colour, and as soft as the sky. The shores of Loch Etive, in their moorish, rocky wildness, their earthly bareness, as they lay in length before us, produced a contrast which, with the pure sea, the brilliant sunshine, the long distance, contributed to the aerial and romantic power with which the mountain island was invested.

Soon after, we came to the ferry. The boat being on the other shore, we had to wait a considerable time, though the water was not wide, and our call was heard immediately. The boatmen moved with surly tardiness, as if glad to make us know they were our masters. At this point the lake was narrowed to the breadth of not a very wide river by a round ear or promontory on the side on which we were, and a low ridge of peat-mossy ground on the other. It was a dreary place, shut out from the beautiful prospect of the Isle of Mull, and Dunstaffnage Castle—so the fortress was called. Four or five men came over with the boat; the horse was unyoked, and being harshly driven over rough stones, which were as slippery as ice, with slimy seaweed, he was in terror before he reached the boat, and they completed the work by beating and pushing him by main force over the ridge of the boat, for there was no open end, or plank, or any other convenience for shipping either horse or carriage. I was very uneasy when we were launched on the water. A blackguard-looking fellow, blind of one eye, which I could not but think had been put out in some strife or other, held him by force like a horse-breaker, while the poor creature fretted, and stamped with his feet against the bare boards, frightening himself more and more with every stroke; and when we were in the middle of the water I would have given a thousand pounds to have been sure that we should reach the other side in safety. The tide was rushing violently in, making a strong eddy with the stream of the loch, so that the motion of the boat and the noise and foam of the waves terrified him still more, and we thought it would be impossible to keep him in the boat, and when we were just far enough from the shore to have been all drowned he became furious, and, plunging desperately, his hind-legs were in the water, then, recovering himself, he beat with such force against the boat-side that we were afraid he should send his feet through. All the while the men were swearing terrible oaths, and cursing the poor beast, redoubling their curses when we reached the landing-place, and whipping him ashore in brutal triumph.

We had only room for half a heartful of joy when we set foot on dry land, for another ferry was to be crossed five miles further. We had intended breakfasting at this house if it had been a decent place; but after this affair we were glad to pay the men off and depart, though I was not well, and needed refreshment. The people made us more easy by assuring us that we might easily swim the horse over the next ferry. The first mile or two of our road was over a peat moss; we then came near to the seashore, and had beautiful views backwards towards the Island of Mull and Dunstaffnage Castle, and forward where the sea ran up between the hills. In this part, on the opposite side of the small bay or elbow of the sea, was a gentleman's house on a hill-side, *{Lochnell House}* and a building on the hill-top which we took for a lighthouse, but were told that it belonged to the mansion, and was only lighted up on rejoicing days—the laird's birthday, for instance. Before we had left the peat-moss to travel close to the sea-shore we delighted ourselves with looking on a range of green hills, in shape like those bordering immediately upon the sea, abrupt but not high; they were, in fact, a continuation of the same; but retiring backwards, and rising from the black peat-moss. These hills were of a delicate green, uncommon in Scotland; a foaming rivulet ran down one part, and near it lay two herdsmen full in the sun, with their dogs, among a troop of black cattle which were feeding near, and sprinkled over the whole range of hills— a pastoral scene, to our eyes the more beautiful from knowing what a delightful prospect it must overlook. We now came under the steeps by the sea-side, which were bold lomond, mouldering scars, or fresh with green grass. Under the brow of one of these rocks was a burying-ground, with many upright grave-stones and hay-cocks between, and fenced round by a wall neatly sodded. Near it were one or two houses, with out-houses under a group of trees, but no chapel. The neatness of the burying-ground would in itself have been noticeable in any part of Scotland where we have been; but it was more interesting from its situation than for its own sake—within the sound of the gentlest waves of the sea, and near so many quiet and beautiful objects. There was a range of hills opposite, which we were here first told were the hills of Morven {*The Morvern Peninsula, opposite the Island of Mull*}, so much sung of by Ossian. We consulted with some men respecting the ferry, who advised us by all means to send our horse round the loch, and go ourselves over in the boat: they were very civil, and seemed to be intelligent men, yet all disagreed about the length of the loch, though we were not two miles from it: one said it was only six miles long, another ten or fifteen, and afterwards a man whom we met told us it was twenty.

We lost sight of the sea for some time, crossing a half-cultivated space, then reached Loch Creran, a large irregular sea loch, with low sloping banks, coppice woods, and uncultivated grounds, with a scattering of corn fields; as it appeared to us, very thinly inhabited: mountains at a distance. We found only women at home at the ferry-house. I was faint and cold, and went to sit by the fire, but, though very much needing refreshment, I had not heart to eat anything there—the house was so dirty, and there were so many wretchedly dirty women and children: yet perhaps I might have got over the dirt, though I believe there are few ladies who would not have been turned sick by it, if there had not been a most disgusting combination of laziness and coarseness in the countenances and manners of the women, though two of them were very handsome. It was a small hut, and four women were living in it: one, the mother of the children and mistress of the house; the others I supposed to be lodgers, or perhaps servants; but there was no work amongst them. They had just taken from the fire a great pan full of potatoes, which they mixed up with milk, all helping themselves out of the same vessel, and the little children put in their dirty hands to dig out of the mess at their pleasure. I thought to myself, 'How light the labour of such a house as this! Little sweeping, no washing of floors, and as to scouring the table, I believe it was a thing never thought of.'

After a long time the ferryman came home; but we had to wait yet another hour for the tide. In the meanwhile our horse took fright in consequence of his terror at the last ferry, ran away with the car, and dashed out umbrellas, greatcoats, etc.; but luckily he was stopped before any serious mischief was done. We had determined, whatever it cost, not to trust ourselves with him again in the boat; but sending him round the lake seemed almost out of the question, there being no road, and probably much difficulty in going round with a horse; so after some deliberation with the ferryman it was agreed that he should swim over. The usual place of ferrying was very broad, but he was led to the point of a peninsula at a little distance. It being an unusual affair,—indeed, the people of the house said that he was the first horse that had ever swum over,—we had several men on board, and the mistress of the house offered herself as an assistant: we supposed for the sake of a share in eighteen-pennyworth of whisky which her husband called for without ceremony, and of which she and the young lasses, who had helped to push the boat into the water, partook as freely as the men. At first I feared for the horse : he was frightened, and strove to push himself under the boat; but I was soon tolerably easy, for he went on regularly and well, and after from six to ten minutes swimming landed in safety on the other side. Poor creature! he stretched out his nostrils and stared wildly while the man was trotting him about to warm him, and when he put him into the car he was afraid of the sound of the wheels. For some time our road was up a glen, the banks chiefly covered with coppice woods, and unpeopled, but, though without grandeur, not a dreary tract.

Came to a moor and descended into a broad vale, which opened to Loch Linnhe, an arm of the sea, the prospect being shut in by high mountains, on which the sun was shining among mists and resting clouds. A village and chapel stood on the opposite hill; the hills sloped prettily down to the bed of the vale, a large level area—the grounds in general cultivated, but not rich. We went perhaps half a mile down the vale, when our road struck right across it towards the village on the hill-side. We overtook a tall, well-looking man, seemingly about thirty years of age, driving a cart, of whom we inquired concerning the road, and the distance to Portnacroish, our baiting-place. We made further inquiries respecting our future journey, which he answered in an intelligent manner, being perfectly acquainted with the geography of Scotland. He told us that the village which we saw before us and the whole tract of country was called Appin. William said that it was a pretty wild place, to which the man replied, 'Sir, it is a very bonny place if you did but see it on a fine day,' mistaking William's praise for a half-censure; I must say, however, that we hardly ever saw a thoroughly pleasing place in Scotland, which had not something of wildness in its aspect of one sort or other. It came from many causes here: the sea, or sea-loch, of which we only saw as it were a glimpse crossing the vale at the foot of it, the high mountains on the opposite shore, the unenclosed hills on each side of the vale, with black cattle feeding on them, the simplicity of the scattered huts, the half-sheltered, half-exposed situation of the village, the imperfect culture of the fields, the distance from any city or large town, and the very names of Morven and Appin, particularly at such a time, when old Ossian's old friends, sunbeams and mists, as like ghosts as any in the mid-afternoon could be, were keeping company with them. William did all he could to efface the unpleasant impression he had made on the Highlander, and not without success, for he was kind and communicative when we walked up the hill towards the village. He had been a great traveller, in Ireland and elsewhere; but I believe that he had visited no place so beautiful to his eyes as his native home, the strath of Appin under the heathy hills.

We arrived at Portnacroish soon after parting from this man. It is a small village—a few huts and an indifferent inn by the side of the loch. Ordered a fowl for dinner, had a fire lighted, and went a few steps from the door up the road, and turning aside into a field stood at the top of a low eminence, from which, looking down the loch to the sea through a long vista of hills and mountains, we beheld one of the most delightful prospects that, even when we dream of fairer worlds than this, it is possible for us to conceive in our hearts. A covering of clouds rested on the long range of the hills of Morven, mists floated very near, to the water on their sides, and were slowly shifting about:

yet the sky was clear, and the sea, from the reflection of the sky, of an ethereal or sapphire blue, which was intermingled in many places, and mostly by gentle gradations, with beds of bright dazzling sunshine; green islands lay on the calm water, islands far greener, for so it seemed, than the grass of other places; and from their excessive beauty, their unearthly softness, and the great distance of many of them, they made us think of the islands of the blessed in the Vision of Mirza—a resemblance more striking from the long tract of mist which rested on the top of the steeps of Morven. The view was endless, and though not so wide, had something of the intricacy of the islands and water of Loch Lomond as we saw them from Inch-ta-vanach; and yet how different! At Loch Lomond we could never forget that it was an inland lake of fresh water, nor here that it was the sea itself, though among multitudes of hills. Immediately below us, on an island a few yards from the shore, stood an old keep or fortress; *{Castle Stalker}* the vale of Appin opened to the water-side, with cultivated fields and cottages. If there were trees near the shore they contributed little to the delightful effect of the scene: it was the immeasurable water, the lofty mist-covered steeps of Morven to the right, the emerald islands without a bush or tree, the celestial colour and brightness of the calm sea, and the innumerable creeks and bays, the communion of land and water as far as the eye could travel. My description must needs be languid; for the sight itself was too fair to be remembered. We sate a long time upon the hill, and pursued our journey at about four o'clock. Had an indifferent dinner, but the cheese was so excellent that William wished to buy the remainder; but the woman would not consent to sell it, and forced us to accept a large portion of it. We had to travel up the loch, leaving behind us the beautiful scene which we had viewed with such delight before dinner. Often, while we were climbing the hill, did we stop to look back, and when we had gone twenty or thirty yards beyond the point where we had the last view of it, we left the car to the care of some children who were coming from school, and went to take another farewell, always in the hope of bearing away a more substantial remembrance. Travelled for some miles along a road which was so smooth it was more like a gravel walk in a gentleman's grounds than a public highway. Probably the country is indebted for this excellent road to Lord Tweeddale, *{George, seventh Marquis of Tweeddale, being in France in 1803, was detained by Bonaparte, and died at Verdun, 9th August 1801—Ed}* now a prisoner in France. His house stands upon an eminence within a mile of Portnacroish, commanding the same prospect which I have spoken of, except that it must lose something in not having the old fortress at the foot of it— indeed, it is not to be seen at all from the house or grounds.

We travelled under steep hills, stony or smooth, with coppice-woods and patches of cultivated land, and houses here and there; and at every hundred yards, I may almost venture to say, a streamlet, narrow as a ribbon, came tumbling down, and, crossing our road, fell into the lake below. On the opposite shore, the hills—namely, the continuation of the hills of Morven—were stern and severe, rising like upright walls from the water's edge, and in colour more resembling rocks than hills, as they appeared to us. We did not see any house or any place where it was likely a house could stand, for many miles; but as the loch was broad we could not perhaps distinguish the objects thoroughly. A little after sunset our road led us from the vale of the loch. We came to a small river, a bridge, a mill, and some cottages at the foot of a hill, and close to the loch. Did not cross the bridge, but went up the brook, having it on our left, and soon found ourselves in a retired valley, scattered over with many grey huts, and surrounded on every side by green hills. The hay grounds in the middle of the vale were unenclosed, which was enough to keep alive the Scottish wildness, here blended with exceeding beauty; for there were trees growing irregularly or in clumps all through the valley, rocks or stones here and there, which, with the people at work, hay-cocks sprinkled over the fields, made the vale look full and populous. It was a sweet time of the evening: the moon was up; but there was yet so much of day that her light was not perceived. Our road was through open fields; the people suspended their work as we passed along, and leaning on their pitchforks or rakes, with their arms at their sides, or hanging down, some in one way, some in another, and no two alike, they formed most beautiful groups the outlines of their figures being much more distinct than by day, and all that might have been harsh or unlovely softened down. The dogs were, as usual, attendant on their masters, and, watching after us, they barked aloud; yet even their barking hardly disturbed the quiet of the place.

I cannot say how long this vale was; it made the larger half of a circle, or a curve deeper than that of half a circle, before it opened again upon the loch. It was less thoroughly cultivated and woody after the last turning—the hills steep and lofty. We met a very tall stout man, a fine figure, in a Highland bonnet, with a little girl, driving home their cow: he accosted us, saying that we were late travellers, and that we had yet four miles to go before we should reach Ballachulish—a long way, uncertain as we were respecting our accommodations. He told us that the vale was called the Strath of Duror, and when we said it was a pretty place, he answered, Indeed it was, and that they lived very comfortably there, for they had a good master, Lord Tweeddale, whose imprisonment he lamented, speaking earnestly of his excellent qualities. At the end of the vale we came close upon a large bay of the loch, formed by a rocky hill, a continuation of the ridge of high hills on the left side of the strath, making a very grand promontory, under which was a hamlet, a cluster of huts, at the water's edge, with their little fleet of fishing-boats at anchor, and behind, among the rocks, a hundred slips of corn, slips and patches, often no bigger than a garden such as a child, eight years old, would make for sport: it might have been the work of a small colony from China. There was something touching to the heart in this appearance of scrupulous industry, and excessive labour of the soil, in a country where hills and mountains, and even valleys, are left to the care of nature and the pleasure of the cattle that feed among them It was, indeed, a very interesting place, the more so being in perfect contrast with the few houses at the entrance of the strath—a sea hamlet, without trees, under a naked stony mountain, yet perfectly sheltered, standing in the middle of a large bay which half the winds that travel over the lake can never visit. The other, a little bowery spot, with its river, bridge, and mill, might have been a hundred miles from the sea-side.

The moon was now shining, and, though it reminded as how far the evening was advanced, we stopped for many minutes before we could resolve to go on; we saw nothing stirring, neither men, women, nor cattle; but the linen was still bleaching by the stony rivulet, which ran near the houses in water-breaks and tiny cataracts.   For the first half mile after we had left this scene there was nothing remarkable; and afterwards we could only see the hills, the sky, the moon, and moonlight water. When we came within, it might be, half a mile of Ballachulish, the place where we were to lodge; the loch narrowed very much, the hills still continuing high. I speak inaccurately, for it split into two divisions, the one along which we went being called Loch Leven.

The road grew very bad, and we had an anxious journey till we saw a light before us, which with great joy we assured ourselves was from the inn; but what was our distress when, ongoing a few steps further, we came to a bridge half broken down, with bushes laid across to prevent travellers from going over. After some perplexity we determined that I should walk on to the house before us— for we could see that the bridge was safe for foot-passengers —and ask for assistance. By great good luck, at this very moment four or five men came along the road towards us and offered to help William in driving the car through the water, which was not very deep at that time, though, only a few days before, the damage had been done to the bridge by a flood.

I walked on to the inn, ordered tea, and was conducted into a lodging room. I desired to have a fire, and was answered with the old scruple about 'giving fire,' with, at the same time, an excuse 'that it was so late,'—the girl, however, would ask the landlady, who was lying-in; the fire was brought immediately, and from that time the girl was very civil. I was not, however, quite at ease, for William stayed long, and I was going to leave my fire to seek after him, when I heard him at the door with the horse and car. The horse had taken fright with the roughness of the river-bed and the rattling of the wheels—the second fright in consequence of the ferry—and the men had been obliged to unyoke him and drag the car through, a troublesome affair for William; but he talked less of the trouble and alarm than of the pleasure he had felt in having met with such true good-will and ready kindness in the Highlanders. They drank their glass of whisky at the door, wishing William twenty good wishes, and asking him twice as many questions,—if he was married, if he had an estate, where he lived, etc. etc. This inn is the ferry-house on the main road up into the

Highlands by Fort-William, and here Coleridge, though unknown to us, had slept three nights before.

Saturday, September 3rd—When we have arrived at an unknown place by moonlight, it is never a moment of indifference when I quit it again with the morning light, especially if the objects have appeared beautiful, or in any other way impressive or interesting. I have kept back, unwilling to go to the window that I might not lose the picture taken to my pillow at night. So it was at Ballachulish: and instantly I felt that the passing away of my own fancies was a loss. The place had appeared exceedingly wild by moonlight; I had mistaken corn fields for naked rocks, and the lake had appeared narrower and the hills more steep and lofty than they really were.

We rose at six o'clock, and took a basin of milk before we set forward on our journey to Glen Coe. It was a delightful morning, the road excellent, and we were in good spirits, happy that we had no more ferries to cross, and pleased with the thought that we were going among the grand mountains which we saw before us at the head of the loch. We travelled close to the water's edge, and were rolling along a smooth road, when the horse suddenly-backed, frightened by the upright shafts of a roller rising from behind the wall of a field adjoining the road. William pulled, whipped, and struggled in vain; we both leapt upon the ground, and the horse dragged the car after him, he going backwards down the bank of the loch, and it was turned over, half in the water, the horse lying on his back, struggling in the harness, a frightful sight! I gave up everything; thought that the horse would be lamed, and the car broken to pieces. Luckily a man came up in the same moment, and assisted William in extricating the horse, and, after an hour's delay, with the help of strings and pocket-handkerchiefs, we mended the harness and set forward again, William leading the poor animal all the way, for the regular beating of the waves frightened him, and any little gushing stream that crossed the road would have sent him off. The village where the blacksmith lived was before us—a few huts under the mountains, and, as it seemed, at the head of the loch; but it runs further up to the left, being narrowed by a hill above the village, near which, at the edge of the water, was a slate quarry, and many large boats with masts, on the water below, high mountains shutting in the prospect, which stood in single, distinguishable shapes, yet clustered together—simple and bold in their forms, and their surfaces of all characters and all colours— somethat looked as if scarified by fire, others green; and there was one that might have been blasted by an eternal frost, its summit and sides for a considerable way down being as white as hoar-frost at eight o'clock on a winter's morning. No clouds were on the hills; the sun shone bright, but the wind blew fresh and cold.

When we reached the blacksmith's shop, I left William to help to take care of the horse, and went into the house. The mistress, with a child in her arms and two or three running about, received me very kindly, making many apologies for the dirty house, which she partly attributed to its being Saturday; but I could plainly see that it was dirt of all days. I sate in the midst of it with great delight, for the woman's benevolent, happy countenance almost converted her slovenly and lazy way of leaving all things to take care of themselves into a comfort and a blessing.

It was not a Highland hut, but a slated house built by the master of the quarry for the accommodation of his blacksmith,—the shell of an English cottage, as if left unfinished by the workmen, without plaster, and with floor of mud. Two beds, with not over-clean bedclothes, were in the room. Luckily for me, there was a good fire and a boiling kettle. The woman was very sorry she had no butter; none was to be had in the village: she gave me oaten and barley bread. We talked over the fire; I answered her hundred questions, and in my turn put some to her. She asked me, as usual, if I was married, how many brothers I had, etc. etc. I told her that William was married, and had a fine boy; to which she replied, 'And the man's a decent man too.' Her next-door neighbour came in with a baby on her arm, to request that I would accept of some fish, which I broiled in the ashes. She joined in our conversation, but with, more shyness than her neighbour, being a very young woman. She happened to say that she was a stranger in that place, and had been bred and born a long way off. On my asking her where, she replied, 'At Leadhillsand;' when I told her that I had been there, a joy lighted up her countenance which I shall never forget, and when she heard that it was only a fortnight before, her eyes filled with tears. I was exceedingly affected with the simplicity of her manners; her tongue was now let loose, and she would have talked for ever of Leadhills, of her mother, of the quietness of the people in general, and the goodness of Mrs. Otto, who, she told me, was a 'varra discreet woman.' She was sure we should be 'well put up' at Mrs. Otto's, and praised her house and furniture; indeed, it seemed she thought all earthly comforts were gathered together under the bleak heights that surround the villages of Wanlockhead and Leadhills: and afterwards, when I said it was a wild country thereabouts, she even seemed surprised, and said it was not half so wild as where she lived now. One circumstance which she mentioned of Mrs. Otto I must record, both in proof of her 'discretion,' and the sobriety of the people at Leadhills, namely, that no liquor was ever drunk in her house after a certain hour of the night—I have forgotten what hour; but it was an early one, I am sure not later than ten.

The blacksmith, who had come in to his breakfast, was impatient to finish our job that he might go out into the hay-field, for, it being a fine day, every plot of hay-ground was scattered over with hay-makers. On my saying that I guessed much of their hay must be spoiled, he told me no, for that they had high winds, which dried it quickly,—the people understood the climate, 'were clever at the work, and got it in with a blink.' He hastily swallowed his breakfast, dry bread and a basin of weak tea without sugar, and held his baby on his knee till he had done.

The women and I were again left to the fireside, and there were no limits to their joy in me, for they discovered another bond of connexion. I lived in the same part of England from which Mr. Rose, the superintendent of the slate-quarries, and his wife, had come. 'Oh!' said Mrs. Stuart—so her neighbour called her, they not giving each other their Christian names, as is common in Cumberland and Westmoreland,—'Oh!' said she, 'what would not I give to see anybody that came from within four or five miles of Leadhills!' They both exclaimed that I must see Mrs. Rose, she would make much of me—she would have given me tea and bread and butter and a good breakfast. I learned from the two women, Mrs. Stuart and Mrs. Duncan—so the other was called—that Stuart had come from Leadhills for the sake of better wages, to take the place of Duncan, who had resigned his office of blacksmith to the quarries, as far as I could learn, in a pet, intending to go to America, that his wife was averse to go, and that the scheme, for this cause and through other difficulties, had been given up. He appeared to be a good-tempered man, and made us a most reasonable charge for mending the car. His wife told me that they must give up the house in a short time to the other blacksmith; she did not know whither they should go, but her husband being a good workman, could find employment anywhere. She hurried me out to introduce me to Mrs. Rose, who was at work in the hay-field; she was exceedingly glad to see one of her country-women, and entreated that I would go up to her house. It was a substantial plain house that would have held half-a-dozen of the common huts. She conducted me into a sitting-room up-stairs, and set before me red and white wine, with the remnant of a loaf of wheaten bread, which she took out of a cupboard in the sitting-room, and some delicious butter. She was a healthy and cheerful-looking woman, dressed like one of our country lasses, and had certainly had no better education than Aggy Ashburner, but she was as a chief in this secluded place, a Madam of the village, and seemed to be treated with the utmost respect.

In our way to and from the house we met several people who interchanged friendly greetings with her, but always as with one greatly superior. She attended me back to the blacksmith's, and would not leave me till she had seen us set forward again on our journey. Mrs. Duncan and Mrs. Stuart shook me cordially, nay, affectionately, by the hand. I tried to prevail upon the former, who had been my hostess, to accept of some money, but in vain; she would not take a farthing, and though I told her it was only to buy something for her little daughter, even seemed grieved that I should think it possible. I forgot to mention that while the blacksmith was repairing the car, we walked to the slate-quarry, where we saw again some of the kind creatures who had helped us in our difficulties the night before. The hovel under which they split their slates stood upon an out-jutting rock, a part of the quarry rising immediately out of the water, and commanded a fine prospect down the loch below Ballachulish, and upwards towards the grand mountains, and the other horn of the vale where the lake was concealed. The blacksmith drove our car about a mile of the road; we then hired a man and horse to take me and the car to the top of Glen Coe, being afraid that if the horse backed or took fright we might be thrown down some precipice. But before we departed we could not resist our inclination to climb up the hill which I have mentioned as appearing to terminate the loch. The mountains, though inferior to those of Glen Coe, on the other side are very-majestic; and the solitude in which we knew the unseen lake was bedded at their feet was enough to excite our longings. We climbed steep after steep, far higher than they appeared to us, and I was going to give up the accomplishment of our aim, when a glorious sight on the mountain before us made me forget my fatigue. A slight shower had come on, its skirts falling upon us, and half the opposite side of the mountain was wrapped up in rainbow light, covered as by a veil with one dilated rainbow: so it continued for some minutes; and the shower and rainy clouds passed away as suddenly as they had come, and the sun shone again upon the tops of all the hills. In the meantime we reached the wished-for point, and saw to the head of the loch. Perhaps it might not be so beautiful as we had imaged it in our thoughts, but it was beautiful enough not to disappoint us,—a narrow deep valley, a perfect solitude, without house or hut. One of the hills was thinly sprinkled with Scotch firs, which appeared to be the survivors of a large forest: they were the first natural wild Scotch firs we had seen. Though thinned of their numbers, and left, comparatively, to a helpless struggle with the elements, we were much struck with the gloom, and even grandeur, of the trees.

Hastened back again to join the car, but were tempted to go a little out of our way to look at a nice white house belonging to the laird of Glen Coe, which stood sweetly in a green field under the hill near some tall trees and coppice woods. At this house the horrible massacre of Glen Coe began, which we did not know when we were there; but the house must have been rebuilt since that time. We had a delightful walk through fields, among copses, and by a river-side: we could have fancied ourselves in some part of the north of England unseen before, it was so much like it, and yet so different. I must not forget one place on the opposite side of the water, where we longed to live—a snug white house on the mountain-side, surrounded by its own green fields and woods, the high mountain above, the loch below, and inaccessible but by means of boats. A beautiful spot indeed it was; but in the retired parts of Scotland a comfortable white house is itself such a pleasant sight, that I believe, without our knowing how or why, it makes us look with a more loving eye on the fields and trees than for their own sakes they deserve.

At about one o'clock we set off, William on our own horse, and I with my Highland driver. He was perfectly acquainted with the country, being a sort of carrier or carrier-merchant or shopkeeper, going frequently to Glasgow with his horse and cart to fetch and carry goods and merchandise. He knew the name of every hill, almost every rock; and I made good use of his knowledge; but partly from laziness, and still more because it was inconvenient, I took no notes, and now I am little better for what he told me. He spoke English tolerably; but seldom understood what was said to him without a 'What's your wull?' We turned up to the right, and were at the foot of the glen—the laird's house cannot be said to be in the glen. The afternoon was delightful,—the sun shone, the mountain-tops were clear, the lake glittered in the great vale behind us, and the stream of Glen Coe flowed down to it glittering among alder-trees. The meadows of the glen were of the freshest green; one new-built stone house in the first reach, some huts, hillocks covered with wood, alder-trees scattered all over. Looking backward, we were reminded of Patter-dale and the head of Ulswater, but forward the greatness of the mountains overcame every other idea.

The impression was, as we advanced up to the head of this first reach, as if the glen were nothing, its loneliness and retirement—as if it made up no part of my feeling: the mountains were all in all. That which fronted us— I have forgotten its name—was exceedingly lofty, the surface stony, nay, the whole mountain was one mass of stone, wrinkled and puckered up together. At the second and last reach—for it is not a winding vale—it makes a quick turning almost at right angles to the first; and now we are in the depths of the mountains; no trees in the glen, only green pasturage for sheep, and here and there a plot of hay-ground, and something that tells of former cultivation. I observed this to the guide, who said that formerly the glen had had many inhabitants, and that there, as elsewhere in the Highlands, there had been a great deal of corn where now the lands were left waste, and nothing fed upon them but cattle. I cannot attempt to describe the mountains. I can only say that I thought those on our right—for the other side was only a continued high ridge or craggy barrier, broken along the top into petty spiral forms—were the grandest I had ever seen. It seldom happens that mountains in a very clear air look exceedingly high, but these, though we could see the whole of them to their very summits, appeared to me more majestic in their own nakedness than our imaginations could have conceived them to be, had they been half hidden by clouds, yet showing some of their highest pinnacles. They were such forms as Milton might be supposed to have had in his mind when he applied to Satan that sublime expression—'His stature reached the sky.'

The first division of the glen, as I have said, was scattered over with rocks, trees, and woody hillocks, and cottages were to be seen here and there. The second division is bare and stony, huge mountains on all sides, with a slender pasturage in the bottom of the valley; and towards the head of it is a small lake or tarn, and near the tarn a single inhabited dwelling, and some unfenced hay-ground—a simple impressive scene! Our road frequently crossed large streams of stones, left by the mountain-torrents, losing all appearance of a road. After we had passed the tarn the glen became less interesting, or rather the mountains, from the manner in which they are looked at; but again, a little higher up, they resume their grandeur. The river is, for a short space, hidden between steep rocks: we left the road, and, going to the top of one of the rocks, saw it foaming over stones, or lodged in dark black dens; birch-trees grew on the inaccessible banks, and a few old Scotch firs towered above them. At the entrance of the glen the mountains had been all without trees, but. here the birches climb very far up the side of one of them opposite to us, half concealing a rivulet, which came tumbling down as white as snow from the very top of the mountain. Leaving the rock, we ascended a hill which terminated the glen. We often stopped to look behind at the majestic company of mountains we had left. Before us was no single paramount eminence, but a mountain waste, mountain beyond mountain, and a barren hollow or basin into which we were descending. We parted from our companion at the door of a whisky hovel, a building which, when it came out of the workmen's hands with its unglassed windows, would, in that forlorn region, have been little better than a howling place for the winds, and was now half unroofed. On seeing a smoke, I exclaimed, 'Is it possible any people can live there?' when at least half a dozen, men, women, and children, came to the door. They were about to rebuild the hut, and I suppose that they, or some other poor creatures, would dwell there through the winter, dealing' out whisky to the starved travellers. The sun was now setting, the air very cold, the sky clear; I could have fancied that it was winter-time, with hard frost. Our guide pointed out King's House to us, our resting-place for the night. We could just distinguish the house at the bottom of the moorish hollow or basin—I call it so, for it was nearly as broad as long—lying before us, with three miles of naked road winding through it, every foot of which we could see. The road was perfectly white, making a dreary contrast with the ground, which was of a dull earthy brown. Long as the line of road appeared before us, we could scarcely believe it to be three miles—I suppose owing to its being unbroken by any one object, and the moor naked as the road itself, but we found it the longest three miles we had yet travelled, for the surface was so stony we had to walk most of the way.

The house looked respectable at a distance—a large square building, cased in blue slates to defend it from storms,—but when we came close to it the outside forewarned us of the poverty and misery within. Scarce a blade of grass could be seen growing upon the open ground; the heath-plant itself found no nourishment there, appearing as if it had but sprung up to be blighted. There was no enclosure for a cow, no appropriated ground but a small plot like a churchyard, in which were a few starveling dwarfish potatoes, which had, no doubt, been raised by means of the dung left by travellers' horses: they had not come to blossoming, and whether they would either yield fruit or blossom I know not. The first thing we saw on entering the door was two sheep hung up, as if just killed from the barren moor, their bones hardly sheathed in flesh. After we had waited a few minutes, looking about for a guide to lead us into some corner of the house, a woman, seemingly about forty years old, came to us in a great bustle, screaming in Erse, with the most horrible guinea-hen or peacock voice I ever heard, first to one person, then another. She could hardly spare time to show us up-stairs, for crowds of men were in the house—drovers, carriers, horsemen, travellers, all of whom she had to provide with supper, and she was, as she told us, the only woman there.

Never did I see such a miserable, such a wretched place,—long rooms with ranges of beds, no other furniture except benches, or perhaps one or two crazy chairs, the floors far dirtier than an ordinary house could be if it were never washed, as dirty as a house after a sale on a rainy day, and the rooms being large, and the walls naked, they looked as if more than half the goods had been sold out. We sate shivering in one of the large rooms for three quarters of an hour before the woman could find time to speak to us again she then promised a fire in another room, after two travellers, who were going a stage further, had finished their whisky, and said we should have supper as soon as possible. She had no eggs, no milk, no potatoes, no loaf-bread, or we should have preferred tea. With length of time the fire was kindled, and, after another hour's waiting, supper came,—a shoulder of mutton so hard that it was impossible to chew the little flesh that might be scraped off the bones, and some sorry soup made of barley and water, for it had no other taste. After supper, the woman, having first asked if we slept on blankets, brought in two pair of sheets, which she begged that I would air by the fire, for they would be dirtied below-stairs. I was very willing, but behold! the sheets were so wet, that it would have been at least a two-hours' job before a far better fire than could be mustered at King's House,—for, that nothing might be wanting to make it a place of complete starvation, the peats were not dry, and if they had not been helped out by decayed wood dug out of the earth along with them, we should have had no fire at all. The woman was civil, in her fierce, wild way. She and the house, upon that desolate and extensive wilderness, and everything we saw, made us think of one of those places of rendezvous which we read of in novels—Ferdinand Count Fathom, or Gil Bias,—where there is one woman to receive the booty, and prepare the supper at night. She told us that she was only a servant, but that she had now lived there five years, and that, when but a 'young lassie,' she had lived there also. We asked her if she had always served the same master, 'Nay, nay, many masters, for they were always changing.' I verily believe that the woman was attached to the place like a cat to the empty house when the family who brought her up are gone to live elsewhere. The sheets were so long in drying that it was very late before we went to bed. We talked over our day's adventures by the fireside, and often looked out of the window towards a huge pyramidal mountain *{Buachailel, the Shepherd of Etive.}* at the entrance of Glen Coe. All between, the dreary waste was clear, almost, as sky, the moon shining full upon it. A rivulet ran amongst stones near the house, and sparkled with light: I could have fancied that there was nothing else, in that extensive circuit over which we looked, that had the power of motion.

In comparing the impressions we had received at Glen Coe, we found that, though the expectations of both had been far surpassed by the grandeur of the mountains, we had, upon the whole, both been disappointed, and from the same cause: we had been prepared for images of terror, had expected a deep, den-like valley with overhanging rocks, such as William has described in these lines, speaking of the Alps:—

Brook and road

Were fellow-travellers in this gloomy Pass,
And with them did we journey several hours
At a slow step.
The immeasurable height
Of woods decaying, never to be decayed!
The stationary blasts of waterfalls;
And everywhere along the hollow rent
Winds thwarting winds, bewilder'd and forlorn;
The torrents shooting from the clear blue sky,
The rocks that mutter'd close upon our ears,
Black drizzling crags that spake by the way-side
As if a voice were in them; the sick sight
And giddy prospect of the raving stream;
The unfetter'd clouds, and region of the heavens,
Tumult and peace, the darkness and the light,
Were all like workings of one mind, the features
Of the same face, blossoms upon one tree,
Characters of the great Apocalypse,
The Types and Symbols of Eternity,
Of first, and last, and midst, and without end.

The place had nothing of this character, the glen being open to the eye of day, the mountains retiring in independent majesty. Even in the upper part of it, where the stream rushed through the rocky chasm, it was but a deep trench in the vale, not the vale itself, and could only be seen when we were close to it.

Glen Croe

Inverary

Inverary Castle

The hill folly

Kilchurn Castle

Loch Etive

Glencoe on the way to the King's House

The King's House at Glencoe

Dunstaffnage Castle

Buachaille, the Shepherd of Etive

FOURTH WEEK

Sunday, September 4th—We had desired to be called at six o'clock, and rose at the first summons. Our beds had proved better than we expected, and we had not slept ill; but poor Coleridge had passed a wretched night here four days before. This we did not know; but since, when he told us of it, the notion of what he must have suffered, with the noise of drunken people about his ears all night, himself sick and tired, has made our discomfort cling to my memory, and given these recollections a twofold interest. I asked if it was possible to have a couple of eggs boiled before our departure: the woman hesitated; she thought I might, and sent a boy into the out-houses to look about, who brought in one egg after long searching. Early as we had risen it was not very early when we set off, for everything at King's House was in unison—equally uncomfortable. As the woman had told us the night before, 'They had no hay, and that was a loss.' There were neither stalls nor bedding in the stable, so that William was obliged to watch the horse while it was feeding, for there were several others in the stable, all standing like wild beasts, ready to devour each other's portion of corn: this, with the slowness of the servant and other hindrances, took up much time, and we were completely starved, for the morning was very cold, as I believe all the mornings in that desolate place are.

When we had gone about a quarter of a mile I recollected that I had left the little cup given me by the kind landlady at Taynuilt, which I had intended that John should hereafter drink out of, in memory of our wanderings. I would have turned back for it, but William pushed me on, unwilling that we should lose so much time, though indeed he was as sorry to part with it as myself.

Our road was over a hill called the Black Mount. For the first mile, or perhaps more, after we left King's House, we ascended on foot; then came upon a new road, one of the finest that was ever trod; and, as we went downwards almost all the way afterwards, we travelled very quickly. The motion was pleasant, the different reaches and windings of the road were amusing; the sun shone, the mountain-tops were clear and cheerful, and we in good spirits, in a bustle of enjoyment, though there never was a more desolate region: mountains behind, before, and on every side; I do not remember to have seen either patch of grass, flower, or flowering heather within three or four miles of King's House. The low ground was not rocky, but black, and full of white frost-bleached stones, the prospect only varied by pools, seen everywhere both near and at a distance, as far as the ground stretched out below us: these were interesting spots, round which the mind assembled living objects, and they shone as bright as mirrors in the forlorn waste. We passed neither tree nor shrub for miles—I include the whole space from Glen Coe—yet we saw perpetually traces of a long decayed forest, pieces of black mouldering wood.

Through such a country as this we had travelled perhaps seven and a half miles this morning, when, after descending a hill, we turned to the right, and saw an unexpected sight in the moorland hollow into which we were entering, a small lake bounded on the opposite side by a grove of Scotch firs, two or three cottages at the head of it, and a lot of cultivated ground with scattered hay-cocks. The road along which we were going, after having made a curve considerably above the tarn, was seen winding through the trees on the other side, a beautiful object, and, luckily for us, a drove of cattle happened to be passing there at the very time, a stream coursing the road, with off-stragglers to the borders of the lake, and under the trees on the sloping ground.

In conning over our many wanderings I shall never forget the gentle pleasure with which we greeted the lake of Inveroran and its few grey cottages: we suffered our horse to slacken his pace, having now no need of the comfort of quick motion, though we were glad to think that one of those cottages might be the public-house where we were to breakfast. A forest—now, as it appeared, dwindled into the small grove bordering the lake—had, not many years ago, spread to that side of the vale where we were: large stumps of trees which had been cut down were yet remaining undecayed, and there were some single trees left alive, as if by their battered black boughs to tell us of the storms that visit the valley which looked now so sober and peaceful. When we arrived at the huts, one of them proved to be the inn, a thatched house without a sign-board. We were kindly received, had a fire lighted in the parlour, and were in such good humour that we seemed to have a thousand comforts about us; but we had need of a little patience in addition to this good humour before breakfast was brought, and at last it proved a disappointment: the butter not eatable, the barley-cakes fusty, the oat-bread so hard I could not chew it, and there were only four eggs in the house, which they had boiled as hard as stones.

Before we had finished breakfast two foot-travellers came in, and seated themselves at our table; one of them was returning, after a long absence, to Fort-William, his native home; he had come from Egypt, and, many years ago, had been on a recruiting party at Penrith, and knew many people there. He seemed to think his own country but a dismal land.

There being no bell in the parlour, I had occasion to go several times and ask for what we wanted in the kitchen, and I would willingly have given twenty pounds to have been able to take a lively picture of it. About seven or eight travellers, probably drovers, with as many dogs, were sitting in a complete circle round a large peat-fire in the middle of the floor, each with a mess of porridge, in a wooden vessel, upon his knee; a pot, suspended from one of the black beams, was boiling on the fire; two or three women pursuing their household business on the outside of the circle, children playing on the floor. There was nothing uncomfortable in this confusion: happy, busy, or vacant faces, all looked pleasant; and even the smoky air, being a sort of natural indoor atmosphere of Scotland, served only to give a softening, I may say harmony, to the whole.

We departed immediately after breakfast, our road leading us, as I have said, near the lake-side and through the grove of firs, which extended backward much further than we had imagined. After we had left it we came again among bare moorish wastes, as before, under the mountains, so that Inveroran still lives in our recollection as a favoured place, a flower in the desert. Descended upon the whole, I believe very considerably, in our way to Tyndrum; but it was a road of long ups and downs, over hills and through hollows of uncultivated ground; a chance farm perhaps once in three miles, a glittering rivulet bordered with greener grass than grew on the broad waste, or a broken fringe of alders or birches, partly concealing and partly pointing out its course.

Arrived at Tyndrum at about two o'clock. It is a cold spot. Though, as I should suppose, situated lower than Inveroran, and though we saw it in the hottest time of the afternoon sun, it had a far colder aspect from the want of trees. We were here informed that Coleridge, who, we supposed, was gone to Edinburgh, had dined at this very house a few days before, in his road to Fort-William. By the help of the cook, who was called in, the landlady made out the very day: it was the day after we parted from him; as she expressed it, the day after the 'great speet,' namely, the great rain. We had a moorfowl and mutton-chops for dinner, well cooked, and a reasonable charge. The house was clean for a Scotch inn, and the people about the doors were well dressed. In one of the parlours we saw a company of nine or ten, with the landlady, seated round a plentiful table,—a sight which made us think of the fatted calf in the alehouse pictures of the Prodigal Son. There seemed to be a whole harvest of meats and drinks, and there was something of festivity and picture-like gaiety even in the fresh-coloured dresses of the people and their Sunday faces. The white table-cloth, glasses, English dishes, etc., were all in contrast with what we had seen at Inveroran: the places were but about nine miles asunder, both among hills; the rank of the people little different, and each house appeared to be a house of plenty.

We were, I think, better pleased with our treatment at this inn than any of the lonely houses on the road, except Taynuilt; but Coleridge had not fared so well, and was dissatisfied, as he has since told us, and the two travellers who breakfasted with us at Inveroran had given a bad account of the house.

Left Tyndrum at about five o'clock; a gladsome afternoon; the road excellent, and we bowled downwards through a pleasant vale, though not populous, or well cultivated, or woody, but enlivened by a river that glittered as it flowed. On the side of a sunny hill a knot of men and women were gathered together at a preaching. We passed by many droves of cattle and Shetland ponies, which accident stamped a character upon places, else unrememberable—not an individual character, but the soul, the spirit, and solitary simplicity of many a Highland region.

We had about eleven miles to travel before we came to our lodging, and had gone five or six, almost always descending, and still in the same vale, when we saw a small lake before us, after the vale had made a bending to the left. It was about sunset when we came up to the lake; the afternoon breezes had died away, and the water was in perfect stillness. One grove-like island, with a ruin that stood upon it overshadowed by the trees, was reflected on the water. This building, which, on that beautiful evening, seemed to be wrapped up in religious quiet, we were informed had been raised for defence by some Highland chieftain. All traces of strength, or war, or danger are passed away, and in the mood in which we were we could only look upon it as a place of retirement and peace. The lake is called Loch Dochart. We passed by two others of inferior beauty, and continued to travel along the side of the same river, the Dochart, through an irregular, undetermined vale,—poor soil and much waste land.

At that time of the evening when, by looking steadily, we could discover a few pale stars in the sky, we saw upon an eminence, the bound of our horizon, though very near to us, and facing the bright yellow clouds of the west, a group of figures that made us feel how much we wanted in not being painters. Two herdsmen, with a dog beside them, were sitting on the hill, overlooking a herd of cattle scattered over a large meadow by the river-side. Their forms, looked at through a fading light, and backed by the bright west, were exceedingly distinct, a beautiful picture in the quiet of a Sabbath evening, exciting thoughts and images of almost patriarchal simplicity and grace. We were much pleased with the situation of our inn, where we arrived between eight and nine o'clock. The river was at the distance of a broad field from the door; we could see it from the upper windows and hear its murmuring; the moon shone, enlivening the large corn fields with cheerful light. We had a bad supper, and the next morning they made us an unreasonable charge; and the servant was uncivil, because, forsooth! we had no wine.

N.B.—The travellers in the morning had spoken highly of this inn, the Suie.

Monday, September 5th—After drinking a bason of milk we set off again at a little after six o'clock—a fine morning—eight miles to Killin—the river Dochart always on our left. The face of the country not very interesting, though not unpleasing, reminding us of some of the vales of the north of England, though meagre, nipped-up, or shrivelled compared with them. There were rocks, and rocky knolls, as about Grasmere and Wythebum, and copses, but of a starveling growth; the cultivated ground poor. Within a mile or two of Killin the land was better cultivated, and, looking down the vale, we had a view of Loch Tay, into which the Dochart falls. Close to the town, the river took up a roaring voice, beating its way over a rocky descent among large black stones: islands in the middle turning the stream this way and that; the whole course of the river very wide. We crossed it by means of three bridges, which make one continued bridge of a great length. On an island below the bridge is a gateway with tall pillars, leading to an old burying-ground belonging to some noble family. *{The burial-place of Macnab of Macnab.}* It has a singular appearance, and the place is altogether uncommon and romantic—a remnant of ancient grandeur: extreme natural wildness—the sound of roaring water, and withal, the ordinary half-village, half-town bustle of an every-day place.

The inn at Killin is one of the largest on the Scotch road: it stands pleasantly, near the chapel, at some distance from the river Dochart, and out of reach of its tumultuous noise; and another broad, stately, and silent stream, which you cannot look at without remembering its boisterous neighbour, flows close under the windows of the inn, and beside the churchyard, in which are many graves. That river falls into the lake at the distance of nearly a mile from the mouth of the Dochart. It is bordered with tall trees and corn fields, bearing plentiful crops, the richest we had seen in Scotland.

After breakfast we walked onwards, expecting that the stream would lead us into some considerable vale; but it soon became little better than a common rivulet, and the glen appeared to be short; indeed, we wondered how the river had grown so great all at once. Our horse had not been able to eat his corn, and we waited a long time in the hope that he would be better. At eleven o'clock, however, we determined to set off, and give him all the ease possible by walking up the hills, and not pushing beyond a slow walk. We had fourteen miles to travel to Kenmore, by the side of Loch Tay. Crossed the same bridge again, and went down the south side of the lake. We had a delightful view of the village of Killin, among rich green fields, corn and wood, and up   towards the two horns of the vale of Tay, the valley of the Dochart, and the other valley with its full-grown river, the prospect terminated by mountains. We travelled through lanes, woods, or open fields, never close to the lake, but always near it, for many miles, the road being carried along the side of a hill, which rose in an almost regularly receding steep from the lake. The opposite shore did not much differ from that down which we went, but it seemed more thinly inhabited, and not so well cultivated. The sun shone, the cottages were pleasant, and the goings-on of the harvest—for all the inhabitants were at work in the corn fields—made the way cheerful. But there is an uniformity in the lake which, comparing it with other lakes, made it appear tiresome. It has no windings: I should even imagine, although it is so many miles long that, from some points not very high on the hills, it may be seen from one end to the other. There are few bays, no lurking-places where the water hides itself in the land, no outjutting points or promontories, no islands; and there are no commanding mountains or precipices. I think that this lake would be the most pleasing in spring-time, or in summer before the corn begins to change colour, the long tracts of hills on each side of the vale having at this season a kind of patchy appearance, for the corn fields in general were very small, mere plots, and of every possible shade of bright yellow. When we came in view of the foot of the lake we perceived that it ended, as it had begun, in pride and loveliness. The village of Kenmore, with its neat church and cleanly houses, stands on a gentle eminence at the end of the water. The view, though not near so beautiful as that of Killin, is exceedingly pleasing. Left our car, and turned out of the road at about the distance of a mile from the town, and after having climbed perhaps a quarter of a mile, we were conducted into a locked-up plantation, and guessed by the sound that we were near the cascade, but could not see it. Our guide opened a door, and we entered a dungeon-like passage, and, after walking some yards in total darkness, found ourselves in a quaint apartment stuck over with moss, hung about with stuffed foxes and other wild animals, and ornamented with a library of wooden books covered with old leather backs, the mock furniture of a hermit's cell. At the end of the room, through a large bow-window, we saw the waterfall, and at the same time, looking down to the left, the village of Kenmore and a part of the lake—a very beautiful prospect.

MEMORANDUM BY THE AUTHOR.

'The transcript of the First Part of this Journal, and the Second as far as page 138, were written before the end of the year 1803. I do not know exactly when I concluded the remainder of the Second Part, but it was resumed on the 2nd of February 1804. The Third Part was begun at the end of the month of April 1805, and finished on the 31st of May.' *{In this interval her dear brother, Captain Wordsworth, had been drowned, as stated in note to page 3, in the wreck of the 'Abergavenny,' on February 5, 1805.}*

April 11th, 1805—I am setting about a task which, however free and happy the state of my mind, I could not have performed well at this distance of time; but now, I do not know that I shall be able to go on with it at all. I will strive, however, to do the best I can, setting before myself a different object from that hitherto aimed at, which was, to omit no incident, however trifling, and to describe the country so minutely that you should, where the objects were the most interesting, feel as if you had been with us. I shall now only attempt to give you an idea of those scenes which pleased us most, dropping the incidents of the ordinary days, of which many have slipped from my memory, and others which remain it would be difficult, and often painful to me, to endeavour to draw out and disentangle from other thoughts. I the less regret my inability to do more, because, in describing a great part of what we saw from the time we left Kenmore, my work would be little more than a repetition of what I have said before, or, where it was not so, a longer time was necessary to enable us to bear away what was most interesting than we could afford to give.

Monday, September 5th—We arrived at Kenmore after sunset.

Tuesday, September 6th—Walked before breakfast in Lord Breadalbane's grounds, which border upon the river Tay. The higher elevations command fine views of the lake; and the walks are led along the river's banks, and shaded with tall trees: but it seemed to us that a bad taste had been at work, the banks being regularly shaven and cut as if by rule and line. One or two of such walks I should well have liked to see; but they are all equally trim, and I could not but regret that the fine trees had not been left to grow out of a turf that cattle were permitted to feed upon. There was one avenue which would well have graced the ruins of an abbey or some stately castle. It was of a very great length, perfectly straight, the trees meeting at the top in a cathedral arch, lessening in perspective,—the boughs the roof, the stems the pillars. I never saw so beautiful an avenue. We were told that some improver of pleasure-grounds had advised Lord B. to cut down the trees, and lay the whole open to the lawn, for the avenue is very near his house. His own better taste, or that of some other person, I suppose, had saved them from the axe. Many workmen were employed in building a large mansion, something like that of Inverary, close to the old house, which was yet standing; the situation, as we thought, very bad, considering that Lord Breadalbane had the command of all the ground at the foot of the lake, including hills both high and low. It is in a hollow, without prospect either of the lake or river, or anything else—seeing nothing, and adorning nothing. After breakfast, left Kenmore, and travelled through the vale of Tay, I believe fifteen or sixteen miles; but in the course of this we turned out of our way to the Falls of Moness, a stream tributary to the Tay, which passes through a narrow glen with very steep banks. A path like a woodman's track has been carried through the glen, which, though the private property of a gentleman, has not been taken out of the hands of Nature, but merely rendered accessible by this path, which ends at the waterfalls. They tumble from a great height, and are indeed very beautiful falls, and we could have sate with pleasure the whole morning beside the cool basin in which the waters rest, surrounded by high rocks and overhanging trees. In one of the most retired parts of the dell, we met a young man coming slowly along the path, intent upon a book which he was reading: he did not seem to be of the rank of a gentleman, though above that of a peasant.

Passed through the village of Aberfeldy at the foot of the glen of Moness. The birks of Aberfeldy are spoken of in some of the Scotch songs, which no doubt grew in the stream of Moness; but near the village we did not see any trees that were remarkable, except a row of laburnums, growing as a common field hedge; their leaves were of a golden colour, and as lively as the yellow blossoms could have been in the spring. Afterwards we saw many laburnums in the woods, which we were told had been 'planted;' though I remember that Withering speaks of the laburnum as one of the British plants, and growing in Scotland. The twigs and branches being stiff were not so graceful as those of our garden laburnums, but I do not think I ever before saw any that were of so brilliant colours in their autumnal decay. In our way to and from Moness we crossed the Tay by a bridge of ambitious and ugly architecture. Many of the bridges in Scotland are so, having eye-holes between the arches, not in the battlements but at the outspreading of the pillar of the arch, which destroys its simplicity, and takes from the appearance of strength and security, without adding anything of lightness. We returned, by the same road, to the village of Weem, where we had left our car. The vale of Tay was very wide, having been so from within a short distance of Kenmore: the reaches of the river are long; and the ground is more regularly cultivated than in any vale we had yet seen—chiefly corn, and very large tracts. Afterwards the vale becomes narrow and less cultivated, the reaches shorter—on the whole resembling the vale of Nith, but we thought it inferior in beauty.

One among the cottages in this narrow-and wilder part of the vale fixed our attention almost as much as a Chinese or a Turk would do passing through the vale of Grasmere. It was a cottage, I believe, little differing in size and shape from all the rest; but it was like a visitor, a stranger come into the Highlands, or a model set up of what may be seen in other countries. The walls were neatly plastered or roughcast, the windows of clean bright glass, and the door was painted—before it a flower-garden, fenced with a curiously-clipped hedge, and against the wall was placed the sign of a spinning-wheel. We could not pass this humble dwelling, so distinguished by an appearance of comfort and neatness, without some conjectures respecting the character and manner of life of the person inhabiting it. Leisure he must have had; and we pleased ourselves with thinking that some self-taught mind might there have been nourished by knowledge gathered from books, and the simple duties and pleasures of rural life.

At Logierait, the village where we dined, the vale widens again, and the Tummel joins the Tay and loses its name; but the Tay falls into the channel of the Tummel, continuing its course in the same direction, almost at right angles to the former course of the Tay. We were sorry to find that we had to cross the Tummel by a ferry, and resolved not to venture in the same boat with the horse. Dined at a little public-house, kept by a young widow, very talkative, and laboriously civil. She took me out to the. back-door, and said she would show me a place which had once been very grand, and, opening a door in a high wall, I entered a ruinous court-yard, in which was a large old mansion, the walls entire and very strong, but the roof broken in. The woman said it had been a palace (14) of one of the kings of Scotland. It was a striking, and even an affecting object, coming upon it, as I did, unawares,—a royal residence shut up and hidden, while yet in its strength, by mean cottages; there was no appearance of violence, but decay from desertion, and I should think that it may remain many years without undergoing further visible change. The woman and her daughter accompanied us to the ferry and crossed the water with us; the woman said, but with not much appearance of honest heart-feeling, that she could not be easy to let us go without being there to know how we sped, so I invited the little girl to accompany her, that she might have a ride in the car. The men were cautious, and the horse got over with less alarm than we could have expected. Our way was now up the vale, along the banks of the Tummel, an impetuous river; the mountains higher than near the Tay, and the vale more wild, and the different reaches more interesting.

When we approached near to Fascally, near the junction of the Garry with the Tummel, the twilight was far advanced, and our horse not being perfectly recovered, we were fearful of taking him on to Blair-Athole—five miles further; besides, the Pass of Killiecrankie was within half a mile, and we were unwilling to go through a place so celebrated in the dark; therefore, being joined by a traveller, we inquired if there was any public-house near; he said there was; and that though the accommodations were not good, we might do well enough for one night, the host and his wife being very honest people. It proved to be rather better than a common cottage of the country; we seated ourselves by the fire, William called for a glass of, whisky, and asked if they could give us beds. The woman positively refused to lodge us, though we had every reason to believe that she had at least one bed for me; we entreated again and again in behalf of the poor horse, but all in vain; she urged, though in an uncivil way, that she had been sitting up the whole of one or two nights before on account of a fair, and that now she wanted to go to bed and sleep; so we were obliged to remount our car in the dark, and with a tired horse we moved on, and went through the Pass of Killiecrankie, hearing only the roaring of the river, and seeing a black chasm with jagged-topped black hills towering above. Afterwards the moon rose, and we should not have had an unpleasant ride if our horse had been in better plight, and we had not been annoyed, as we were almost at every twenty yards, by people coming from a fair held that day near Blair—no pleasant prognostic of what might be our accommodation at the inn, where we arrived between ten and eleven o'clock, and found the house in an uproar; but we were civilly treated, and were glad, after eating a morsel of cold beef, to retire to rest, and I fell asleep in spite of the noisy drunkards below stairs, who had outstayed the fair.

Wednesday, September 7th—Rose early, and went before breakfast to the Duke of Athol's gardens and pleasure-grounds, where we completely tired ourselves with a three-hours' walk. Having been directed to see all the waterfalls, we submitted ourselves to the gardener, who dragged us from place to place, calling our attention to, it might be, half-a-dozen—I cannot say how many—dripping streams, very pretty in themselves, if we had had the pleasure of discovering them; but they were generally robbed of their grace by the obtrusive ornaments which were first seen. The whole neighbourhood, a great country, seems to belong to the Duke of Athol. In his domain are hills and mountains, glens and spacious plains, rivers and innumerable torrents; but near Blair are no old woods, and the plantations, except those at a little distance from the house, appear inconsiderable, being lost to the eye in so extensive a circuit.

The castle stands on low ground, and far from the Garry, commanding a prospect all round of distant mountains, a bare and cold scene, and, from the irregularity and width of it, not so grand as one should expect, knowing the great height of some of the mountains. Within the Duke's park are three glens, the glen of the river Tilt and two others, which, if they had been planted more judiciously, would have been very sweet retirements; but they are choked up, the whole hollow of the glens—I do not speak of the Tilt, for that is rich in natural wood—being closely planted with trees, and those chiefly firs; but many of the old fir-trees are, as single trees, very fine. On each side of the glen is an ell-wide gravel walk, which the gardener told us was swept once a week. It is conducted at the top of the banks, on each side, at nearly equal height, and equal distance from the stream; they lead you up one of these paths, and down the other—very wearisome, as you will believe—mile after mile! We went into the garden, where there was plenty of fruit—gooseberries, hanging as thick as possible upon the trees, ready to drop off; I thought the gardener might have invited us to refresh ourselves with some of his fruit after our long fatigue. One part of the garden was decorated with statues,' images,' as poor Mr. Gill used to call those at Eacedown, dressed in gay-painted clothes; and in a retired corner of the grounds, under some tall trees, appeared the figure of a favourite old gamekeeper of one of the former Dukes, in the attitude of pointing his gun at the game—'reported to be a striking likeness,' said the gardener. Looking at some of the tall larches, with long hairy twigs, very beautiful trees, he told us that they were among the first which had ever been planted in Scotland, that a Duke of Athol had brought a single larch from London in a pot, in his coach, from which had sprung the whole family that had overspread Scotland. This, probably, might not be accurate, for others might afterwards have come, or seed from other trees. He told us many anecdotes of the present Duke, which I wish I could perfectly remember. He is an indefatigable sportsman, hunts the wild deer on foot, attended by twelve Highlanders in the Highland dress, which he himself formerly used to wear; he will go out at four o'clock in the morning, and not return till night. His fine family, 'Athol's honest men, and Athol's bonny lasses,' to whom Burns, in his bumpers, drank health and long life, are dwindled away: of nine, I believe only four are left: the mother of them is dead in a consumption, and the-Duke married again. We rested upon the heather seat which Burns was so loth to quit that moonlight evening when he first went to Blair Castle, and had a pleasure in thinking that he had been under the same shelter, and viewed the little waterfall opposite with some of the happy and pure feelings of his better mind. The castle has been modernized, which has spoiled its appearance. It is a large irregular pile, not handsome, but I think may have been picturesque, and even noble, before it was docked of its battlements and whitewashed.

The most interesting object we saw at Blair was the chapel, shaded by trees, in which the body of the impetuous Dundee lies buried. This quiet spot is seen from the windows of the inn, whence you look, at the same time, upon a high wall and a part of the town—a contrast which, I know not why, made the chapel and its grove appear more peaceful, as if kept so for some sacred purpose. We had a very nice breakfast, which we sauntered over after our weary walk.

Being come to the most northerly point of our destined course, we took out the map, loth to turn our backs upon the Highlands, and, looking about for something which we might yet see, we fixed our eyes upon two or three spots not far distant, and sent for the landlord to consult with him. One of them was Loch Rannoch, a fresh-water lake, which he told us was bordered by a natural pine forest, that its banks were populous, and that the place being very remote, we might there see much of the simplicity of the Highlander's life. The landlord said that we must take a guide for the first nine or ten miles; but afterwards the road was plain before us, and very good, so at about ten o'clock we departed, having engaged a man to go with us. The Falls of Bruar, which we wished to visit for the sake of Burns, are about three miles from Blair, and our road was in the same direction for two miles.

After having gone for some time under a bare hill, we were told to leave the car at some cottages, and pass through a little gate near a brook which crossed the road. We walked upwards at least three quarters of a mile in the hot sun, with the stream on our right, both sides of which to a considerable height were planted with firs and larches intermingled—children of poor Burns's song; for his sake we wished that they had been the natural trees of Scotland, birches, ashes, mountain-ashes, etc.; however, sixty or seventy years hence they will be no unworthy monument to his memory. At present, nothing can be uglier than the whole chasm of the hill-side with its formal walks. I do not mean to condemn them, for, for aught I know, they are as well managed as they could be; but it is not easy to see the use of a pleasure-path leading to nothing, up a steep and naked hill in the midst of an unlovely tract of country, though by the side of a tumbling stream of clear water. It does not surely deserve the name of a pleasure-path. It is three miles from the Duke of Athol's house, and I do not believe that one person living within five miles of the place would wish to go twice to it. The falls are high, the rocks and stones fretted and gnawed by the-water. I do not wonder at the pleasure which Burns received from this stream; I believe we should have been much pleased if we had come upon it as he did. At the bottom of the hill we took up our car, and, turning back, joined the man who was to be our guide.

Crossed the Garry, and went along a moor without any road but straggling cart-tracks. Soon began to ascend a high hill, and the ground grew so rough—road there was none—that we were obliged to walk most of the way. Ascended to a considerable height, and commanded an extensive prospect bounded by lofty mountains, and having crossed the top of the fell we parted with our guide, being in sight of the vale into which we were to descend, and to pursue upwards till we should come to Loch Rannoch, a lake, as described to us, bedded in a forest of Scotch pines.

When left to ourselves we sate down on the hillside, and looked with delight into the deep vale below, which was exceedingly green, not regularly fenced or cultivated, but the level area scattered over with bushes and trees, and through that level ground glided a glassy river, not in serpentine windings, but in direct turnings backwards and forwards, and then flowed into the head of the Lake of Tummel; but I will copy a rough sketch which i made while we sate upon the hill, which, imperfect as it is, will give a better idea of the course of the river, which I must add is more curious than beautiful, than my description. The ground must be often overflowed in winter, for the water seemed to touch the very edge of its banks. At this time the scene was soft and cheerful, such as invited us downwards, and made us proud of our adventure. Coming near to a cluster of huts, we turned thither, a few steps out of our way, to inquire about the road; these huts were on the hill, placed side by side, in a figure between a square and a circle, as if for the sake of mutual shelter, like haystacks in a farmyard—no trees near them. We called at one of the doors, and three hale, stout men came out, who could speak very little English, and stared at us with an almost savage look of wonder. One of them took much pains to set us forward, and went a considerable way down the hill till we came in sight of the cart road, which we were to follow; but we had not gone far before we were disheartened. It was with the greatest difficulty William could lead the horse and car over the rough stones, and to sit in it was impossible; the road grew worse and worse, therefore we resolved to turn back, having no reason to expect anything better, for we had been told that after we should leave the untracked ground all would be fair before us. We knew ourselves where we stood to be about eight miles distant from the point where the river Tummel, after having left the lake, joins the Garry at Fascally near the Pass of Killiecrankie, therefore we resolved to make our way thither, and endeavour to procure a lodging at the same public-house where it had been refused to us the night before. The road was likely to be very bad; but, knowing the distance, we thought it more prudent than to venture further with nothing before us but uncertainty. We were forced to unyoke the horse, and turn the car ourselves, owing to the steep banks on either side of the road, and after much trouble we got him in again, and set our faces down the vale towards Loch Tummel, William leading the car and I walking by his side. For the first two or three miles we looked down upon the lake, our road being along the side of the hill directly above it. On the opposite side another range of hills rose up in the same manner,—farm-houses thinly scattered among the copses near the water, and cultivated ground in patches. The lake does not wind, nor are the shores much varied by bays,—the mountains not commanding; but the whole a pleasing scene. Our road took us out of sight of the water, and we were obliged to procure a guide across a high moor, where it was impossible that the horse should drag us at all, the ground being exceedingly rough and untracked: of course fatiguing for foot-travellers, and on foot we must travel. After some time, the river Tummel again served us for a guide, when it had left the lake. It was no longer a gentle stream, a mirror to the sky, but we could hear it roaring at a considerable distance between steep banks of rock and wood. We had to cross the Garry by a bridge, a little above the junction of the two rivers; and were now not far from the public-house, to our great joy, for we were very weary with our laborious walk. I do not think that I had walked less than sixteen miles, and William much more, to which add the fatigue of leading the horse, and the rough roads, and you will not wonder that we longed for rest. We stopped at the door of the house, and William entered as before, and again the woman refused to lodge us, in a most inhuman manner, giving no other reason than that she would not do it. We pleaded for the poor horse, entreated, soothed, and flattered, but all in vain, though the night was cloudy and dark. We begged to sit by the fire till morning, and to this she would not consent; indeed, if it had not been for the sake of the horse, I would rather have lain in a barn than on the best of feather-beds in the house of such a cruel woman.

We were now, after our long day's journey, five miles from the inn at Blair, whither we, at first, thought of returning; but finally resolved to go to a public-house which we had seen in a village we passed through, about a mile above the ferry over the Tummel, having come from that point to Blair, for the sake of the Pass of Killiecrankie and Blair itself, and had now the same road to measure back again. We were obliged to leave the Pass of Killiecrankie unseen; but this disturbed us little at a time when we had seven miles to travel in the dark, with a poor beast almost sinking with fatigue, for he had not rested once all day. We went on spiritless, and at a dreary pace. Passed by one house which we were half inclined to go up to and ask for a night's lodging; and soon after, being greeted by a gentle voice from a poor woman, whom, till she spoke, though we were close to her, we had not seen, we stopped, and asked if she could tell us where we might stay all night, and put up our horse. She mentioned the public-house left behind, and we told our tale, and asked her if she had no house to which she could take us. 'Yes, to be sure she had a house, but it was only a small cottage;' and she had no place for the horse, and how we could lodge in her house she could not tell; but we should be welcome to whatever she had, so we turned the car, and she walked by the side of it, talking to us in a tone of human kindness which made us friends at once.

I remember thinking to myself, as I have often done in a stage-coach, though never with half the reason to prejudge favourably, what sort of countenance and figure shall we see in this woman when we come into the light? And indeed it was an interesting moment when, after we had entered her house, she blew the embers on the hearth, and lighted a candle to assist us in taking the luggage out of the car. Her husband presently arrived, and he and William took the horse to the public-house. The poor woman hung the kettle over the fire. We had tea and sugar of our own, and she set before us barley cakes, and milk which she had just brought in; I recollect she said she 'had been west to fetch it.' The Highlanders always direct you by east and west, north and south—very confusing to strangers. She told us that it was her business to 'keep the gate' for Mr.-,who lived at-, just below,—that is, to receive messages, take in letters, etc. Her cottage stood by the side of the road leading to his house, within the gate, having, as we saw in the morning, a dressed-up porter's lodge outside; but within was nothing but the naked walls, unplastered, and floors of mud, as in the common huts. She said that they lived rent-free in return for their services; but spoke of her place and Mr.- with little respect, hinting that he was very proud, and indeed, her appearance and subdued manners, and that soft voice which had prepossessed us so much in her favour, seemed to belong to an injured and oppressed being. We talked a great deal with her, and gathered some interesting facts from her conversation, which I wish I had written down while they were fresh in my memory. They had only one child, yet seemed to be very poor, not discontented, but languid, and willing to suffer rather than rouse-to any effort. Though it was plain she despised and hated her master, and had no wish to conceal it, she hardly appeared to think it worthwhile to speak ill of him. We were obliged to sit up very late while our kind hostess was preparing our beds. William lay upon the floor on some hay, without sheets; my bed was of chaff; I had plenty of covering, and a pair of very nice strong clean sheets,—she said with some pride that she had good linen. I believe the sheets had been of her own spinning, perhaps when she was first married, or before, and she probably will keep them to the end of her life of poverty.

Thursday, September 8th—Before breakfast we walked to the Pass of Killiecrankie. A very fine scene; the river Garry forcing its way down a deep chasm between rocks, at the foot of high rugged hills covered with wood, to a great height. The Pass did not, however, impress us with awe, or a sensation of difficulty or danger, according to our expectations; but, the road being at a considerable height on the side of the hill, we at first only looked into the dell or chasm. It is much grander seen from below, near the river's bed. Everybody knows that this Pass is famous in military history. When we were travelling in Scotland an invasion was hourly looked for, and one could not but think with some regret of the times when from the now depopulated

Highlands forty or fifty thousand men might have been poured down for the defence of the country, under such leaders as the Marquis of Montrose or the brave man who had so distinguished himself upon the ground where we were standing. I will transcribe a sonnet suggested to William by this place, and written in October 1803:—

> *Six thousand Veterans practised in War's game,*
> *Tried men, at Killiecrankie were array'd*
> *Against an equal host that wore the Plaid,*
> *Shepherds and herdsmen. Like a whirlwind came*
> *The Highlanders; the slaughter spread like flame,*
> *And Garry, thundering down his mountain road,*
> *Was stopp'd, and could not breathe beneath the load*
> *Of the dead bodies. 'Twas a day of shame*
> *For them whom precept and the pedantry*
> *Of cold mechanic battle do enslave.*
> *Oh! for a single hour of that Dundee*
> *Who on that day the word of onset gave:*
> *Like conquest might the men of England*
> *And her Foes find a like inglorious grave.*

We turned back again, and going down the hill below the Pass, crossed the same bridge we had come over the night before, and walked through Lady Perth's grounds by the side of the Garry till we came to the Tummel, and then walked up to the cascade of the Tummel. The fall is inconsiderable, scarcely more than an ordinary 'wear;' but it makes a loud roaring over large stones, and the whole scene is grand—hills, mountains, woods, and rocks.- is a very pretty place, all but the house. Stoddart's print gives no notion of it. The house stands upon a small plain at the junction of the two rivers, a close deep spot, surrounded by high hills and woods. After we had breakfasted William fetched the car, and, while we were conveying the luggage to the outside of the gate, where it stood, Mr. - *mal apropos* came very near to the door, called the woman out, and railed at her in the most abusive manner for 'harbouring' people in that way. She soon slipped from him, and came back to us: I wished that William should go and speak to her master, for I was afraid that he might turn the poor woman away; but she would not suffer it, for she did not care whether they stayed or not. In the meantime, Mr. - continued scolding her husband; indeed, he appeared to be not only proud, but very ignorant, insolent, and low-bred. The woman told us that she had sometimes lodged poor travellers who were passing along the road, and permitted others to cook their victuals in her house, for which Mr. -had reprimanded her before; but, as she said, she did not value her place, and it was no matter. In sounding forth the dispraise of Mr. - , I ought not to omit mentioning that the poor woman had great delight in talking of the excellent qualities of his mother, with whom she had been a servant, and lived many years. After having interchanged good wishes we parted with our charitable hostess, who, telling us her name, entreated us, if ever we came that way again, to inquire for her. We travelled down the Tummel till it is lost in the Tay, and then, in the same direction, continued our course along the vale of Tay, which is very wide for a considerable way, but gradually narrows, and the river, always a fine stream, assumes more dignity and importance. Two or three miles before we reached Dunkeld, we observed whole hill-sides, the property of the Duke of Athol, planted with fir-trees till they are lost among the rocks near the tops of the hills. In forty or fifty years these plantations will be very fine, being carried from hill to hill, and not bounded by a visible artificial fence. Reached Dunkeld at about three o'clock. It is a pretty, small town, with a respectable and rather large ruined abbey, which is greatly injured by being made the nest of a modern Scotch kirk, with sash windows,—very incongruous with the noble antique tower,—a practice which we afterwards found is not uncommon in Scotland. Sent for the Duke's gardener after dinner, and walked with him into the pleasure-grounds, intending to go to the Falls of the Bran, a mountain stream which here joins the Tay. After walking some time on a shaven turf under the shade of old trees, by the side of the Tay, we left the pleasure-grounds, and crossing the river by a ferry, went up a lane on the hill opposite till we came to a locked gate by the road-side, through which we entered into another part of the Duke's pleasure-grounds bordering on the Bran, the glen being for a considerable way—for aught I know, two miles thridded by gravel walks. The walks are quaintly enough intersected, here and there by a baby garden of fine flowers among the rocks and stones. The waterfall, which we came to see, warned us by a loud roaring that we must expect it; we were first, however, conducted into a small apartment, where the gardener desired us to look at a painting of the figure of Ossian, which, while he was telling us the story of the young artist who performed the work, disappeared, parting in the middle, flying asunder as if by the touch of magic, and lo! we are at the entrance of a splendid room, which was almost dizzy and alive with waterfalls, that tumbled in all directions—the great cascade, which was opposite to the window that faced us, being reflected in innumerable mirrors upon the ceiling and against the walls. We both laughed heartily, which, no doubt, the gardener considered as high commendation; for he was very eloquent in pointing out the beauties of the place. We left the Bran, and pursued our walk through the plantations, where we readily forgave the Duke his little devices for their sakes. They are already no insignificant woods, where the trees happen to be oaks, birches, and others natural to the soil; and under their shade the walks are delightful. From one hill, through different openings under the trees, we looked up the vale of Tay to a great distance, a magnificent prospect at that time of the evening; woody and rich—corn, green fields, and cattle, the winding Tay, and distant mountains. Looked down the river to the town of Dunkeld, which lies low, under irregular hills, covered with wood to their rocky summits and bounded by higher mountains, which are bare. The hill of Birnam, no longer Birnam 'wood,' was pointed out to us. After a very long walk we parted from our guide when it was almost dark, and he promised to call on us in the morning to conduct us to the gardens.

Friday, September 9th—According to appointment, the gardener came with his keys in his hand, and we attended him whithersoever he chose to lead, in spite of past experience at Blair. We had, however, no reason to repent, for we were repaid for the trouble of going through the large gardens by the apples and pears of which he gave us liberally, and the walks through the woods on that part of the grounds opposite to where we had been the night before were very delightful. The Duke's house is neither large nor grand, being just an ordinary gentleman's house, upon a green lawn, and whitewashed, I believe. The old abbey faces the house on the east side, and appears to stand upon the same green lawn, which, though close to the town, is entirely excluded from it by high walls and trees.

We had been undetermined respecting our future course when we came to Dunkeld, whether to go on directly to Perth and Edinburgh, or to make a circuit and revisit the Trossachs. We decided upon the latter plan, and accordingly, after breakfast, set forward towards Crief, where we intended to sleep, and the next night at Callander. The first part of our road, after having crossed the ferry, was up the glen of the Bran. Looking backwards, we saw Dunkeld very pretty under the hills, and surrounded by rich cultivated ground, but we had not a good distant view of the abbey.

Left our car, and went about a hundred yards from the road to see the Rumbling Brig, which, though well worth our going out of the way even much further, disappointed us, as places in general do which we hear much spoken of as savage, tremendous, etc.,—and no wonder, for they are usually described by people to whom rocks are novelties. The gardener had told us that we should pass through the most populous glen in Scotland, the glen of Amulree. It is not populous in the usual way, with scattered dwellings; but many clusters of houses, hamlets such as we had passed near the Tummel, which had a singular appearance, being like small encampments, were generally without trees, and in high situations—every house the same as its neighbour, whether for men or cattle. There was nothing else remarkable in the glen. We halted at a lonely inn at the foot of a steep barren moor, which we had to cross; then, after descending considerably, came to the narrow glen, which we had approached with no little curiosity, not having been able to procure any distinct description of it.

At Dunkeld, when we were hesitating what road to take, we wished to know whether that glen would be worth visiting, and accordingly put several questions to the waiter, and, among other epithets used in the course of interrogation, we stumbled upon the word 'grand,' to which he replied, 'No, I do not think there are any gentlemen's seats in it.' However, we drew enough from this describer and the gardener to determine us finally to go to Callander, the Narrow Glen being in the way.

Entered the glen at a small hamlet at some distance from the head, and, turning aside a few steps, ascended a hillock which commanded a view to the top of it—a very sweet scene, a green valley, not very narrow, with a few scattered trees and huts, almost invisible in a misty gleam of afternoon light. At this hamlet we crossed a bridge, and the road led us down the glen, which had become exceedingly narrow, and so continued to the end: the hills on both sides heathy and rocky, very steep, but continuous; the rocks not single or overhanging, not scooped into caverns or sounding with torrents: there are no trees, no houses, no traces of cultivation, not one outstanding object. It is truly a solitude, the road even making it appear still more so: the bottom of the valley is mostly smooth and level, the brook not noisy: everything is simple and undisturbed, and while we passed through it the whole place was shady, cool, clear, and solemn. At the end of the long valley we ascended a hill to a great height, and reached the top, when the sun, on the point of setting, shed a soft yellow light upon every eminence. The prospect was very extensive; over hollows and plains, no towns, and few houses visible—a prospect, extensive as it was, in harmony with the secluded dell, and fixing its own peculiar character of removedness from the world, and the secure possession of the quiet of nature more deeply in our minds. The following poem was written by William on hearing of a tradition relating to it, which we did not know when we were there:—

In this still place remote from men
 Sleeps Ossian, in the Narrow Glen,
In this still place where murmurs on
But one meek streamlet, only one.
He sung of battles and the breath
Of stormy war, and violent death,
And should, methinks, when all was pass'd
Have rightfully been laid at last
Where rocks were rudely heap'd, and rent
As by a spirit turbulent;
Where sights were rough, and sounds were wild,
And everything unreconciled,
In some complaining, dim retreat
Where fear and melancholy meet;
But this is calm; there cannot be
A more entire tranquillity.

Does then the Bard sleep here indeed?
Or is it but a groundless creed?
What matters it? I blame them not
Whose fancy in this lonely spot
Was moved, and in this way express'd
Their notion of its perfect rest.
A convent, even a hermit's cell
Would break the silence of this Dell;
It is not quiet, is not ease,
But something deeper far than these;
The separation that is here
Is of the grave; and of austere
And happy feelings of the dead:
And therefore was it rightly said
That Ossian, last of all his race,
Lies buried in this lonely place.

Having descended into a broad cultivated vale, we saw nothing remarkable. Observed a gentleman's house, {*Monzie probably}* which stood pleasantly among trees. It was dark some time before we reached Crieff, a small town, though larger than Dunkeld.

Saturday, September 10th—Rose early, and departed without breakfast. We were to pass through one of the most celebrated vales of Scotland, Strath Erne. We found it a wide, long, and irregular vale, with many gentlemen's seats under the hills, woods, copses, frequent cottages, plantations, and much cultivation, yet with an intermixture of barren ground; indeed, except at Killin and Dunkeld, there was always something which seemed to take from the composure and simplicity of the cultivated scenes. There is a struggle to overcome the natural barrenness, and the end not attained, an appearance of something doing, or imperfectly done, a passing with labour from one state of society into another. When you look from an eminence on the fields of Grasmere Vale, the heart is satisfied with a simple undisturbed pleasure, and no less, on one of the green or heathy dells of Scotland, where there is no appearance of change to be, or having been, but such as the seasons make. Strath Erne is so extensive a vale that, had it been in England, there must have been much inequality, as in Wensly Dale; but at Wensly there is a unity, a softness, a melting together, which in the large vales of Scotland I never perceived. The difference at Strath Erne may come partly from the irregularity, the undefined outline, of the hills which enclose it; but it is caused still more by the broken surface, I mean broken as to colour and produce, the want of hedgerows, and also the great number of new fir plantations. After some miles it becomes much narrower as we approach nearer the mountains at the foot of the lake of the same name, Loch Erne.

Breakfasted at a small public-house, a wretchedly dirty cottage, but the people were civil, and though we had nothing but barley cakes, we made a good breakfast, for there were plenty of eggs. Walked up a high hill to view the seat of Mr. Dundas, now Lord Melville—a spot where, if he have gathered much wisdom from his late disgrace or his long intercourse with the world, he may spend his days as quietly as he need desire. It is a secluded valley, not rich, but with plenty of wood : there are many pretty paths through the woods, and moss huts in different parts. After leaving the cottage where we breakfasted the country was very pleasing, yet still with a want of richness; but this was less perceived, being huddled up in charcoal woods, and the vale narrow. Loch Erne opens out in a very pleasing manner, seen from a hill along which the road is carried through a wood of low trees; but it does not improve afterwards, lying directly from east to west without any perceivable bendings; and the shores are not much broken or varied, not populous, and the mountains not sufficiently commanding to make up for the deficiencies. Dined at the head of the lake, I scarcely know its length, but should think not less than four or five miles, and it is wide in proportion. The inn is in a small village—a decent house.

Walked about half a mile along the road to Tyndrum, which is through a bare glen, {*Glen Ogle*} and over a mountain pass. It rained when we pursued our journey again, and continued to rain for several hours. The road which we were to take was up another glen, down which came a stream that fell into the lake on the opposite side at the head of it, so, after having crossed the main vale, a little above the lake, we entered into the smaller glen. The road delightfully smooth and dry—one gentleman's house very pleasant among large coppice woods. After going perhaps three miles up this valley, we turned to the left into another, which seemed to be much more beautiful. It was a level valley, not—like that which we had passed—a wide sloping cleft between the hills, but having a quiet, slow-paced stream, which flowed through level green grounds tufted with trees intermingled with cottages. The tops of the hills were hidden by mists, and the objects in the valley seen through misty rain, which made them look exceedingly soft, and indeed partly concealed them, and we always fill up what we are left to guess at with something as beautiful as what we see. This valley seemed to have less of the appearance of barrenness or imperfect cultivation than any of the same character we had passed through; indeed, we could not discern any traces of it. It is called Strath Eyer. 'Strath' is generally applied to a broad vale; but this, though open, is not broad.

We next came to a lake, called Loch Lubnaig, a name which signifies 'winding.' In shape it somewhat resembles Ulswater, but is much narrower and shorter, being only four miles in length. The character of this lake is simple and grand. On the side opposite to where we were is a range of steep craggy mountains, one of which—like Place Fell—encroaching upon the bed of the lake, forces it to make a considerable bending. I have forgotten the name of this precipice: it is a very remarkable one, being almost perpendicular, and very rugged. We, on the other side, travelled under steep and rocky hills which were often covered with low woods to a considerable height; there were one or two farm-houses, and a few cottages. A neat white dwelling *{Ardhullary},* on the side of the hill over against the bold steep of which I have spoken, had been the residence of the famous traveller Bruce, who, all his travels ended, had arranged the history of them in that solitude—as deep as any Abyssinian one—among the mountains of his native country, where he passed several years. Whether he died there or not we did not learn; but the manner of his death was remarkable and affecting, —from a fall down-stairs in his own house, after so many dangers through which fortitude and courage had never failed to sustain him. The house stands sweetly, surrounded by coppice-woods and green fields. On the other side, I believe, were no houses till we came near to the outlet, where a few low huts looked very beautiful, with their dark brown roofs, near a stream which hurried down the mountain, and after its turbulent course travelled a short way over a level green, and was lost in the lake.

Within a few miles of Callander we come into a grand region; the mountains to a considerable height were covered with wood, enclosing us in a narrow passage; the stream on our right, generally concealed by wood, made a loud roaring; at one place, in particular, it fell down the rocks in a succession of cascades. The scene is much celebrated in Scotland, and is called the Pass of Leny. It was nearly dark when we reached Callander. We were wet and cold, and glad of a good fire. The inn was comfortable; we drank tea; and after tea the waiter presented us with a pamphlet descriptive of the neighbourhood of Callander, which we brought away with us, and I am very sorry I lost it.

To Tyndrum

Tyndrum

To Dalmally

Tummel

Pass at Killiecrankie

Blair Castle

Dunkeld

FIFTH WEEK

Sunday, September 11th—Immediately after breakfast, the morning being fine, we set off with cheerful spirits towards the Trossachs, intending to take up our lodging at the house of our old friend the ferryman. A boy accompanied us to convey the horse and car back to Callander from the head of Loch Achray. The country near Callander is very pleasing; but, as almost everywhere else, imperfectly cultivated. We went up a broad vale, through which runs the stream from Loch Ketterine, and came to Loch Vennachar, a larger lake than Loch Achray, the small one which had given us such unexpected delight when we left the Pass of the Trossachs. Loch Vennachar is much larger, but greatly inferior in beauty to the image which we had conceived of its neighbour, and so the reality proved to us when we came up to that little lake, and saw it before us in its true shape in the cheerful sunshine. The Trossachs, overtopped by Ben Ledi and other high mountains, enclose the lake at the head; and those houses which we had seen before, with their corn fields sloping towards the water, stood very prettily under low woods. The fields did not appear so rich as when we had seen them through the veil of mist; but yet, as in framing our expectations we had allowed for a much greater difference, so we were even a second time surprised with pleasure at the same spot.

Went as far as these houses of which I have spoken in the car, and then walked on, intending to pursue the road up the side of Loch Ketterine along which Coleridge had come; but we had resolved to spend some hours in the neighbourhood of the Trossachs, and accordingly coasted the head of Loch Achray, and pursued the brook between the two lakes as far as there was any track. Here we found, to our surprise—for we had expected nothing but heath and rocks, like the rest of the neighbourhood of the Trossachs—a secluded farm, a plot of verdant ground with a single cottage and its company of out-houses. We turned back, and went to the very point from which we had first looked upon Loch Achray when we were here with Coleridge. It was no longer a visionary scene: the sun shone into every crevice of the hills, and the mountain-tops were clear. After some time we went into the pass from the Trossachs, and were delighted to behold the forms of objects fully revealed, and even surpassing in loveliness and variety what we had conceived. The mountains, I think, appeared not so high; but on the whole we had not the smallest disappointment; the heather was fading, though still beautiful.

Sate for half-an-hour in Lady Perth's shed, and scrambled over the rocks and through the thickets at the head of the lake. I went till I could make my way no further, and left William to go to the top of the hill, whence he had a distinct view, as on a map, of the intricacies of the lake and the course of the river. Returned to the huts, and, after having taken a second dinner of the food we had brought from Callander, set our faces towards the head of Loch Ketterine. I can add nothing to my former description of the Trossachs, except that we departed with our old delightful remembrances endeared, and many new ones. The path or road—for it was neither the one nor the other, but something between both—is the pleasantest I have ever travelled in my life for the same length of way,— now with marks of sledges or wheels, or none at all, bare or green, as it might happen; now a little descent, now a level; sometimes a shady lane, at others an open track through green pastures; then again it would lead us into thick coppice-woods, which often entirely shut out the lake, and again admitted it by glimpses. We have never had a more delightful walk than this evening. Ben Lomond and the three pointed-topped mountains of Loch Lomond, which we had seen from the Garrison, were very majestic under the clear sky, the lake perfectly calm, the air sweet and mild. I felt that it was much more interesting to visit a place where we have been before than it can possibly be the first time, except under peculiar circumstances. The sun had been set for some time, when, being within a quarter of a mile of the ferryman's hut, our path having led us close to the shore of the calm lake, we met two neatly dressed women, without hats, who had probably been taking their Sunday evening's walk. One of them said to us in a friendly, soft tone of voice, 'What! you are stepping westward!' I cannot describe how affecting this simple expression was in that remote place, with the western sky in front, yet glowing with the departed sun. William

wrote the following poem long after, in remembrance of his feelings
and mine:—

> *'What! you are stepping westward!' Yea,*
> *'Twould be a wildish destiny*
> *If we, who thus together roam*
> *In a strange land, and far from home,*
> *Were in this place the guests of chance:*
> *Yet who would stop, or fear to advance,*
> *Though home or shelter he had none,*
> *With such a sky to lead him on?*
>
> *The dewy ground was dark and cold,*
> *Behind all gloomy to behold,*
> *And stepping westward seem'd to be*
> *A kind of heavenly destiny;*
> *I liked the greeting, 'twas a sound*
> *Of something without place or bound;*
> *And seem'd to give me spiritual right*
> *To travel through that region bright.*
>
> *The voice was soft; and she who spake*
> *Was walking by her native Lake;*
> *The salutation was to me*
> *The very sound of courtesy;*
> *Its power was felt, and while my eye*
> *Was fix'd upon the glowing sky,*
> *The echo of the voice enwrought*
> *A human sweetness with the thought*
> *Of travelling through the world that lay*
> *Before me in my endless way*

We went up to the door of our boatman's hut as to a home, and
scarcely less confident of a cordial welcome than if we had been
approaching our own cottage at Grasmere. It had been a very pleasing
thought, while we were walking by the side of the beautiful lake that,
few hours as we had been there, there was a home for us in one of its
quiet dwellings. Accordingly, so we found it; the good woman, who
had been at a preaching by the lake-side, was in her holiday dress at
the door, and seemed to be rejoiced at the sight of us. She led us into
the hut in haste to supply our wants; we took once more a refreshing

meal by her fireside, and, though not so merry as the last time, we were not less happy, bating our regrets that Coleridge was not in his old place. I slept in the same bed as before, and listened to the household stream, which now only made a very low murmuring.

Monday, September 12th—Rejoiced in the morning to see the sun shining upon the hills when I first looked out through the open window-place at my bed's head. We rose early, and after breakfast, our old companion, who was to be our guide for the day, rowed us over the water to the same point where Coleridge and I had sate down and eaten our dinner, while William had gone to survey the unknown coast. We intended to cross Loch Lomond, follow the lake to Glenfalloch, above the head of it, and then come over the mountains to Glengyle, and so down the glen, and passing Mr. Macfarlane's house, back again to the ferry-house, where we should sleep. So, a third time we went through the mountain hollow, now familiar ground. The inhabitants had not yet got in all their hay, and were at work in the fields; our guide often stopped to talk with them, and no doubt was called upon to answer many inquiries respecting us two strangers.

At the ferry-house of Inversneyde we had not the happy sight of the Highland girl and her companion, but the good woman received us cordially, gave me milk, and talked of Coleridge, who, the morning after we parted from him, had been at her house to fetch his watch, which he had forgotten two days before. He has since told me that he questioned her respecting the miserable condition of her hut, which, as you may remember, admitted the rain at the door, and retained it in the hollows of the mud floor: he told her how easy it would be to remove these inconveniences, and to contrive something, at least, to prevent the wind from entering at the window-places, if not a glass window for light and warmth by day. She replied that this was very true, but if they made any improvements the laird would conclude that they were growing rich, and would raise their rent.

The ferryman happened to be just ready at the moment to go over the lake with a poor man, his wife and child. The little girl, about three years old, cried all the way, terrified by the water. When we parted from this family, they going down the lake, and we up it, I could not but think of the difference in our condition to that poor woman, who, with her husband, had been driven from her home by want of work, and was now going a long journey to seek it elsewhere: every step was painful toil, for she had either her child to bear or a heavy burthen. I walked as she did, but pleasure was my object, and if toil came along with it, even that was pleasure,—pleasure, at least, it would be in the remembrance.

We were, I believe, nine miles from Glenfalloch when we left the boat. To us, with minds at ease, the walk was delightful; it could not be otherwise, for we passed by a continual succession of rocks, woods, and mountains; but the houses were few, and the ground cultivated only in small portions near the water, consequently there was not that sort of variety which leaves distinct separate remembrances, but one impression of solitude and greatness. While the Highlander and I were plodding on together side by side, interspersing long silences with now and then a question or a remark, looking down to the lake he espied two small rocky islands, and pointing to them, said to me, 'It will be gay and dangerous sailing there in stormy weather when the water is high.' *{This is none other than the well-known Scottish word 'gay', indifferently, tolerable, considerable.—Ed}.* In giving my assent I could not help smiling, but I afterwards found that a like combination of words is not uncommon in Scotland, for, at Edinburgh, William being afraid of rain, asked the ostler what he thought, who, looking up to the sky, pronounced it to 'be gay and dull,' and therefore rain might be expected. The most remarkable object we saw was a huge single stone, I believe three or four times the size of Bowder Stone. The top of it, which on one side was sloping like the roof of a house, was covered with heather. William climbed up the rock, which would have been no easy task but to a mountaineer, and we constructed a rope of pocket-handkerchiefs, garters, plaids, coats, etc., and measured its height. It was so many times the length of William's walking-stick, but, unfortunately, having lost the stick, we have lost the measure. The ferryman told us that a preaching was held there once in three months by a certain minister— I think of Arrochar—who engages, as a part of his office, to perform the service. The interesting feelings we had connected with the Highland Sabbath and Highland worship returned here with double force. The rock, though on one side a high perpendicular wall, in no place overhung so as to form a shelter, in no place could it be more than a screen from the elements. Why then had it been selected for such a purpose? Was it merely from being a central situation and a conspicuous object? Or did there belong to it some inheritance of superstition from old times? It is impossible to look at the stone without asking, How came it hither? Had then that obscurity and unaccountableness, that mystery of power which is about it, any influence over the first persons who resorted hither for worship, or have they now on those who continue to frequent it ? The lake is in front of the perpendicular wall, and behind, at some distance, and totally detached from it, is the continuation of the ridge of mountain which forms the vale of Loch Lomond—a magnificent temple, of which this spot is a noble Sanctum Sanctorum.

We arrived at Glenfalloch at about one or two o'clock. It is no village; there being only scattered huts in the glen, which may be four miles long, according to my remembrance: the middle of it is very green, and level, and tufted with trees. Higher up, where the glen parts into two very narrow ones, is the house of the laird; I daresay a pretty place. The view from the door of the public-house is exceedingly beautiful; the river flows smoothly into the lake, and the fields were at that time as green as possible. Looking backward, Ben Lomond very majestically shuts in the view. The top of the mountain, as seen here, being of a pyramidal form, it is much grander than with the broken outline, and stage above stage, as seen from the neighbourhood of Luss. We found nobody at home at the inn, but the ferryman shouted, wishing to have a glass of whisky, and a young woman came from the hay-field, dressed in a white bed gown, without hat or cap. There was no whisky in the house, so he begged a little whey to drink with the fragments of our cold meat brought from Callander. After a short rest in a cool parlour we set forward again, having to cross the river and climb up a steep mountain on the opposite side of the valley. I observed that the people were busy bringing in the hay before it was dry into a sort of 'fauld' or yard, where they intended to leave it, ready to be gathered into the house with the first threatening of rain, and if not completely dry brought out again. Our guide bore me in his arms over the stream, and we soon came to the foot of the mountain. The most easy rising, for a short way at first, was near a naked rivulet which made a fine cascade in one place. Afterwards, the ascent was very laborious, being frequently almost perpendicular.

It is one of those moments which I shall not easily forget, when at that point from which a step or two would have carried us out of sight of the green fields of Glenfalloch, being at a great height on the mountain, we sate down, and heard, as if from the heart of the earth, the sound of torrents ascending out of the long hollow glen. To the eye all was motionless, a perfect stillness. The noise of waters did not appear to come this way or that, from any particular quarter: it was everywhere, almost, one might say, as if 'exhaled' through the whole surface of the green earth. Glenfalloch, Coleridge has since told me, signifies the Hidden Vale; but William says if we were to name it from our recollections of that time, we should call it the Vale of Awful Sound. We continued to climb higher and higher; but the hill was no longer steep, and afterwards we pursued our way along the top of it with many small ups and downs. The walk was very laborious after the climbing was over, being often exceedingly stony, or through swampy moss, rushes, or rough heather. As we proceeded, continuing our way at the top of the mountain, encircled by higher mountains at a great distance, we were passing, without notice, a heap of scattered stones round which was a belt of green grass—green, and as it seemed rich, where all else was either poor heather and coarse grass, or unprofitable rushes and spongy moss. The Highlander made a pause, saying, 'This place is much changed since I was here twenty years ago.' He told us that the heap of stones had been a hut where a family was then living, who had their winter habitation in the valley, and brought their goats thither in the summer to feed on the mountains, and that they were used to gather them together at night and morning to be milked close to the door, which was the reason why the grass was yet so green near the stones. It was affecting in that solitude to meet with this memorial of manners passed away; we looked about for some other traces of humanity, but nothing else could we find in that place. We ourselves afterwards espied another of those ruins, much more extensive—the remains, as the man told us, of several dwellings. We were astonished at the sagacity with which our Highlander discovered the track, where often no track was visible to us, and scarcely even when he pointed it out. It reminded us of what we read of the Hottentots and other savages. He went on as confidently as if it had been a turnpike road—the more surprising, as when he was there before it must have been a plain track, for he told us that fishermen from Arrochar carried herrings regularly over the mountains by that way to Loch Ketterine when the glens were much more populous than now.

Descended into Glengyle, above Loch Ketterine, and passed through Mr. Macfarlane's grounds, that is, through the whole of the glen, where there was now no house left but his. We stopped at his door to inquire after the family, though with little hope of finding them at home, having seen a large company at work in a hay-field, whom we conjectured to be his whole household—as it proved, except a servant-maid, who answered our inquiries. We had sent the ferryman forward from the head of the glen to bring the boat round from the place where he left it to the other side of the lake. Passed the same farm-house we had such good reason to remember, and went up to the burying-ground that stood so sweetly near the water-side. The ferryman had told us that Rob Roy's grave was there, (15) so we could not pass on without going up to the spot. There were several tomb-stones, but the inscriptions were either worn-out or unintelligible to us, and the place choked up with nettles and brambles. You will remember the description I have given of the spot. I have nothing here to add, except the following poem which it suggested to William:—

A famous Man is Robin Hood,
The English Ballad-singer's joy,
And Scotland boasts of one as good,
    She has her own Rob Roy!

Then clear the weeds from off his grave,
And let us chaunt a passing stave
In honour of that Outlaw brave.

Heaven gave Rob Roy a daring heart
And wondrous length and strength of arm,
Nor craved he more to quell his foes,
    Or keep his friends from harm.

Yet Robin was as wise as brave,
As wise in thought as bold in deed,
For in the principles of things
    He sought his moral creed.

Said generous Rob, 'What need of books'
Burn all the statutes and their shelves:
They stir us up against our kind,
    And worse, against ourselves.'

We have a passion; make a law,
Too false to guide us or control:
And for the law itself we fight

In bitterness of soul.'

And puzzled, blinded thus, we lose
Distinctions that are plain and few:
These find I graven on my heart:
    That tells me what to do.'

The Creatures see of flood and field,
And those that travel on the wind!
With them no strife can last; they live
 In peace, and peace of mind.'

For why? Because the good old rule
Suffices them, the simple plan
That they should take who have the power,
    And they should keep who can.

A lesson which is quickly learn'd,
A signal this which all can see!
Thus nothing here provokes the strong
    To tyrannous cruelty,

And freakishness of mind is check'd;
He tamed who foolishly aspires,
While to the measure of their might
    All fashion their desires.

All kinds and creatures stand and fall
By strength of prowess or of wit,
'Tis God's appointment who must sway,
    And who is to submit.

'Since then,' said Robin, 'right is plain,
And longest life is but a day;

To have my ends, maintain my rights,
    I'll take the shortest way.'

And thus among these rocks he lived
Through summer's heat and winter's snow;
The Eagle, he was lord above,
    And Rob was lord below.

So was it—would at least have been
But through untowardness of fate;
For polity was then too strong:
    He came an age too late.

Or shall we say an age too soon?
For were the bold man living now,
How might he flourish in his pride
    With buds on every bough?

Then Rents and Land-marks, Rights of chase,
Sheriffs and Factors, Lairds and Thanes,
Would all have seem'd but paltry things
    Not worth a moment's pains.

Rob Roy had never linger'd here,
To these few meagre vales confined,
But thought how wide the world, the times
    How fairly to his mind.

And to his Sword he would have said,
'Do thou my sovereign will enact
From land to land through half the earth;
    Judge thou of law and fact.'

'Tis fit that we should do our part;

Becoming that mankind should learn
That we are not to be surpass'd
    In fatherly concern'

Of old things all are over old,
Of good things none are good enough;
I'll shew that I can help to frame
    A world of other stuff.'

I, too, will have my Kings that take
From me the sign of life and death,
Kingdoms shall shift about like clouds
    Obedient to my breath'

And if the word had been fulfill'd
As might have been, then, thought of joy!
France would have had her present boast,
    And we our brave Rob Roy.

Oh! say not so, compare them not;
I would not wrong thee, Champion brave!
Would wrong thee nowhere; least of all
    Here, standing by thy Grave.

For thou, although with some wild thoughts,
Wild Chieftain of a savage Clan,
Hadst this to boast of—thou didst love
    The Liberty of Man.

And had it been thy lot to live
With us who now behold the light,
Thou wouldst have nobly stirr'd thyself,
    And battled for the right.

For Robin was the poor man's stay;
The poor man's heart, the poor man's hand,
And all the oppress'd who wanted strength
    Had Robin's to command.

Bear witness many a pensive sigh
Of thoughtful Herdsman when he strays
Alone upon Loch Veol's heights,
    And by Loch Lomond's Braes.

And far and near, through vale and hill,
Are faces that attest the same;
Kindling with instantaneous joy
    At sound of Rob Roy's name.

Soon after we saw our boat coming over the calm water. It was late in the evening, and I was stiff and weary, as well I might, after such a long and toilsome walk, so it was no poor gratification to sit down and be conscious of advancing in our journey without further labour. The stars were beginning to appear, but the brightness of the west was not yet gone;—the lake perfectly still, and when we first went into the boat we rowed almost close to the shore under steep crags hung with birches: it was like a new-discovered country of which we had not dreamed, for in walking down the lake, owing to the road in that part being carried at a considerable height on the hill-side, the rocks and the indentings of the shore had been hidden from us. At this time, those rocks and their images in the calm water composed one mass, the surfaces of both equally distinct, except where the water trembled with the motion of our boat. Having rowed a while under the bold steeps, we launched out further when the shores were no longer abrupt. We hardly spoke to each other as we moved along receding from the west, which diffused a solemn animation over the lake. The sky was cloudless; and everything seemed at rest except our solitary boat, and the mountain-streams,—seldom heard, and but faintly. I think I have rarely experienced a more elevated pleasure than during our short voyage of this night. The good woman had long been looking out for us, and had prepared everything for our refreshment; and as soon as we had finished supper, or rather tea, we went to bed. William, I doubt not, rested well, and, for my part, I slept as soundly on my chaff bed as ever I have done in childhood after the long day's playing of a summer's holiday.

Tuesday, 13th September—Again a fine morning. I strolled into the green field in which the house stands while the woman was preparing breakfast, and at my return found one of her neighbours sitting by the fire, a feeble paralytic old woman. After having inquired concerning our journey the day before, she said, 'I have travelled far in my time,' and told me she had married an English soldier who had been stationed at the Garrison; they had had many children, who were all dead or in foreign countries; and she had returned to her native place, where now she had lived several years, and was more comfortable than she could ever have expected to be, being very kindly dealt with by all her neighbours. Pointing to the ferryman and his wife, she said they were accustomed to give her a day of their labour in digging peats, in common with others, and in that manner she was provided with fuel, and, by like voluntary contributions, with other necessaries. While this infirm old woman was relating her story in a tremulous voice, I could not but think of the changes of things, and the days of her youth, when the shrill fife, sounding from the walls of the Garrison, made a merry noise through the echoing hills. I asked myself, if she were to be carried again to the deserted spot after her course of life, no doubt a troublesome one, would the silence appear to her the silence of desolation or of peace? After breakfast we took a final leave of our hostess, and, attended by her husband, again set forward on foot. My limbs were a little stiff, but the morning being uncommonly fine I did not fear to aim at the accomplishment of a plan we had laid of returning to Callander by a considerable circuit We were to go over the mountains from Loch Ketterine, a little below the ferry-house on the same side of the water, descending to Loch Voil, a lake from which issues the stream that flows through Strath Eyer into Loch Lubnaig. Our road, as is generally the case in passing from one vale into another, was through a settling between the hills, not far from a small stream. We had to climb considerably, the mountain being much higher than it appears to be, owing to its retreating in what looks like a gradual slope from the lake, though we found it steep enough in the climbing. Our guide had been born near Loch Voil, and he told us that at the head of the lake, if we would look about for it, we should see the burying-place of a part of his family, the MacGregors, a clan who had long possessed that district, a circumstance which he related with no unworthy pride of ancestry. We shook hands with him at parting, not without a hope of again entering his hut in company with others whom we loved.

Continued to walk for some time along the top of the hill, having the high mountains of Loch Voil before us, and Ben Lomond and the steeps of Loch Ketterine behind. Came to several deserted mountain huts or shiels, and rested for some time beside one of them, upon a hillock of its green plot of monumental herbage. William here conceived the notion of writing an ode upon the affecting subject of those relics of human society found in that grand and solitary region. The spot of ground where we sate was even beautiful, the grass being uncommonly verdant, and of a remarkably soft and silky texture.

After this we rested no more till we came to the foot of the mountain, where there was a cottage, at the door of which a woman invited me to drink some whey: this I did, while William went to inquire respecting the road at a new stone house a few steps further. He was told to cross the brook, and proceed to the other side of the vale, and that no further directions were necessary, for we should find ourselves at the head of the lake, and on a plain road which would lead us downward. We waded the river and crossed the vale, perhaps half a mile or more. The mountains all round are very high; the vale pastoral and unenclosed, not many dwellings, and but few trees; the mountains in general smooth near the bottom. They are in large, unbroken masses, combining with the vale to give an impression of bold simplicity.

Near the head of the lake, at some distance from us, we discovered the burial-place of the MacGregors, and did not view it without some interest, with its ornamental balls on the four corners of the wall, which, I daresay, have been often looked at with elevation of heart by our honest friend of Loch Ketterine. The lake is divided right across by a narrow slip of flat land, making a small lake at the head of the large one. The whole may be about five miles long.

As we descended, the scene became more fertile, our way being pleasantly varied—through coppices or open fields, and passing farmhouses, though always with an intermixture of uncultivated ground. It was harvest-time, and the fields were quietly—might I be allowed to say pensively?—enlivened by small companies of reapers. It is not uncommon in the more lonely parts of the Highlands to see a single person so employed. The following poem was suggested to William by a beautiful sentence in Thomas Wilkinson's 'Tour in Scotland:'(16)

Behold her single in the field,
Yon solitary Highland Lass,
Reaping and singing by herself—
Stop here, or gently pass.
Alone she cuts and binds the grain,
And sings a melancholy strain.
Oh! listen, for the Vale profound
Is overflowing with the sound.

No nightingale did ever chaunt
So sweetly to reposing bands
Of travellers in some shady haunt
Among Arabian Sands;
No sweeter voice was ever heard
In spring-time from the cuckoo-bird
Breaking the silence of the seas
Among the farthest Hebrides.

Will no one tell me what she sings?
Perhaps the plaintive numbers flow
For old unhappy far-off things,
And battles long ago;—
Or is it some more humble lay—
Familiar matter of to-day—
Some natural sorrow, loss, or pain
That has been, and may be again?

Whate'er the theme, the Maiden sung
As if her song could have no ending;
I saw her singing at her work,
And o'er the sickle bending;
I listen'd till I had my fill,
And as I mounted up the hill
The music in my heart I bore
Long after it was heard no more

Towards the foot of the lake, on the opposite side which was more barren than that on which we travelled, was a bare road up a steep hill, which leads to Glen Finlas, formerly a royal forest. It is a wild and rocky glen, as we had been told by a person who directed our notice to its outlet at Loch Achray. The stream which passes through it falls into that lake near the head. At the end of Loch Voil the vale is wide and populous—large pastures with many cattle, large tracts of corn. We walked downwards a little way, and then crossed over to the same road along which we had travelled from Loch Erne to Callander, being once again at the entrance of Strath Eyer. It might be about four or five o'clock in the afternoon; we were ten miles from Callander, exceedingly tired, and wished heartily for the poor horse and car. Walked up Strath Eyer, and saw in clear air and sunshine what had been concealed from us when we travelled before in the mist and rain. We found it less woody and rich than it had appeared to be, but, with all deductions, a very sweet valley.

Not far from Loch Lubnaig, though not in view of it, is a long village, with two or three public-houses, and being in despair of reaching Callander that night without overfatigue we resolved to stop at the most respectable-looking house, and, should it not prove wretched indeed, to lodge there, if there were beds for us: at any rate, it was necessary to take some refreshment. The woman of the house spoke with gentleness and civility, and had a good countenance, which reconciled me to stay, though I had been averse to the scheme, dreading the dirt usual in Scotch public-houses by the way-side. She said she had beds for us, and clean sheets, and we desired her to prepare them immediately. It was a two-storied house, light built, though in other respects no better than the huts, and—as all the slated cottages are—much more uncomfortable in appearance, except that there was a chimney in the kitchen. At such places it is fit that travellers should make up their minds to wait at least an hour longer than the time necessary to prepare whatever meal they may have ordered, which we, I may truly say, did with most temperate philosophy. I went to talk with the mistress, who was making barley cakes, which she wrought out with her hands as thin as the oaten bread we make in Cumberland. I asked her why she did not use a rolling-pin, and if it would not be much more convenient, to which she returned me no distinct answer, and seemed to give little attention to the question: she did not know, or that was what they were used to, or something of the sort. It was a tedious process, and I thought could scarcely have been managed if the cakes had been as large as ours; but they are considerably smaller, which is a great loss of time in the baking.

This woman, whose common language was the Gaelic, talked with me a very good English, asking many questions, yet without the least appearance of an obtrusive or impertinent curiosity; and indeed I must say that I never, in those women with whom I conversed, observed anything on which I could put such a construction. They seemed to have a faith ready for all; and as a child, when you are telling him stories, asks for 'more, more,' so they appeared to delight in being amused without effort of their own minds. Among other questions she asked me the old one over again; if I was married; and when I told her that I was not, she appeared surprised, and, as if recollecting herself, said to me, with a pious seriousness and perfect simplicity, 'To be sure, there is a great promise for virgins in Heaven;' and then she began to tell how long she had been married, that she had had a large family and much sickness and sorrow, having lost several of her children. We had clean sheets and decent beds.

Wednesday, September 14th—Rose early, and departed before breakfast. The morning was dry, but cold. Travelled, as before, along the shores of Loch Lubnaig, and along the pass of the roaring stream of Leny, and reached Callander at a little past eight o'clock. After breakfast set off towards Stirling, intending to sleep there; the distance eighteen miles. We were now entering upon a populous and more cultivated country, having left the mountains behind, therefore I shall have little to tell; for what is most interesting in such a country is not to be seen in passing through it as we did. Half way between Callander and Stirling is the village of Doune, and a little further on we crossed a bridge over a pleasant river, the Teith. Above the river stands a ruined castle of considerable size, upon a woody bank. We wished to have had time to go up to the ruin. Long before we reached the town of Stirling, saw the castle, single, on its stately and commanding eminence. The rock or hill rises from a level plain; the print in Stoddart's book does indeed give a good notion of its form.

The surrounding plain appears to be of a rich soil, well cultivated. The crops of ripe corn were abundant. We found the town quite full; not a vacant room in the inn, it being the time of the assizes: there was no lodging for us, and hardly even the possibility of getting anything to eat in a bye-nook of the house. Walked up to the castle. The prospect from it is very extensive, and must be exceedingly grand on a fine evening or morning, with the light of the setting or rising sun on the distant mountains, but we saw it at an unfavourable time of day, the mid-afternoon, and were not favoured by light and shade. The Forth makes most intricate and curious turnings, so that it is difficult to trace them, even when you are overlooking the whole. It flows through a perfect level, and in one place cuts its way in the form of a large figure of eight. Stirling is the largest town we had seen in Scotland, except Glasgow. It is an old irregular place; the Streets towards the castle on one side very steep. On the other, the hill or rock rises from the fields. The architecture of a part of the castle is very fine, and the whole building in good repair: some parts indeed, are modern. At Stirling we bought Burns's Poems in one volume, for two shillings. Went on to Falkirk; ten or eleven miles. I do not recollect anything remarkable after we were out of sight of Stirling Castle, except the Carron iron-works, seen at a distance;—the sky above them was red with a fiery light. In passing through a turnpike gate we were greeted by a Highland drover, who, with many others, was coming from a fair at Falkirk, the road being covered all along with horsemen and cattle. He spoke as if we had been well known to him, asking us how we had fared on our journey. We were at a loss to conceive why he should interest himself about us, till he said he had passed us on the Black Mountain, near King's House. It was pleasant to observe the effect of solitary places in making men friends, and to see so much kindness, which had been produced in such a chance encounter, retained in a crowd. No beds in the inns at Falkirk—every room taken up by the people come to the fair. Lodged in a private house, a neat clean place —kind treatment from the old man and his daughter.

Thursday, September 15th—Breakfasted at Linlithgow, a small town. The house is yet shown from which the Regent Murray was shot. The remains of a royal palace, where Queen Mary was born, are of considerable extent; the banks of gardens and fish-ponds may yet be distinctly traced, though the whole surface is transformed into smooth pasturage where cattle graze. The castle stands upon a gentle eminence, the prospect not particularly pleasing, though not otherwise; it is bare and wide. The shell of a small, ancient church is standing, into which are crammed modern pews, galleries, and pulpit—very ugly, and discordant with the exterior. Nothing very interesting till we came to Edinburgh. Dined by the way at a small town or village upon a hill, the back part of the houses on one side overlooking an extensive prospect over flat corn fields. I mention this for the sake of a pleasant hour we passed sitting on the bank, where we read some of Burns's poems in the volume which we had bought at Stirling.

Arrived at Edinburgh a little before sunset. As we approached, the castle rock resembled that of Stirling—in the same manner appearing to rise from a plain of cultivated ground, the Firth of Forth being on the other side, and not visible. Drove to the White Hart in the Grass-market, an inn which had been mentioned to us, and which we conjectured would better suit us than one in a more fashionable part of the town. It was not noisy, and tolerably cheap. Drank tea, and walked up to the Castle, which luckily was very near. Much of the daylight was gone, so that except it had been a clear evening, which it was not, we could not have seen the distant prospect.

Friday, September 16th—The sky the evening before, as you may remember the ostler told us, had been 'gay and dull,' and this morning it was downright dismal: very dark, and promising nothing but a wet day, and before breakfast was over the rain began, though not heavily. We set out upon our walk, and went through many streets to Holyrood House, and thence to the hill called Arthur's Seat, a high hill, very rocky at the top, and below covered with smooth turf, on which sheep were feeding. We climbed up till we came to St. Anthony's Well and Chapel, as it is called, but it is more like a hermitage than a chapel, — a small ruin, which from its situation is exceedingly interesting, though in itself not remarkable. We sate down on a stone not far from the chapel, overlooking a pastoral hollow as wild and solitary as any in the heart of the Highland mountains: there, instead of the roaring of torrents, we listened to the noises of the city, which were blended in one loud indistinct buzz,—a regular sound in the air, which in certain moods of feeling, and at certain times, might have a more tranquillizing effect upon the mind than those which we are accustomed to hear in such places. The castle rock looked exceedingly large through the misty air: a cloud of black smoke overhung the city, which combined with the rain and mist to conceal the shapes of the houses,—an obscurity which added much to the grandeur of the sound that proceeded from it. It was impossible to think of anything that was little or mean, the goings-on of trade, the strife of men, or every-day city business:—the impression was one, and it was visionary; like the conceptions of our childhood of Bagdad or Balsora when we have been reading the Arabian Nights' Entertainments. Though the rain was very heavy we remained upon the hill for some time, then returned by the same road by which we had come, through green flat fields, formerly the pleasure-grounds of Holyrood House, on the edge of which stands the old roofless chapel, of venerable architecture. It is a pity that it should be suffered to fall down, for the walls appear to be yet entire. Very near to the chapel is Holyrood House, which we could not but lament has nothing ancient in its appearance, being sash-windowed and not an irregular pile. It is very like a building for some national establishment— a hospital for soldiers or sailors. You have a description of it in Stoddart's Tour, therefore I need not tell you what we saw there. When we found ourselves once again in the streets of the city, we lamented over the heavy rain, and indeed before leaving the hill, much as we were indebted to the accident of the rain for the peculiar grandeur and affecting wildness of those objects we saw, we could not but regret that the Firth of Forth was entirely hidden from us, and all distant objects, and we strained our eyes till they ached, vainly trying to pierce through the thick mist. We walked industriously through the streets, street after street, and, in spite of wet and dirt, were exceedingly delighted. The old town, with its irregular houses, stage above stage, seen as we saw it, in the obscurity of a rainy day, hardly resembles the work of men, it is more like a piling up of rocks, and I cannot attempt to describe what we saw so imperfectly, but must say that, high as my expectations had been raised, the city of Edinburgh far surpassed all expectation. Gladly would we have stayed another day, but could not afford more time, and our notions of the weather of Scotland were so dismal, notwithstanding we ourselves had been so much favoured, that we had no hope of its mending. So at about six o'clock in the evening we departed, intending to sleep at an inn in the village of Roslin, about five miles from Edinburgh. The rain continued till we were almost at Roslin; but then it was quite dark, so we did not see the castle that night.

Saturday, September 17ᵗʰ —The morning very fine. We rose early and walked through the glen of Roslin, past Hawthornden, and considerably further, to the house of Mr. Walter Scott at Lasswade. Roslin Castle stands upon a woody bank above a stream, the North Esk, too large, I think, to be called a brook, yet an inconsiderable river. We looked down upon the ruin from higher ground. Near it stands the chapel, a most elegant building, a ruin, though the walls and roof are entire. I never passed through a more delicious dell than the glen of Roslin, though the water of the stream is dingy and muddy. The banks are rocky on each side, and hung with pine wood. About a mile from the castle, on the contrary side of the water, upon the edge of a very steep bank, stands Hawthornden, the house of Drummond the poet, whither Ben Jonson came on foot from London to visit his friend. We did hear to whom the house at present belongs, and some other particulars, but I have a very indistinct recollection of what was told us, except that many old trees had been lately cut down. After Hawthornden the glen widens, ceases to be rocky, and spreads out into a rich vale, scattered over with gentlemen's seats.

Arrived at Lasswade before Mr. and Mrs. Scott had risen, and waited some time in a large sitting-room. Breakfasted with them, and stayed till two o'clock, and Mr. Scott accompanied us back almost to Roslin, having given us directions respecting our future journey, and promised to meet us at Melrose two days after. *{See Lockhart's Life of Scott for an account of this visit, vol. i. p. 402-7. Mr. L. says, 'I have drawn up the account of this meeting from my recollection, partly of Mr. W.'s conversation, partly from that of his sister's charming "Diary," which he was so kind as to read to me on the 16th May 1836.'—Ed.}*

We ordered dinner on our return to the inn, and went to view the inside of the chapel of Roslin, which is kept locked up, and so preserved from the injuries it might otherwise receive from idle boys;

but as nothing is done to keep it together, it must in the end fall. The architecture within is exquisitely beautiful. The stone, both of the roof and walls, is sculptured with leaves and flowers, so delicately wrought that I could have admired them for hours, and the whole of their groundwork is stained by time with the softest colours. Some of those leaves and flowers were tinged perfectly green, and at one part the effect was most exquisite: three or four leaves of a small fern, resembling that which we call adder's tongue, grew round a cluster of them at the top of a pillar, and the natural product and the artificial were so intermingled that at first it was not easy to distinguish the living plant from the other, they being of an equally determined green, though the fern was of a deeper shade.

We set forward again after dinner. The afternoon was pleasant. Travelled through large tracts of ripe corn, interspersed with larger tracts of moorland—the houses at a considerable distance from each other, no longer thatched huts, but farm-houses resembling those of the farming counties in England, having many corn-stacks close to them. Dark when we reached Peebles; found a comfortable old-fashioned public-house, had a neat parlour, and drank tea.

Loch Katrine

Road to Inversnaid

Hotel at old boatman's hut

View from Inversnaid across Loch Lomond

Proposed grave of Rob Roy

Stirling

Edinburgh Castle

Holyrood Palace

Roslin Inn

Vale of Roslin

Much altered Roslin Chapel

SIXTH WEEK

Sunday, September 18th—The town of Peebles is on the banks of the Tweed. After breakfast walked up the river to Neidpath Castle, about a mile and a half from the town. The castle stands upon a green hill, overlooking the Tweed, a strong square-towered edifice, neglected and desolate, though not in ruin, the garden overgrown with grass, and the high walls that fenced it broken down. The Tweed winds between green steeps, upon which, and close to the river side, large flocks of sheep pasturing; higher still are the grey mountains; but I need not describe the scene, for William has done it better than I could do in a sonnet which he wrote the same day; the five last lines, at least, of his poem will impart to you more of the feeling of the place than it would be possible for me to do:—

> Degenerate Douglass! thou unworthy Lord
> Whom mere despite of heart could so far please,
> And love of havoc (for with such disease
> Fame taxes him) that he could send forth word
> To level with the dust a noble horde,
> A brotherhood of venerable trees,
> Leaving an ancient Dome and Towers like these
> Beggar'd and outraged!
> Many hearts deplored
> The fate of those old trees; and oft with pain
> The Traveller at this day will stop and gaze
> On wrongs which Nature scarcely seems to heed;
> For shelter'd places, bosoms, nooks, and bays,
> And the pure mountains, and the gentle Tweed,
> And the green silent pastures yet remain.

Was spared any regret for the fallen woods when we were there, not then knowing the history of them. The soft, low mountains, the castle, and the decayed pleasure-grounds, the scattered trees which have been left in different parts, and the road carried in a very beautiful line along the side of the hill, with the Tweed murmuring through the unfenced green pastures spotted with sheep, together composed an harmonious scene, and I wished for nothing that was not there. When we were with Mr. Scott he spoke of cheerful days he had spent in that castle not many years ago, when it was inhabited by Professor

Ferguson and his family, whom the Duke of Queensberry, its churlish owner, forced to quit it. We discovered a very fine echo within a few yards of the building.

The town of Peebles looks very pretty from the road in returning: it is an old town, built of grey stone, the same as the castle. Well-dressed people were going to church. Sent the car before, and walked ourselves, and while going along the main street William was called aside in a mysterious manner by a person who gravely examined him— whether he was an Irishman or a foreigner, or what he was; I suppose our car was the occasion of suspicion at a time when everyone was talking of the threatened invasion. We had a day's journey before us along the banks of the Tweed, a name which has been sweet to my ears almost as far back as I can remember anything. After the first mile or two our road was seldom far from the river, which flowed in gentleness, though perhaps never silent; the hills on either side high and sometimes stony, but excellent pasturage for sheep. In some parts the vale was wholly of this pastoral character, in others we saw extensive tracts of corn ground, even spreading along whole hill-sides, and without visible fences, which is dreary in a flat country; but there is no dreariness on the banks of the Tweed,—the hills, whether smooth or stony, uncultivated or covered with ripe corn, had the same pensive softness. Near the corn tracts were large farm-houses, with many corn-stacks; the stacks and house and out-houses together, I recollect, in one or two places upon the hills, at a little distance, seemed almost as large as a small village or hamlet. It was a clear autumnal day, without wind, and, being Sunday, the business of the harvest was suspended, and all that we saw, and felt, and heard, combined to excite one sensation of pensive and still pleasure.

Passed by several old halls yet inhabited, and others in ruin; but I have hardly a sufficiently distinct recollection of any of them to be able to describe them, and I now at this distance of time regret that I did not take notes. In one very sweet part of the vale a gate crossed the road, which was opened by an old woman who lived in a cottage close to it; I said to her, 'You live in a very pretty place?' 'Yes,' she replied, 'the water of Tweed is a bonny water.' The lines of the hills are flowing and beautiful, the reaches of the vale long; in some places appear the remains of a forest, in others you will see as lovely a combination of forms as any traveller who goes in search of the picturesque need desire, and yet perhaps without a single tree; or at least if trees there are, they shall be very few, and he shall not care whether they are there or not.

The road took us through one long village, but I do not recollect any other; yet I think we never had a mile's length before us without a house, though seldom several cottages together. The loneliness of the scattered dwellings, the more stately edifices decaying or in ruin, or, if inhabited, not in their pride and freshness, aided the general effect of the gently varying scenes, which was that of tender pensiveness; no bursting torrents when we were there, but the murmuring of the river was heard distinctly, often blended with the bleating of sheep. In one place we saw a shepherd lying in the midst of a flock upon a sunny knoll, with his face towards the sky; happy picture of shepherd life.

The transitions of this vale were all gentle except one, a scene of which a gentleman's house was the centre, standing low in the vale, the hills above it covered with gloomy fir plantations, and the appearance of the house itself, though it could scarcely be seen, was gloomy. There was an allegorical air—a person fond of Spenser will understand me—in this uncheerful spot, single in such a country,
'The house was hearsed about with a black wood.'
We have since heard that it is the residence of Lord Traquair, a Roman Catholic nobleman, of a decayed family.

We left the Tweed when we were within about a mile and a half or two miles of Clovenford, where we were to lodge. Turned up the side of a hill, and went along sheep-grounds till we reached the spot—a single stone house, without a tree near it or to be seen from it. On our mentioning Mr. Scott's name the woman of the house showed us all possible civility, but her slowness was really amusing. I should suppose it is a house little frequented, for there is no appearance of an inn. Mr. Scott, who she told me was a very clever gentleman, 'goes there in the fishing season;' but indeed Mr. Scott is respected everywhere: I believe that by favour of his name one might be hospitably entertained throughout all the borders of Scotland. We dined and drank tea—did not walk out, for there was no temptation; a confined barren prospect from the window. At Clovenford, being so near to the Yarrow, we could not but think of the possibility of going thither, but came to the conclusion of reserving the pleasure for some future time, in consequence of which, after our return, William wrote the poem which I shall here transcribe:

From Stirling Castle we had seen
The lazy Forth unravell'd,
Had trod the banks of Clyde and Tay,
And with the Tweed had travell'd.
And when we came to Clovenford,
Then said my winsome Marrow,
Whate'er betide we'll turn aside
And see the Braes of Yarrow.'

'Let Yarrow Folk frae Selkirk Town,
Who have been buying, selling,
Go back to Yarrow:—'tis their own,
Each Maiden to her dwelling.
On Yarrow's banks let herons feed,
Hares couch, and rabbits burrow,
But we will downwards with the Tweed,
Nor turn aside to Yarrow.

' There's Gala Water, Leader Haughs,
Both lying right before us;
And Dryburgh, where with chiming Tweed
The lintwhites sing in chorus.
There's pleasant Teviot Dale, a land
Made blithe with plough and harrow,
Why throw away a needful day,
To go in search of Yarrow?

'What's Yarrow but a river bare,
That glides the dark hills under
There are a thousand such elsewhere,
As worthy of your wonder.'
Strange words they seem'd of slight and scorn,

My true-love sigh'd for sorrow,
And look'd me in the face to think
I thus could speak of Yarrow.

'Oh! green,' said I, 'are Yarrow's Holms,
And sweet is Yarrow flowing,
Fair hangs the apple frae the rock,
But we will leave it growing.
O'er hilly path and open Strath
We'll wander Scotland thorough,
But though so near we will not turn
Into the Dale of Yarrow.

' Let beeves and home-bred kine partake
The sweets of Burnmill Meadow,
The swan on still St. Mary's Lake
Float double, swan and shadow.
We will not see them, will not go,
To-day nor yet to-morrow;
Enough if in our hearts we know
There's such a place as Yarrow.
Be Yarrow stream unseen, unknown,
It must, or we shall rue it,
We have a vision of our own,
Ah! why should we undo it?
The treasured dreams of times long past,
We'll keep them, "winsome Marrow,"
For when we're there, although 'tis fair,
'Twill be another Yarrow.'

If care with freezing years should come,
And wandering seem but folly,
Should we be loth to stir from home,

And yet be melancholy,	*That earth has something yet to*
Should life be dull and spirits low,	*show—*
'Twill soothe us in our sorrow	*The bonny Holms of Yarrow.'*

The next day we were to meet Mr. Scott, and again join the Tweed. I wish I could have given you a better idea of what we saw between Peebles and this place. I have most distinct recollections of the effect of the whole day's journey; but the objects are mostly melted together in my memory, and though I should recognise them if we revisit the place, I cannot call them out so as to represent them to you with distinctness. William, in attempting in verse to describe this part of the Tweed, says of it,

More pensive in sunshine
Than others in moonshine.

which perhaps may give you more power to conceive what it is than all I have said.

Monday, September 19th—We rose early, and went to Melrose, six miles, before breakfast. After ascending a hill, descended, and overlooked a dell, on the opposite side of which was an old mansion, surrounded with trees and steep gardens, a curious and pleasing, yet melancholy spot; for the house and gardens were evidently going to decay, and the whole of the small dell, except near the house, was unenclosed and uncultivated, being a sheep-walk to the top of the hills. Descended to Gala Water, a pretty stream, but much smaller than the Tweed, into which the brook flows from the glen I have spoken of. Near the Gala is a large modern house, the situation very pleasant, but the old building which we had passed put to shame the fresh colouring and meagre outline of the new one. Went through a part of the village of Galashiels, pleasantly situated on the bank of the stream; a pretty place it once has been, but a manufactory is established there; and a townish bustle and ugly stone houses are fast taking place of the brown-roofed thatched cottages, of which a great number yet remain, partly overshadowed by trees. Left the Gala, and, after crossing the open country, came again to the Tweed, and pursued our way, as before, near the river, perhaps for a mile or two, till we arrived at Melrose. The valley for this short space was not so pleasing as before, the hills more broken, and though the cultivation was general, yet the scene was not rich, while it had lost its pastoral simplicity. At Melrose the vale opens out wide; but the hills are high all round—single distinct risings. After breakfast we went out, intending to go to the Abbey, and in the street met Mr. Scott, who gave us a cordial greeting, and conducted us thither himself. He was here on his own ground, for he is familiar with all that is known of the authentic history of Melrose and the popular tales connected with it. He pointed out many pieces of beautiful sculpture in obscure corners which would have escaped our notice. The Abbey has been built of a pale red stone; that part which was first erected of a very durable kind, the sculptured flowers and leaves and other minute ornaments being as perfect in many places as when first wrought. The ruin is of considerable extent, but unfortunately it is almost surrounded by insignificant houses, so that when you are close to it you see it entirely separated from many rural objects, and even when viewed from a distance the situation does not seem to be particularly happy, for the vale is broken and disturbed, and the Abbey at a distance from the river, so that you do not look upon them as companions of each other. And surely this is a national barbarism: within these beautiful walls is the ugliest church that was ever beheld—if it had been hewn out of the side of a hill it could not have been more dismal; there was no neatness, nor even decency, and it appeared to be so damp, and so completely excluded from fresh air; that it must be dangerous to sit in it; the floor is unpaved, and very rough. What a contrast to the beautiful and graceful order apparent in every part of the ancient design and workmanship! Mr. Scott went with us into the gardens and orchard of a Mr. Riddel, from which we had a very sweet view of the Abbey through trees, the town being entirely excluded. Dined with Mr. Scott at the inn; he was now travelling to the assizes at Jedburgh in his character of Sheriff of Selkirk, and on that account, as well as for his own sake, he was treated with great respect, a small part of which was vouchsafed to us as his friends, though I could not persuade the woman to show me the beds, or to make any sort of promise till she was assured from the Sheriff himself that he had no objection to sleep in the same room with William.

Tuesday, September 20th—Mr. Scott departed very early for Jedburgh, and we soon followed, intending to go by Dryburgh to Kelso. It was a fine morning. We went without breakfast, being told that there was a public-house at Dryburgh. The road was very pleasant, seldom out of sight of the Tweed for any length of time, though not often close to it. The valley is not so pleasantly defined as between Peebles and Clovenford, yet so soft and beautiful, and in many parts pastoral, but that peculiar and pensive simplicity which I have spoken of before was wanting, yet there was a fertility chequered with wildness which to many travellers would be more than a compensation. The reaches of the vale were shorter, the turnings more rapid, the banks often clothed with wood. In one place was a lofty scar, at another a green promontory, a small hill skirted by the river, the hill above irregular and green, and scattered over with trees. We wished we could have brought the ruins of Melrose to that spot, and mentioned this to Mr. Scott, who told us that the monks had first fixed their abode there, and raised a temporary building of wood. The monastery of Melrose was founded by a colony from Rievaux Abbey in Yorkshire, which building it happens to resemble in the colour of the stone, and I think partly in the style of architecture, but is much smaller, that is, has been much smaller, for there is not at Rievaux any one single part of the ruin so large as the remains of the church at Melrose, though at Rievaux a far more extensive ruin remains. It is also much grander, and the situation at present much more beautiful, that ruin not having suffered like Melrose Abbey from the encroachments of a town. The architecture at Melrose is, I believe, superior in the exactness and taste of some of the minute ornamental parts; indeed, it is impossible to conceive anything more delicate than the workmanship, especially in the imitations of flowers.

We descended to Dryburgh after having gone a considerable way upon high ground. A heavy rain when we reached the village, and there was no public-house. A well-dressed, well-spoken woman courteously—shall I say charitably?—invited us into her cottage, and permitted us to make breakfast; she showed us into a neat parlour, furnished with prints, a mahogany table, and other things which I was surprised to see, for her husband was only a day-labourer, but she had been Lady Buchan's waiting-maid, which acccounted for these luxuries and for a noticeable urbanity in her manners. All the cottages in this neighbourhood, if I am not mistaken, were covered with red tiles, and had chimneys. After breakfast we set out in the rain to the ruins of Dryburgh Abbey, which are near Lord Buchan's house, and, like Bothwell Castle, appropriated to the pleasure of the owner. We rang a bell at the gate, and, instead of a porter, an old woman came to open it through a narrow side-alley cut in a thick plantation of evergreens. On entering, saw the thatch of her hut just above the trees, and it looked very pretty, but the poor creature herself was a figure to frighten a child,—bowed almost double, having a hooked nose and overhanging eyebrows, a complexion stained brown with smoke, and a cap that might have been worn for months and never washed. No doubt she had been cowering over her peat fire, for if she had emitted smoke by her breath and through every pore, the odour could not have been stronger. This ancient woman, by right of office, attended us to show off the curiosities, and she had her tale as perfect, though it was not quite so long a one, as the gentleman Swiss, whom I remember to have seen at Blenheim with his slender wand and dainty white clothes. The house of Lord Buchan and the Abbey stand upon a large flat peninsula, a green holm almost covered with fruit-trees. The ruins of Dryburgh are much less extensive than those of Melrose, and greatly inferior both in the architecture and stone, which is much mouldered away. Lord Buchan has trained pear-trees along the walls, which are bordered with flowers and gravel walks, and he has made a pigeon-house, and a fine room in the ruin, ornamented with a curiously-assorted collection of busts of eminent men, in which lately a ball was given; yet, deducting for all these improvements, which are certainly much less offensive than you could imagine, it is a very sweet ruin, standing so enclosed in wood, which the towers overtop, that you cannot know that it is not in a state of natural desolation till you are close to it. The opposite bank of the Tweed is steep and woody, but unfortunately many of the trees are firs. The old woman followed us after the fashion of other guides, but being slower of foot than a younger person, it was not difficult to slip away from the scent of her poor smoke-dried body. She was sedulous in pointing out the curiosities, which, I doubt not, she had a firm belief were not to be surpassed in England or Scotland.

Having promised us a sight of the largest and oldest yew-tree ever seen, she conducted us to it; it was a goodly tree, but a mere dwarf compared with several of our own country—not to speak of the giant of Lorton. We returned to the cottage, and waited some time in hopes that the rain would abate, but it grew worse and worse, and we were obliged to give up our journey to Kelso, taking the direct road to Jedburgh.

We had to ford the Tweed, a wide river at the crossing-place. It would have been impossible to drive the horse through, for he had not forgotten the fright at Connel Ferry, so we hired a man to lead us. After crossing the water, the road goes up the bank, and we had a beautiful view of the ruins of the Abbey, peering above the trees of the woody peninsula, which, in shape, resembles that formed by the Tees at Eickburn, but is considerably smaller. Lord Buchan's house is a very neat, modest building, and almost hidden by trees. It soon began to rain heavily. Crossing the Teviot by a stone bridge—the vale in that part very wide—there was a great deal of ripe corn, but a want of trees, and no appearance of richness. Arrived at Jedburgh half an hour before the Judges were expected out of Court to dinner.

We gave in our passport—the name of Mr. Scott, the Sheriff—and were very civilly treated, but there was no vacant room in the house except the Judge's sitting-room, and we wanted to have a fire, being exceedingly wet and cold. I was conducted into that room, on condition that I would give it up the moment the Judge came from Court. After I had put off my wet clothes I went up into a bedroom, and sate shivering there, till the people of the inn had procured lodgings for us in a private house.

We were received with hearty welcome by a good woman, who, though above seventy years old, moved about as briskly as if she was only seventeen. Those parts of the house which we were to occupy were neat and clean; she showed me every corner, and, before I had been ten minutes in the house, opened her very drawers that I might see what a stock of linen she had; then asked me how long we should stay, and said she wished we were come for three months. She was a most remarkable person; the alacrity with which she ran up-stairs when we rung the bell, and guessed at, and strove to prevent, our wants was surprising; she had a quick eye, and keen strong features, and a joyousness in her motions, like what used to be in old Molly when she was particularly elated. I found afterwards that she had been subject to fits of dejection and ill-health: we then conjectured that her overflowing gaiety and strength might in part be attributed to the same cause as her former dejection. Her husband was deaf and infirm, and sate in a chair with scarcely the power to move a limb—an affecting contrast! The old woman said they had been a very hard-working pair; they had wrought like slaves at their trade—her husband had been a currier; and she told me how they had portioned off their daughters with money, and each a feather-bed, and that in their old age they had laid out the little they could spare in building and furnishing that house, and she added with pride that she had lived in her youth in the family of Lady Egerton, who was no high lady, and now was in the habit of coming to her house whenever she was at Jedburgh, and a hundred other things; for when she once began with Lady Egerton, she did not know how to stop, nor did I wish it, for she was very entertaining. Mr. Scott sate with us an hour or two, and repeated a part of the Lay of the Last Minstrel. When he was gone our hostess came to see if we wanted anything, and to wish us good-night. On all occasions her manners were governed by the same spirit: there was no withdrawing one's attention from her. We were so much interested that William, long afterwards, thought it worthwhile to express in verse the sensations which she had excited, and which then remained as vividly in his mind as at the moment when we lost sight of Jedburgh:—

Age! twine thy brows with fresh spring flowers,
And call a train of laughing Hours;
And bid them dance, and bid them sing,
And Thou, too, mingle in the Ring!
Take to thy heart a new delight!
If not, make merry in despite
That one should breathe who scorns thy power—
But dance! for under Jedborough Tower
A Matron dwells who, tho' she bears
Our mortal complement of years,
Lives in the light of youthful glee,
And she will dance and sing with thee.

Nay! start not at that Figure—there!
Him who is rooted to his Chair!
Look at him, look again; for He
Hath long been of thy Family.
With legs that move not, if they can,
And useless arms, a Trunk of Man,
He sits, and with a vacant eye;
A Sight to make a Stranger sigh!
Deaf, drooping, such is now his doom;
His world is in that single room—
Is this a place for mirthful cheer?
Can merry-making enter here?
The joyous Woman is the Mate
Of him in that forlorn estate;
He breathes a subterraneous damp;

But bright as Vesper shines her
lamp,
He is as mute as Jedborough Tower,
She jocund as it was of yore
With all its bravery on, in times
When all alive with merry chimes
Upon a sun-bright morn of May
It roused the Vale to holiday.

I praise thee, Matron! and thy due
Is praise, heroic praise and true.
With admiration I behold
Thy gladness unsubdued and bold:
Thy looks, thy gestures, all present
The picture of a life well spent;
This do I see, and something more,
A strength unthought of heretofore.
Delighted am I for thy sake,
And yet a higher joy partake:
Our human nature throws away
Its second twilight, and looks gay,
A Land of promise and of pride
Unfolding, wide as life is wide.

Ah! see her helpless Charge!
enclosed
Within himself as seems, composed;
To fear of loss and hope of gain,
The strife of happiness and pain—
Utterly dead! yet in the guise
Of little Infants when their eyes
Begin to follow to and fro
Repaid thee for that sore distress
By no untimely joyousness;
Which makes of thine a blissful state;
And cheers thy melancholy Mate!

The persons that before them go,
He tracks her motions, quick or
slow.
Her buoyant spirits can prevail
Where common cheerfulness would
fail.
She strikes upon him with the heat
Of July suns; he feels it sweet;
An animal delight, though dim!
'Tis all that now remains for him!

I look'd, I scann'd her o'er and o'er,
And, looking, wondered more and
more:
When suddenly I seem'd to espy
A trouble in her strong black eye,
A remnant of uneasy light,
A flash of something over-bright!
Not long this mystery did detain
My thoughts.   She told in pensive
strain
That she had borne a heavy yoke,
Been stricken by a twofold stroke;
Ill health of body, and had pined
Beneath worse ailments of the mind.

So be it!—but let praise ascend
To Him who is our Lord and Friend!
Who from disease and suffering
As bad almost as Life can bring,
Hath call'd for thee a second
Spring;

Wednesday, September 21ˢᵗ—The house where we lodged was airy, and even cheerful, though one of a line of houses bordering on the churchyard, which is the highest part of the town, overlooking a great portion of it to the opposite hills. The kirk is, as at Melrose, within the walls of a conventual church; but the ruin is much less beautiful, and the church a very neat one. The churchyard was full of graves, and exceedingly slovenly and dirty; one most indecent practice I observed: several women brought their linen to the flat table-tombstones, and, having spread it upon them, began to batter as hard as they could with a wooden roller, a substitute for a mangle.

After Mr. Scott's business in the Courts was over, he walked with us up the Jed—'sylvan Jed' it has been properly called by Thomson—for the banks are yet very woody, though wood in large quantities has been felled within a few years. There are some fine red scars near the river, in one or two of which we saw the entrances to caves, said to have been used as places of refuge in times of insecurity.

Walked up to Ferniehurst, an old hall, in a secluded situation, now inhabited by farmers; the neighbouring ground had the wildness of a forest, being irregularly scattered over with fine old trees. The wind was tossing their branches, and sunshine dancing among the leaves, and I happened to exclaim, 'What a life there is in trees!' on which Mr. Scott observed that the words reminded him of a young lady who had been born and educated on an island of the Orcades, and came to spend a summer at Kelso and in the neighbourhood of Edinburgh. She used to say that in the new world into which she was come nothing had disappointed her so much as trees and woods; she complained that they were lifeless, silent, and, compared with the grandeur of the ever-changing ocean, even insipid. At first I was surprised, but the next moment I felt that the impression was natural. Mr. Scott said that she was a very sensible young woman, and had read much. She talked with endless rapture and feeling of the power and greatness of the ocean; and with the same passionate attachment returned to her native island without any probability of quitting it again. The valley of the Jed is very solitary immediately under Ferniehurst; we walked down the river, wading almost up to the knees in fern, which in many parts overspread the forest-ground. It made me think of our walks at Allfox-den, and of our own park—though at Ferniehurst is no park at present—and the slim fawns that we used to startle from their couching-places among the fern at the top of the hill. We were accompanied on our walk by a young man from the Braes of Yarrow, an acquaintance of Mr. Scott's, (*W.Laidluw See Scott's Life,vol. i*)who, having been much delighted with some of William's poems which he had chanced to see in a newspaper, had wished to be introduced to him; he, lived in the most retired part of the dale of Yarrow, where he had a farm : he was fond of reading, and well informed, but at first meeting as shy as any of our Grasmere lads, and not less rustic in his appearance. He had been in the Highlands, and gave me such an account of Loch Rannoch as made us regret that we had not persevered in our journey thither, especially as he told us that the bad road ended at a very little distance from the place where we had turned back, and that we should have come into another good road, continued all along the shore of the lake. He also mentioned that there was a very fine view from the steeple at Dunkeld. The town of Jedburgh, in returning along the road, as it is seen through the gently winding narrow valley, looks exceedingly beautiful on its low eminence, surmounted by the conventual tower, which is arched over, at the summit, by light stone-work resembling a coronet; the effect at a distance is very graceful. The hills all round are high, and rise rapidly from the town, which though it stands considerably above the river, yet, from every side except that on which we walked, appears to stand in a bottom.

We had our dinner sent from the inn, and a bottle of wine, that we might-not disgrace the Sheriff, who supped with us in the evening,— stayed late, and repeated some of his poem.

Thursday, September 22nd—After breakfast, the minister, Dr. Somerville, called upon us with Mr. Scott, and we went to the manse, a very pretty house, with pretty gardens, and in a beautiful situation, though close to the town. Dr. Somerville and his family complained bitterly of the devastation that had been made among the woods within view from their windows, which looked up the Jed. He conducted us to the church, which under his directions has been lately repaired, and is a very neat place within. Dr. Somerville spoke of the dirt and other indecencies in the churchyard, and said that he had taken great pains to put a stop to them, but wholly in vain. The business of the assizes closed this day, and we went into Court to hear the Judge pronounce his charge, which was the most curious specimen of old woman's oratory and newspaper-paragraph loyalty that was ever heard. When all was over they returned to the inn in procession, as they had come, to the sound of a trumpet, the Judge first, in his robes of red, the Sheriffs next, in large cocked hats, and inferior officers following, a show not much calculated to awe the beholders. After this we went to the inn. The landlady and her sister inquired if we had been comfortable, and lamented that they had not had it in their power to pay us more attention. I began to talk with them, and found out that they were from Cumberland: they knew Captain and Mrs. Wordsworth, who had frequently been at Jedburgh, Mrs. Wordsworth's sister having married a gentleman of that neighbourhood. They spoke of them with great pleasure. I returned to our lodgings to take leave of the old woman, who told me that I had behaved ' very discreetly,' and seemed exceedingly sorry that we were leaving her so soon. She had been out to buy me some pears, saying that I must take away some 'Jedderd' pears. We learned afterwards that Jedburgh is famous in Scotland for pears, which were first cultivated there in the gardens of the monks.

Mr. Scott was very glad to part from the Judge and his retinue, to travel with us in our car to Hawick; his servant drove his own gig. The landlady, very kindly, had put up some sandwiches and cheesecakes for me, and all the family came out to see us depart. Passed the monastery gardens, which are yet gardens, where there are many remarkably large old pear-trees. We soon came into the vale of Teviot, which is open and cultivated, and scattered over with hamlets, villages, and many gentlemen's seats, yet, though there is no inconsiderable quantity of wood, you can never, in the wide and cultivated parts of the Teviot, get rid of the impression of barrenness, and the fir plantations, which in this part are numerous, are for ever at war with simplicity. One beautiful spot I recollect of a different character, which Mr. Scott took us to see a few yards from the road. A stone bridge crossed the water at a deep and still place, called Home's Pool, from a contemplative schoolmaster, who had lived not far from it, and was accustomed to walk thither, and spend much of his leisure near the river. The valley was here narrow and woody. Mr Scott pointed out to us Ruberslaw, Minto Crags, and every other remarkable object in or near the vale of Teviot, and we scarcely passed a house for which he had not some story. Seeing us look at one, which stood high on the hill on the opposite side of the river, he told us that a gentleman lived there who, while he was in India, had been struck with the fancy of making his fortune by a new speculation, and so set about collecting the gods of the country, with infinite pains and no little expense, expecting that he might sell them for an enormous price. Accordingly, on his return they were offered for sale, but no purchasers came. On the failure of this scheme, a room was hired in London in which to exhibit them as a show; but alas! nobody would come to see; and this curious assemblage of monsters is now, probably, quietly lodged in the vale of Teviot. The latter part of this gentleman's history is more affecting:—he had an only daughter, whom he had accompanied into Spain two or three years ago for the recovery of her health, and so for a time saved her from a consumption, which now again threatened her, and he was about to leave his pleasant residence, and attend her once more on the same errand, afraid of the coming winter.

We passed through a village, whither Leyden, Scott's intimate friend, the author of Scenes of Infancy, was used to walk over several miles of moorland country every day to school, a poor barefooted boy. He is now in India, applying himself to the study of Oriental literature, and, I doubt not, it is his dearest thought that he may come and end his days upon the banks of Teviot, or some other of the Lowland streams—for he is, like Mr. Scott, passionately attached to the district of the Borders. Arrived at Hawick to dinner; the inn is a large old house with walls above a yard thick, formerly a gentleman's house. Did not go out this evening.

Friday, September 23rd—Before breakfast, walked with Mr. Scott along a high road for about two miles, up a bare hill. Hawick is a small town. From the top of the hill we had an extensive view over the moors of Liddisdale, and saw the Cheviot Hills. We wished we could have gone with Mr. Scott into some of the remote dales of this country, where in almost every house he can find a home and a hearty welcome. But after breakfast we were obliged to part with him, which we did with great regret: he would gladly have gone with us to Langholm, eighteen miles further. Our way was through the vale of Teviot, near the banks of the river. Passed Branxholm Hall, one of the mansions belonging to the Duke of Buccleuch, which we looked at with particular interest for the sake of the Lay of the Last Minstrel. Only a very small part of the original building remains: it is a large strong house, old, but not ancient in its appearance—stands very near the river-side; the banks covered with plantations.

A little further on, met the Edinburgh coach with several passengers, the only stage-coach that had passed us in Scotland. Coleridge had come home by that conveyance only a few days before. The quantity of arable land gradually diminishes, and the plantations become fewer, till at last the river flows open to the sun, mostly through unfenced and unfilled grounds, a soft pastoral district, both the hills and the valley being scattered over with sheep. Here and there was a single farm-house, or cluster of houses, and near them a portion of land covered with ripe corn.

Near the head of the vale of Teviot, where that stream is but a small rivulet, we descended towards another valley, by another small rivulet. Hereabouts Mr. Scott had directed us to look about for some old stumps of trees, said to be the place where Johnny Armstrong was hanged; but we could not find them out. The valley into which we were descending, though, for aught I know, it is unnamed in song, was to us more interesting than the Teviot itself. Not a spot of tilled ground was there to break in upon its pastoral simplicity; the same soft yellow green spread from the bed of the streamlet to the hill-tops on each side, and sheep were feeding everywhere. It was more close and simple than the upper end of the vale of Teviot, the valley being much narrower, and the hills equally high and not broken into parts, but on each side a long range. The grass, as we had first seen near Crawfordjohn, had been mown in the different places of the open ground, where it might chance to be best; but there was no part of the surface that looked perfectly barren, as in those tracts.

We saw a single stone house a long way before us, which we conjectured to be, as it proved, Moss Paul, the inn where we were to bait. The scene, with this single dwelling, was melancholy and wild, but not dreary, though there was no tree nor shrub; the small streamlet glittered, the hills were populous with sheep; but the gentle bending of the valley, and the correspondent softness in the forms of the hills, were of themselves enough to delight the eye. At Moss Paul we fed our horse;—several travellers were drinking whisky. We neither ate nor drank, for we had, with our usual foresight and frugality in travelling, saved the cheese-cakes and sandwiches which had been given us by our countrywoman at Jedburgh the day before. After Moss Paul, we ascended considerably, then went down other reaches of the valley, much less interesting, stony and barren. The country afterwards not peculiar, I should think, for I scarcely remember it.

Arrived at Langholm at about five o'clock. The town, as we approached, from a hill, looked very pretty, the houses being roofed with blue slates, and standing close to the river Esk, here a large river, that scattered its waters wide over a stony channel. The inn neat and comfortable—exceedingly clean: I could hardly believe we were still in Scotland.

After tea walked out; crossed a bridge, and saw, at a little distance up the valley, Langholm House, a villa of the Duke of Buccleuch: it stands upon a level between the river and a steep hill, which is planted with wood. Walked a considerable way up the river, but could not go close to it on account of the Duke's plantations, which are locked up. When they ended, the vale became less cultivated; the view through the vale towards the hills very pleasing, though bare and cold.

Saturday, September 24th—Rose very early and travelled about nine miles to Longtown, before breakfast, along the banks of the Esk. About half a mile from Langholm crossed a bridge. At this part of the vale, which is narrow, the steeps are covered with old oaks and every variety of trees. Our road for some time through the wood, then came to. a more open country, exceedingly rich and populous; the banks of the river frequently rocky, and hung with wood; many gentlemen's houses. There was the same rich variety while the river continued to flow through Scottish grounds; but not long after we had passed through the last turnpike gate in Scotland and the first in England —but a few yards asunder—the vale widens, and its aspect was cold, and even dreary, though Sir James Graham's plantations are very extensive. His house, a large building, stands in this open part of the vale. Long-town was before us, and ere long we saw the well-remembered guide-post, where the circuit of our six weeks' travels had begun, and now was ended.

We did not look along the white line of the road to Solway Moss without some melancholy emotion, though we had the fair prospect of the Cumberland mountains full in view, with the certainty, barring accidents, of reaching our own dear home the next day. Breakfasted at the Graham's Arms. The weather had been very fine from the time of our arrival at Jedburgh, and this was a very pleasant day. The sun shone fair on Carlisle's walls when we first saw them from the top of the opposite hill. Stopped to look at the place on the sand near the bridge where Hatfield had been executed. Put up at the same inn as before, and were recognised by the woman who had waited on us. Everybody spoke of Hatfield as an injured man. After dinner went to a village six miles further, where we slept.

Sunday, September 25th 1803—A beautiful autumnal day. Breakfasted at a public-house by the road-side; dined at Threlkeld; arrived at home between eight and nine o'clock, where we found Mary in perfect health, Joanna Hutchinson with her, and little John asleep in the clothes-basket by the fire.

SONNET
COMPOSED BETWEEN DALSTON AND GRASMERE,
SEPTEMBER 25TH, 1803.

FLY, some kind spirit, fly to Grasmere Vale!
Say that we come, and come by this day's light
Glad tidings!—spread them over field and height,
But, chiefly, let one Cottage hear the tale!
There let a mystery of joy prevail,
The kitten frolic with unruly might,
And Rover whine as at a second sight
Of near-approaching good, that will not fail:
And from that Infant's face let joy appear;
Yea let our Mary's one companion child,
That hath her six weeks' solitude beguiled
With intimations manifold and dear,
While we have wander'd over wood and wild—
Smile on its Mother now with bolder cheer!

Neidpath Castle

Peebles

Hawthornden

Abbotsford, home of Walter Scott

Walter Scott
Dorothy met him 17th September 1803

NOTES

NOTE 1—*'Hatfield was condemned'*—PAGE 34. James Hatfield, indicted for having, in the Lake District, under the assumed name of Hon. Alexander Augustus Hope, brother of the Earl of Hopetoun, forged certain bills of exchange. He was condemned to death at Carlisle on August 16, 1803. His atrocious treatment of a beautiful girl, known in the district as 'Mary of Buttermere' had drawn more than usual attention to the criminal.

NOTE 2— *'In Captain Wordsworth's ship'*—PAGE 34. The 'Brother John' here alluded to was a sailor. He was about two years and eight months younger than the poet, who found in him quite a congenial spirit. He perished, with nearly all his crew, in the 'Earl of Abergavenny,' East-Indiaman, which he commanded, and which, owing to the incompetency of a pilot, was in his last outward voyage, wrecked on the Shambles of the Bill of Portland on the night of Friday, February 5, 1805. His brother William speaks of him in verse, as 'a silent poet,' and in prose describes him as 'meek, affectionate, silently enthusiastic, loving all quiet things, and a poet in everything but words.' Allusions to this sailor-brother occur in several of the poems, as in those lines beginning 'When to the attractions of the busy world,' to be found among the 'Poems on the Naming of Places,' also in the 'Elegiac Stanzas suggested by a Picture of Peele Castle in a Storm,' and in other poems.

NOTE 3—*'There is no stone to mark the spot.'*—PAGE 36. 'The body of Burns was not allowed to remain long in this place. To suit the plan of a rather showy mausoleum, his remains were removed into a more commodious spot of the same kirkyard on the 5th July 1815. The coffin was partly dissolved away; but the curling locks of the poet were as glossy, and seemed as fresh, as on the day of his death.'—Life of Burns, by Allan Cunningham.

NOTE 4—*'They had a large library'*—PAGE 46.The following account of this library is taken from Dr. John Brown's delightful tract, 'The Enterkin.' The author will excuse wholesale appropriation to illustrate a journal which, I believe, will be dear to him, and to all who feel as he does:—'The miners at Leadhills are a reading, a hard-reading people; and to anyone looking into the catalogue of their "Reading Society," selected by the men themselves for their own uses and tastes, this will be manifest. We have no small gratification in holding their diploma of honorary membership—signed by the preses and clerk, and having the official seal, significant of the craft of the place— of this, we venture to say, one of the oldest and best village libraries in the kingdom, having been founded in 1741, when the worthy miners of that day, headed by James Wells and clerked by William Wright, did, on the 23d November, "condescend upon certain articles and laws"—as grave and thorough as if they were the constitution of a commonwealth, and as sturdily independent as if no Earl were their superior and master. "It is hereby declared that no right is hereby given, nor shall at any time be given, to the said Earl of Hopetoun, or his aforesaids, or to any person or persons whatever, of disposing of any books or other effects whatever belonging to the Society, nor of taking any concern with the Society's affairs," etc. As an indication of the wild region and the distances travelled, one of the rules is, "that every member not residing in Leadhills shall be provided with a bag sufficient to keep out the rain." Here is the stiff, covenanting dignity cropping out—"Every member shall (at the annual meeting) deliver what he hath to say to the preses; and if two or more members attempt to speak at a time, the preses shall determine who shall speak first;" and "members guilty of indecency, or unruly, obstinate behaviour are to be punished by fine, suspension, or exclusion, according to the nature of the transgression." The Westminster Divines could not have made a tighter job.'

NOTE 5— *'The first view of the Clyde'*—PAGE 55. This was not their first view of the Clyde. They had been travelling within sight of it without knowing it for full twenty miles before this, ever since coming down the Daer Water from Leadhills to Elvanfoot. They there reached the meeting-place of that water with a small stream that flows from Ericstane. These two united become the Clyde.

NOTE 6— *'wished Joanna had been there to laugh'*—PAGE 63. Joanna Hutchinson, Mrs. Wordsworth's sister. Among the 'Poems on the Naming of Places,' is one addressed to her, in 1800, in which the following well-known lines occur:—

As it befell,
One summer morning we had
walked abroad
At break of day, Joanna and myself
'Twas that delightful season when
the broom,
Full-flowered, and visible on every
steep,
Along the copses runs in veins of
gold.
Our pathway led us on to Rotha's
banks,
And when we came in front of that
tall rock
That eastward looks, I there stopped
short and stood
Tracing the lofty barrier with my eye
From base to summit; such delight I
found

To note in shrub and tree, in stone
and flower
That intermixture of delicious hues,
Along so vast a surface, all at once,
In one impression, by connecting
force
Of their own beauty, imaged in the
heart.
When I had gazed perhaps two
minutes' space,
Joanna, looking in my eyes, beheld
That ravishment of mine, and
laughed aloud;
The Rock, like something starting
from a sleep,
Took up the Lady's voice and
laughed again;
That ancient woman seated on Helm
Crag

Was ready with her cavern;
Hammarscar,
And the tall Steep of Silverhaw, sent
forth
A noise of laughter; southern
Loughrigg heard,
And Fairfield answered with a
mountain tone;
Helvellyn far into the clear blue sky

Carried the Lady's voice,—old
Skiddaw blew
His speaking-trumpet;—back out of
the clouds
Of Glaramara southward came the
voice;
And Kirkstone tossed it from his
misty head.'

In his comments made on his Poems late in life, Wordsworth said of this one:—'The effect of her laugh is an extravagance; though the effect of the reverberation of voices in some parts of the mountains is very striking. There is, in the "Excursion," an allusion to the bleat of a lamb thus re-echoed, and described without any exaggeration, as I heard it, on the side of Stickle Tarn, from the precipice that stretches on to Langdale Pikes.'

NOTE 7— *'With two bells hanging in the open air'*—PAGE 82. 'When I wrote this account of the village of Luss, I fully believed I had a perfect recollection of the two bells, as I have described them; but I am half tempted to think they have been a creation of my own fancy, though no image that I know I have actually seen is at this day more vividly impressed upon my mind.'—MS. note, Author, 1806.

NOTE 8— *'Her countenance corresponded with the unkindness of denying us a fire on a cold night.'*—PAGE 84. The writer, inhospitably as she had been treated, was more fortunate than a distinguished French traveller, who arrived at Luss at night, a few years earlier. The hostess made signs to him that he should not speak, hustled him into a stable, and said solemnly, 'The Justiciary Lords do me the honour to lodge here when they are on this circuit. There is one of them here at present he is asleep, and nobody must disturb him.' And forthwith she drove him out into the rain and darkness, saying, 'How can I help it? Make no noise, his Lordship must not be disturbed. Everyone should pay respect to the law. God bless you. Farewell' And on they had to go fifteen miles to Tarbet.— St. Fond's Travels, vol. i p. 233.

NOTE 9— *'could not help smiling when I saw him lying by the roadside.'*— PAGE 91. 'The ferryman happened to mention that a fellow-countryman of his had lately come from America—a wild sort of genius. This reminded us of our friend whom we had met at Loch Lomond, and we found that it was the same person. He was the brother of the Lady of Glengyle, who had made a gentleman of him by new-clothing him from head to foot. "But," said the ferryman, "when the clothes are worn out, and his sister is tired of supplying him with pocket-money (which will probably be very soon), he will be obliged to betake himself again to America." The Lady of Glengyle has a house not far from the ferry-house, but she now lives mostly at Callander for the sake of educating her son.'—Author's MS., 1806.

NOTE 10—*'In a word, the Trossachs beggar all description.'* PAGE 106. The world believes, and will continue to believe, that Scott was the first 'Sassenach' who discovered the Trossachs, as it was his Poem which gave them world-wide celebrity. It would probably be as impossible to alter this impression, as it would be to substitute for Shakespeare's Macbeth and Lady Macbeth the very different versions of the facts and characters which historical research has brought to light. And yet it would be interesting, to those who care for truth and fact, to inquire, did time allow, what first brought the Trossachs into notice, and who first did so. That they had, as I have said in the Preface, some fame before Scott's Poem appeared, is clear, else a stranger like Wordsworth would never have gone so far out of his way to search for them. Pending a thorough examination of the question, it may be worth while here to note the following facts. Miss Wordsworth refers in the text to some work on the Trossachs, from which the words at the head of this note are taken. I was under the impression that the work referred to was the well-known 'Sketches descriptive of Picturesque Scenery on the Southern Confines of Perthshire,' by the Rev. Patrick Graham, minister of Aberfoyle, but it is satisfactory to find that Mr. Graham was not alone in his admiration of Highland scenery in those early days. A neighbour of his, the Rev. James Robertson, who was presented to the parish of Callander in 1768, wrote a description of the Trossachs in Sir John Sinclair's Statistical Account, and from the fact of his using the very sentence quoted by Miss Wordsworth, I have no doubt he was the author of the little pamphlet Miss Spence in her 'Caledonian Excursion,' 1811, says that the Honourable Mrs. Murray told the minister of Callander that Scott ought to have dedicated 'The Lady of the Lake' to her as the discoverer of the Trossachs — 'Pray, Madam,' said the good doctor, 'when did you write your Tour?' 'In the year 1794.' *{If this is not a misprint, the Lady had antedated her tour by two years, as she made it in 1796 and published it in 1799.}*

'Then, Madam, it is no presumption in me to consider that I was the person who in 1790 made the Trossachs first known, for except to the natives and a few individuals in this neighbourhood, this remarkable place had never been heard of.' Mr. Robertson died in 1812. There were thus at least two notices of the Trossachs published before Mr. Graham's Sketches: these were not published till 1806. The Lady of the Lake was first published in 1810.

NOTE 11—*'Dutch myrtle'*—PAGE 106. This seems to be the name by which Miss Wordsworth knew the plant which Lowlanders generally call bog myrtle, Border men gale, or sweet gale, and Highlanders roid (pronounced as roitch). Botanists, I believe, know it as Myrica Gale, a most fragrant plant or shrub, growing generally in moist and mossy ground. Perhaps nothing more surely brings back the feeling that you are in the very Highlands than the first scent of this plant caught on the breeze.

NOTE 12—*'Bonnier than Loch Lomond'*—PAGE 109. As an illustration of local jealousy, I may mention that when Mr. Jamieson, the editor of the fifth edition of Burt's Letters, was in the Highlands in 1814, four years after the publication of Scott's Poem, and eleven after the Wordsworths' visit, he met a savage looking fellow on the top of Ben Lomond, the image of 'Red Murdoch,' who told him that he had been a guide to the mountain for more than forty years, but now 'a Walter Scott' had spoiled his trade. 'I wish,' said he, 'I had him in a ferry over Loch Lomond; I should be after sinking the boat, if I drowned myself into the bargain, for ever since he wrote his "Lady of the Lake," as they call it, everybody goes to see that filthy hole, Loch Ketterine. The devil confound his ladies and his lakes!'

NOTE 13—*'For poor Ann Tyson's sake'*—Page 140. The dame with whom Wordsworth lodged at Hawkshead. Of her he has spoken with affectionate tenderness in the 'Prelude:'—

'The thoughts of gratitude shall fall like dew
upon thy grave, good creature!'

Her garden, its brook, and dark pine tree, and the stone table under it, were all dear to his memory, and the chamber in which he,

'Had lain awake on summer nights to watch
The moon in splendour couched among the leaves
Of a tall ash that near our cottage stood.'

She lived to above fourscore; unmarried, and loving her young inmates as her children, and beloved by them as a mother.

'Childless, yet by the strangers to her blood
Honoured with little less than filial love.'
Wordsworth's Life, vol. i. 39.

NOTE 14 – *'The woman said it had been a palace'* – PAGE 177. A mistake. The old mansion here described was the building formerly used as a prison house of the Regality of Athole in which the dukes and formerly the Earls of Athole confined their criminals during the ages when they in common with all the other Scottish Barons exercised the right of heritable jurisdiction. This right was abolished after the '45 and then like this, like all other baronial prison houses fell into decay. Nearly 70 years ago it has now wholly disappeared having been used up, no doubt, as material for the neighbouring buildings. There was, however, at Logierait, a Royal Castle, from which the place itself and the large adjacent parish take their names-Lag-an raith, the hollow of the castle,- while the neighbouring small hamlet and railway station on the other side of the Tummel are called Ball-na-luig - the town of the hollow. The castle stood on a high knoll overlooking the church and in at Logierait, commanding a view of the junction of the Tummel and the Tay immediately underneath, and of the whole of southern Athole, so far as Dunkeld. This knoll is now crowned by a high Celtic cross, memorial to the late Duke of Athole. Immediately around it are seen lying here and there blocks of solid masonry, the sole remnants of the Castle in which Robert II is said to have dwelt during his visits to Athole. Traces of the castle moat are still discernible.

NOTE 15—*'Rob Roy's grave was there'*—PAGE 201. Regarding this Wordsworth says, 'I have since been told that I was misinformed as to the burial-place of Rob Roy; if so, I may plead in excuse that I wrote on apparent good authority, namely, that of a well-educated lady who lived at the head of the lake, within a mile or less of the point indicated as containing the remains of one so famous in that neighbourhood.' The real burial-place of Rob Roy is the Kirkton of Balquhidder, at the lower end of Loch Voil. The grave is covered by a rude, grey slab, on which a long claymore is roughly engraved. The Guidebook informs us that the arms on his tombstone are a Scotch pine, the badge of Clan Gregor, crossed by a sword, and supporting a crown, this last to denote the relationship claimed by the Gregarach with the Royal Stuarts. When I last saw the tombstone, as far as I remember, I observed nothing but the outline of the long sword.

NOTE 16—*'Thomas Wilkinson's "Tour in Scotland"'*—PAGE 206. Probably one of Wilkinson's poems, of which Wordsworth speaks occasionally in his letters. 'The present Lord Lonsdale has a neighbour, a Quaker, an amiable, inoffensive man, and a little of a poet too, who has amused himself upon his own small estate upon the Emont, in twining pathways along the banks of the river, making little cells and bowers with inscriptions of his own writing.'— Letter-to Sir G. Beaumont, Oct. 17, 1805. Wordsworth wrote the poem, 'To a Spade of a Friend,' composed ' while we were labouring together in his pleasure-grounds,' commencing—'Spade with which Wilkinson hath tilled his land, And shaped these pleasant walks by Emont's side,' in memory of this friend.—See Life, vol. i pp. 55, 323, 349.

ITINERARY DISTANCES FROM PLACE TO PLACE

	MILES		MILES
Grasmere to Keswick, . .	13	Brownhill (pretty good),	12
Hesket Newmarket (road very-bad), ...	15	Leadhills (tolerable), . .	19
		Douglass Mill (very bad), .	12
Carlisle (bad road) . .	14	Lanark (baddish), ...	9
Longtown (newly mended, not good), ...	8	Hamilton (tolerable), . .	15
		Glasgow (tolerable), . .	11
Annan (good), ...	14	Dumbarton (very good), .	15
Dumfries (good), ...	15	Luss (excellent), ...	13

Tarbet (not bad), ...	8	Loch Erne Head (tolerable),	20
Arrochar (good), ...	2	Callander (most excellent),	14
Cairndow (middling), .	12	Trossachs, ...	16
Inverary (very good), .	10	Ferryman's House (about 8)	8
Dalmally (tolerable), .	16	Callander to Falkirk	
Taynuilt (excellent), .	13	(bad-dish road),	27
Portnacroish (tolerable), .	15	Edinburgh (good),	24
Ballachulish(part most excellent)	12	Roslin (good),	6
King's House (bad) .	12	Peebles (good), .	16
Tyndrum (good), ...	18	Clovenford (tolerable),.	16
Suie (road excellent), .	13	Melrose (tolerable),	8
Killin (tolerable),	7	Dryburgh (good) .	4
Kenmore (baddish),	15	Jedburgh (roughish), .	10
Blair (bad), ...	23	Hawick (good), .	12
Fascally (wretchedly bad), .	18	Langholm (very good),	24
Dunkeld (bad), .	12	Longtown (good),	12
Ambletree (hilly—good), .	10	Carlisle, ...	8
Crieff (hilly—goodish),	11	Grasmere, ...	36

APPENDIX

Holly abounds Glen Etive
{Original painting by S. Borland}

Near Glencoe with Ben Nevis to the left
{Kathleen Morison "The Mermaid of Glencoe"
on Stob Coire Sgreamhach}

241

Looking down to the King's House from Buachaille Etive Mor with Rannoch Moor and Glen Orchy in the distance. The climbers are from the Royal Air Force Leuchars Mountain Rescue Team. Dorothy was very familiar with this topography in 1803.

Buachaille Etive Beag in snow. Dorothy would be aware of its nature in winter